MILLENNIUM

THE GIRL WITH THE DRAGON TATTOO

Titan
COMICS

THE GIRL WITH THE DRAGON TATTOO

9781785861734
Published by Titan Comics
A division of Titan Publishing Group Ltd.
144 Southwark St., London, SE1 0UP

MILLENNIUM: THE GIRL WITH THE DRAGON TATTOO

Originally published as *Millennium Vol.1: Les hommes qui n'aimaient pas les femmes*
EDITIONS DUPUIS S.A. © DUPUIS 2013, By Runberg, Homs. All rights reserved. The name *Hard Case Crime* and the Hard Case Crime logo are trademarks of Winterfall LLC. Hard Case Crime Comics are produced with editorial guidance from Charles Ardai

Millennium © 2017 Stieg Larsson and Moggliden AB
Lettering by Phillippe Glogowski

A CIP catalogue record for this title is available from the British Library

10 9 8 7 6 5 4 3 2 1
First Published September 2017
Printed in Spain.
Titan Comics.

TITAN COMICS
EDITOR: TOM WILLIAMS
DESIGNER: OZ BROWN

Senior Comics Editor: Andrew James
Titan Comics Editorial: Amoona Saohin, Lauren McPhee,
Jonathan Stevenson, Lauren Bowes
Senior Production Controller: Jackie Flook
Production Supervisor: Maria Pearson
Production Controller: Peter James
Art Director: Oz Browne
Senior Sales Manager: Steve Tothill
Press Officer: Will O'Mullane
Direct Sales & Marketing Manager: Ricky Claydon
Commercial Manager: Michelle Fairlamb
Ads & Marketing Assistant: Tom Miller
Publishing Manager: Darryl Tothill
Publishing Director: Chris Teather
Operations Director: Leigh Baulch
Executive Director: Vivian Cheung
Publisher: Nick Landau

WWW.TITAN-COMICS.COM
Follow us on Twitter @ComicsTitan
Visit us at facebook.com/comicstitan

MILLENNIUM

THE GIRL WITH THE DRAGON TATTOO

CHAPTER 1

WRITTEN BY
SYLVAIN RUNBERG

ARTWORK BY
HOMS

TRANSLATED BY
RACHEL ZERNER

BASED ON THE NOVEL
TRILOGY BY
STIEG LARSSON

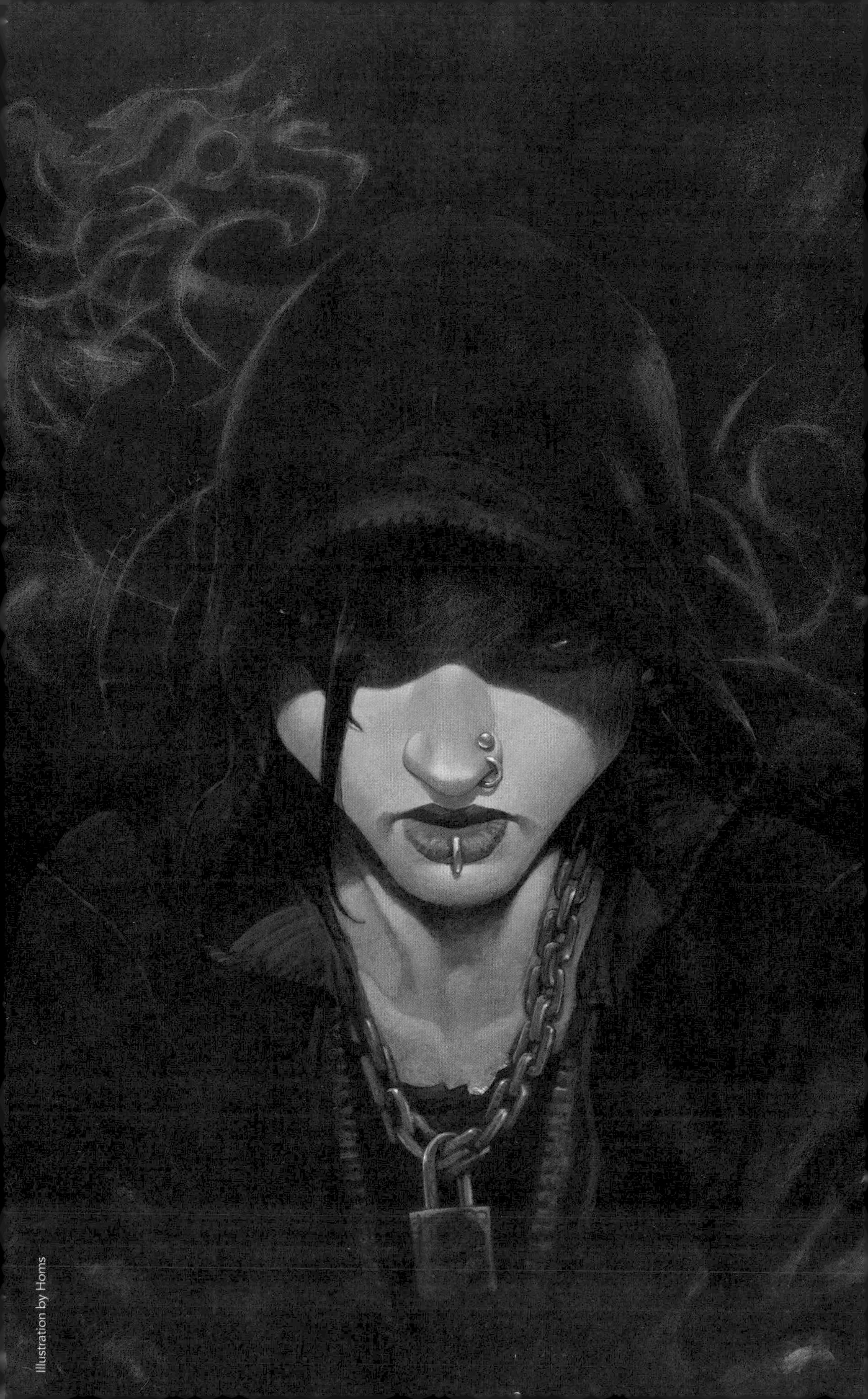

Illustration by Homs

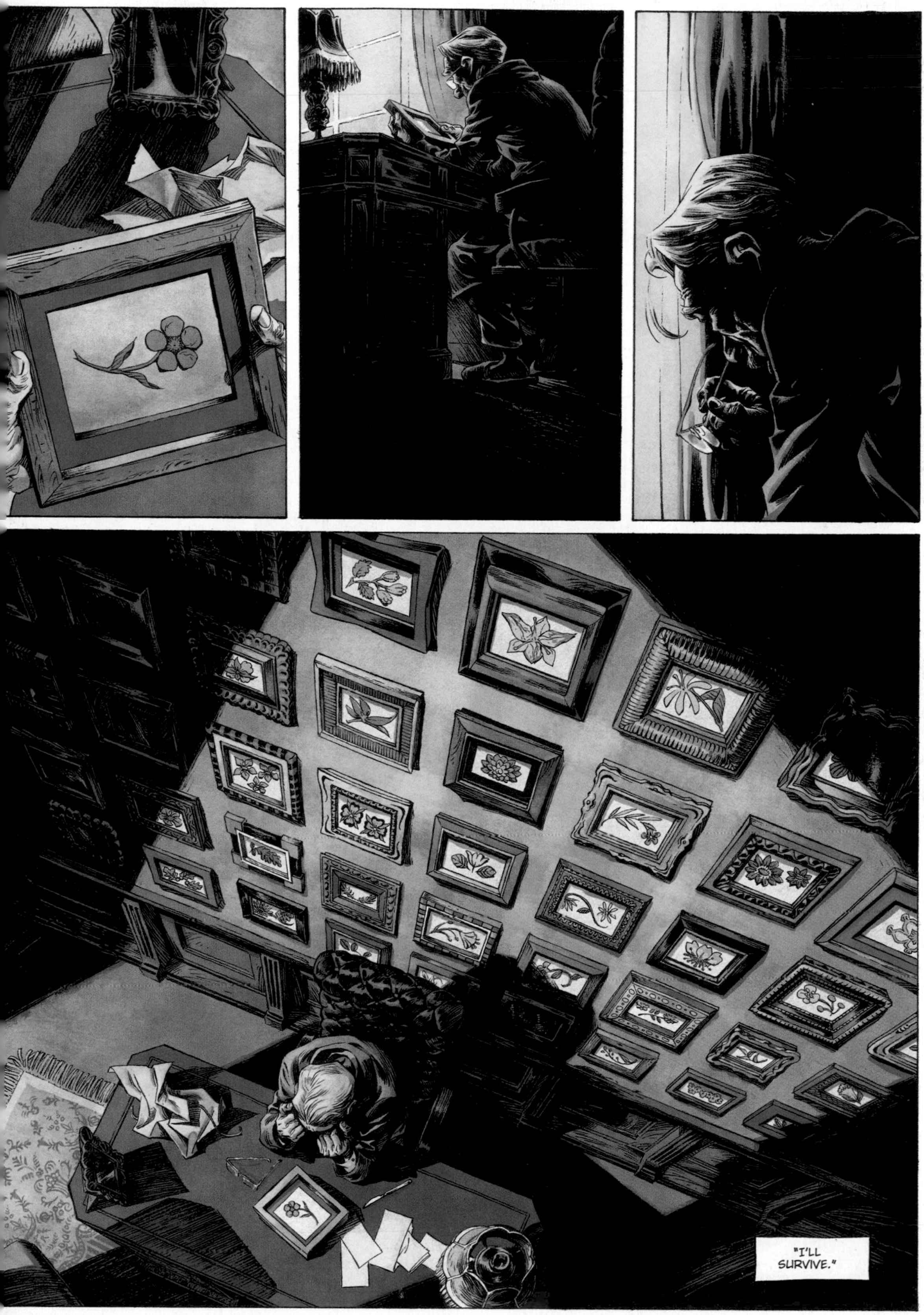
"I'LL SURVIVE."

YOU'LL *SURVIVE?*

IS THAT *REALLY* ALL YOU HAVE TO SAY ABOUT YOUR CONVICTION, MR. BLOMKVIST?

IF YOU WANT MORE MATERIAL FOR YOUR ARTICLE, I SUGGEST YOU GO JOIN YOUR COLLEAGUES OVER THERE...

I'M SURE THAT *HANS-ERIK WENNERSTRÖM* HAS A LOT TO TELL YOU.

TODAY, THE JUSTICE SYSTEM OF THIS COUNTRY HAS DEMONSTRATED THAT IT *WORKS* -- AND THAT WE CANNOT GO AROUND UNJUSTLY ACCUSING HONEST CITIZENS!

NATURALLY, I'M *DELIGHTED* WITH THIS VERDICT. NOW, I'M OFF TO REJOIN MY FAMILY, WHO HAVE SUFFERED TERRIBLY FROM THE VICIOUS CLAIMS MADE BY MIKAEL BLOMKVIST...

THEN MAYBE WE CAN REDISCOVER THE PEACE AND QUIET THAT HAS BEEN TORN FROM US BY A MAN WE ALL *THOUGHT* TO BE AN EXEMPLARY JOURNALIST. THAT *MASK* HAS CERTAINLY FALLEN TODAY!

A 300,000 KRONA FINE AND *THREE MONTHS* IN PRISON -- MIKAEL BLOMKVIST'S CONVICTION WAS ISSUED WITHOUT APPEAL.

IT'S A STAGGERING BLOW FOR THE JOURNALIST WHOSE WORK, IN THE MAGAZINE *MILLENNIUM* HAS ENRAPTURED SWEDEN FOR YEARS.

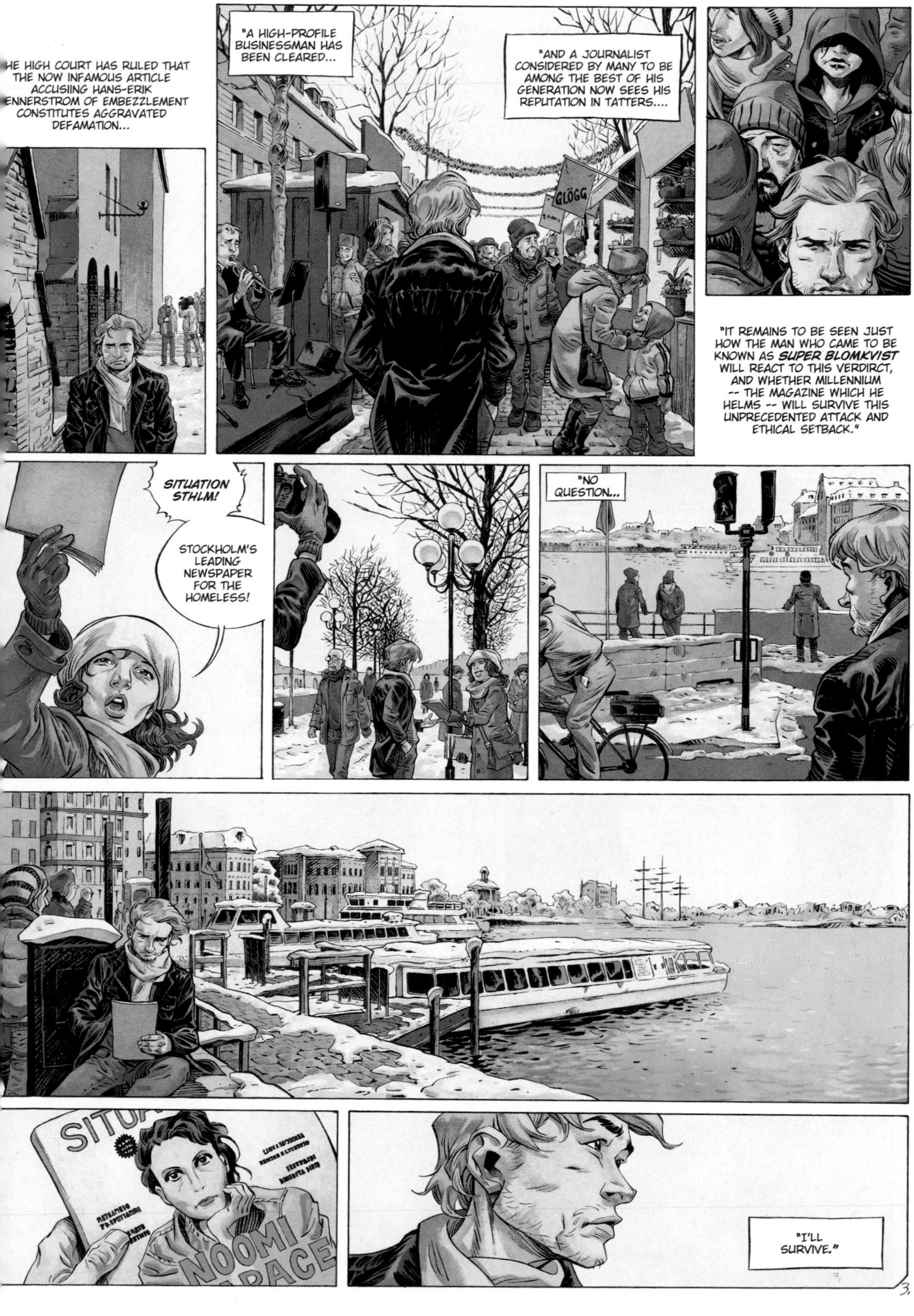

HE HIGH COURT HAS RULED THAT THE NOW INFAMOUS ARTICLE ACCUSIING HANS-ERIK ENNERSTROM OF EMBEZZLEMENT CONSTITUTES AGGRAVATED DEFAMATION...
"A HIGH-PROFILE BUSINESSMAN HAS BEEN CLEARED...
"AND A JOURNALIST CONSIDERED BY MANY TO BE AMONG THE BEST OF HIS GENERATION NOW SEES HIS REPUTATION IN TATTERS....
GLÖGG
"IT REMAINS TO BE SEEN JUST HOW THE MAN WHO CAME TO BE KNOWN AS ***SUPER BLOMKVIST*** WILL REACT TO THIS VERDIRCT, AND WHETHER MILLENNIUM -- THE MAGAZINE WHICH HE HELMS -- WILL SURVIVE THIS UNPRECEDENTED ATTACK AND ETHICAL SETBACK."
SITUATION STHLM!
STOCKHOLM'S LEADING NEWSPAPER FOR THE HOMELESS!
"NO QUESTION...
NOOMI
"I'LL SURVIVE."

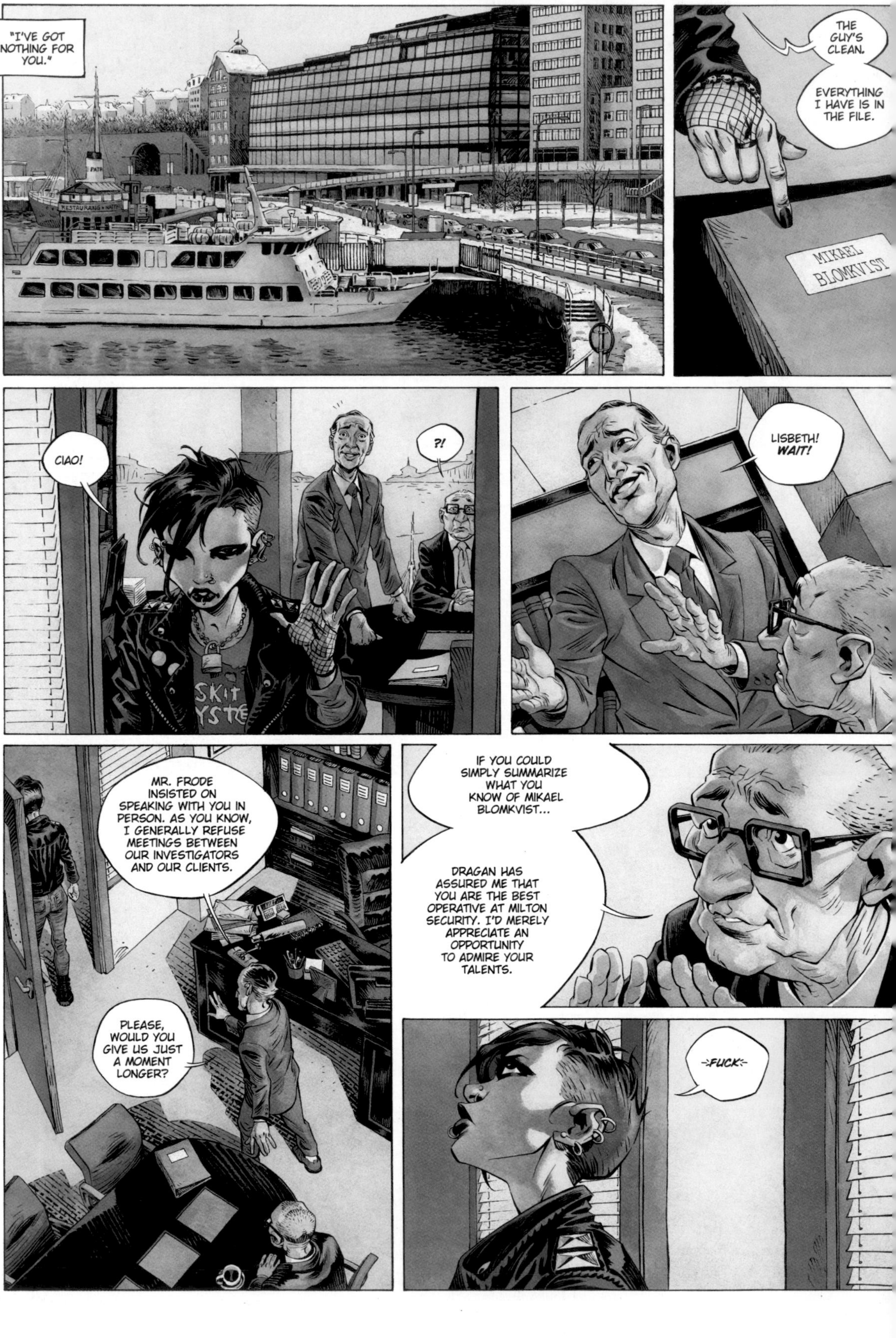
"I'VE GOT NOTHING FOR YOU."
THE GUY'S CLEAN.
EVERYTHING I HAVE IS IN THE FILE.
MIKAEL BLOMKVIST
CIAO!
?!
LISBETH! WAIT!
MR. FRODE INSISTED ON SPEAKING WITH YOU IN PERSON. AS YOU KNOW, I GENERALLY REFUSE MEETINGS BETWEEN OUR INVESTIGATORS AND OUR CLIENTS.
PLEASE, WOULD YOU GIVE US JUST A MOMENT LONGER?
IF YOU COULD SIMPLY SUMMARIZE WHAT YOU KNOW OF MIKAEL BLOMKVIST...
DRAGAN HAS ASSURED ME THAT YOU ARE THE BEST OPERATIVE AT MILTON SECURITY. I'D MERELY APPRECIATE AN OPPORTUNITY TO ADMIRE YOUR TALENTS.
FUCK

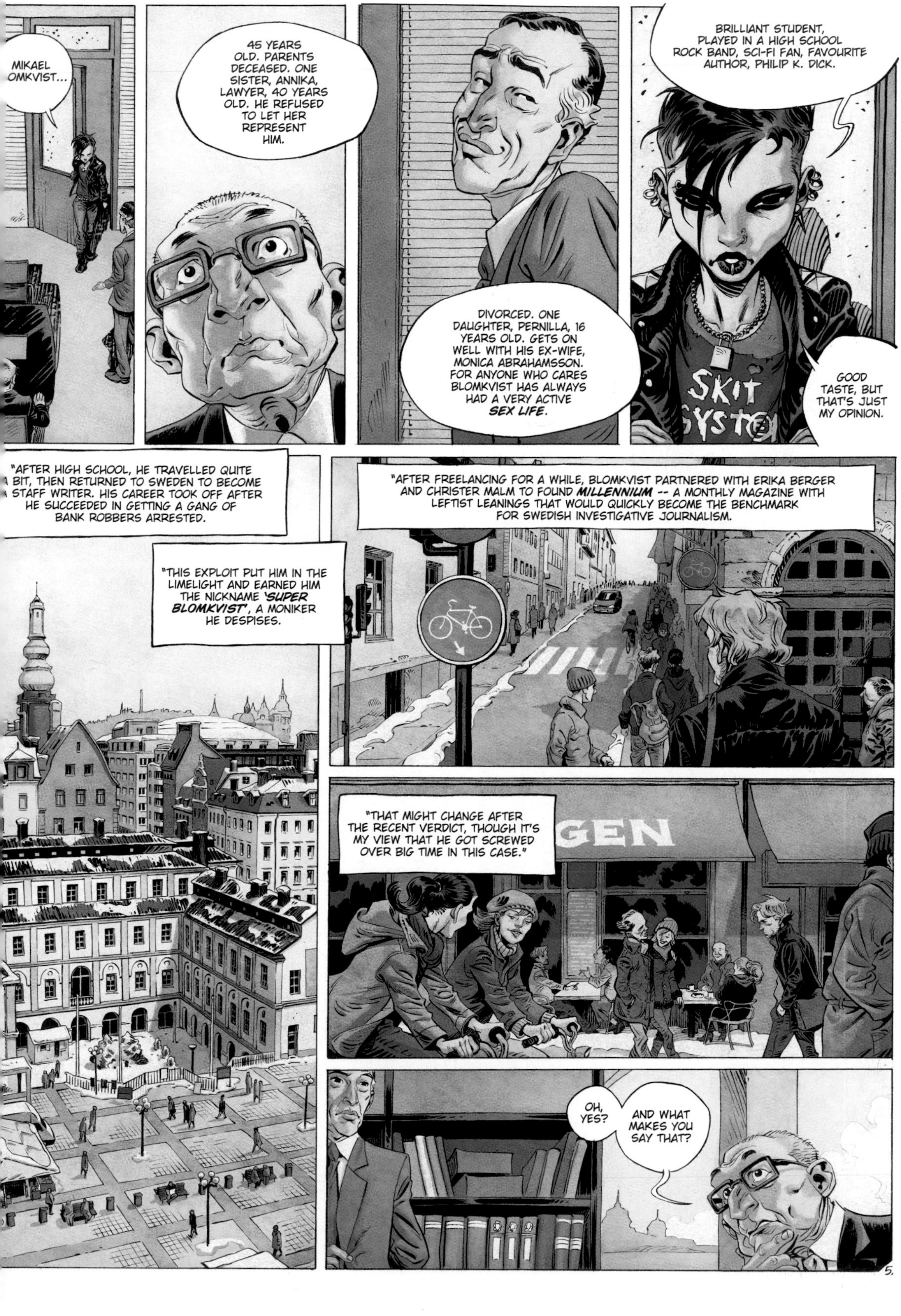
MIKAEL ...OMKVIST...
45 YEARS OLD. PARENTS DECEASED. ONE SISTER, ANNIKA, LAWYER, 40 YEARS OLD. HE REFUSED TO LET HER REPRESENT HIM.
DIVORCED. ONE DAUGHTER, PERNILLA, 16 YEARS OLD. GETS ON WELL WITH HIS EX-WIFE, MONICA ABRAHAMSSON. FOR ANYONE WHO CARES BLOMKVIST HAS ALWAYS HAD A VERY ACTIVE SEX LIFE.
BRILLIANT STUDENT, PLAYED IN A HIGH SCHOOL ROCK BAND, SCI-FI FAN, FAVOURITE AUTHOR, PHILIP K. DICK.
SKIT SYSTE
GOOD TASTE, BUT THAT'S JUST MY OPINION.
"AFTER HIGH SCHOOL, HE TRAVELLED QUITE A BIT, THEN RETURNED TO SWEDEN TO BECOME A STAFF WRITER. HIS CAREER TOOK OFF AFTER HE SUCCEEDED IN GETTING A GANG OF BANK ROBBERS ARRESTED.
"THIS EXPLOIT PUT HIM IN THE LIMELIGHT AND EARNED HIM THE NICKNAME 'SUPER BLOMKVIST', A MONIKER HE DESPISES.
"AFTER FREELANCING FOR A WHILE, BLOMKVIST PARTNERED WITH ERIKA BERGER AND CHRISTER MALM TO FOUND MILLENNIUM -- A MONTHLY MAGAZINE WITH LEFTIST LEANINGS THAT WOULD QUICKLY BECOME THE BENCHMARK FOR SWEDISH INVESTIGATIVE JOURNALISM.
"THAT MIGHT CHANGE AFTER THE RECENT VERDICT, THOUGH IT'S MY VIEW THAT HE GOT SCREWED OVER BIG TIME IN THIS CASE."
GEN
OH, YES?
AND WHAT MAKES YOU SAY THAT?

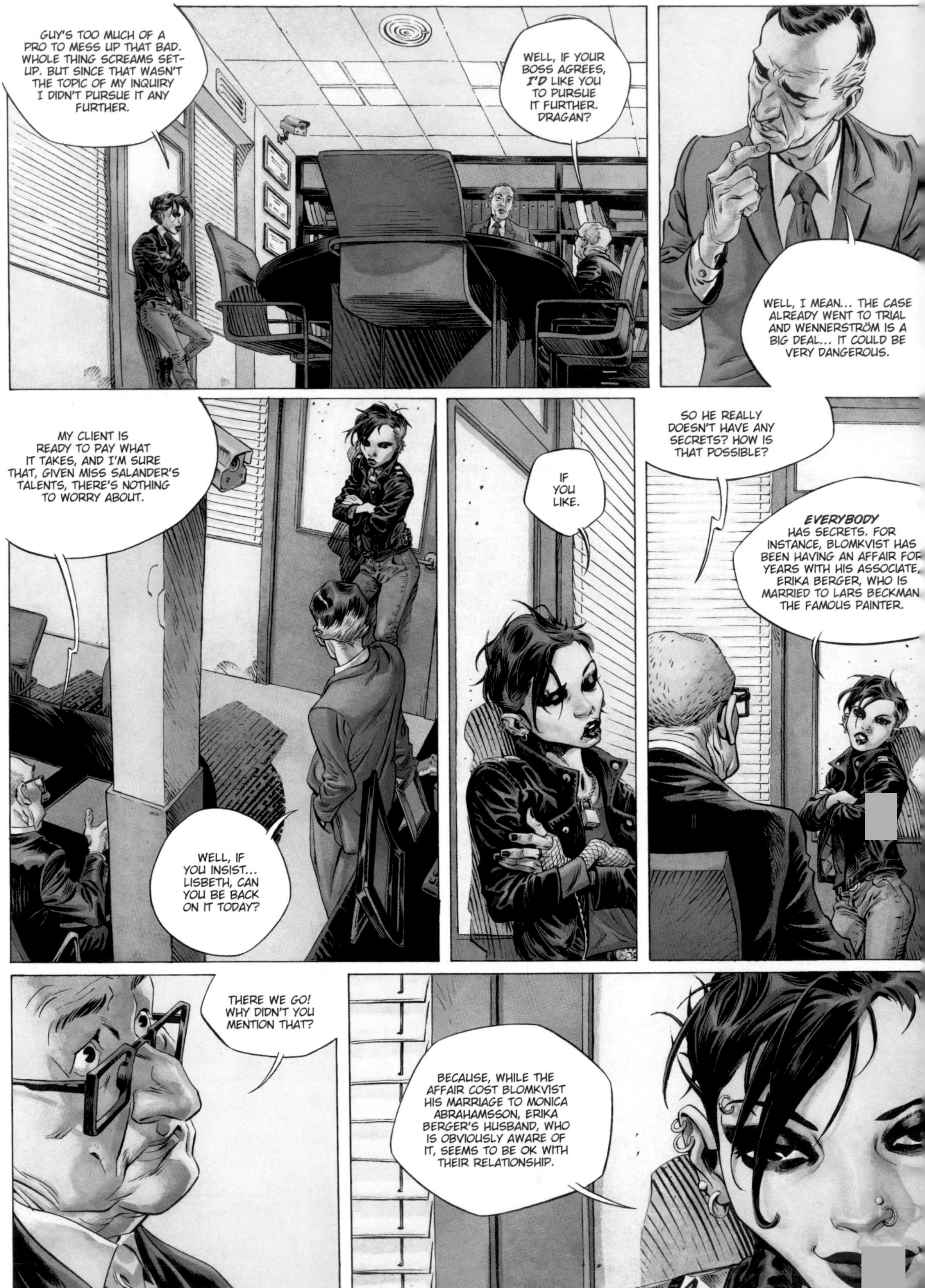

GUY'S TOO MUCH OF A PRO TO MESS UP THAT BAD. WHOLE THING SCREAMS SET-UP. BUT SINCE THAT WASN'T THE TOPIC OF MY INQUIRY I DIDN'T PURSUE IT ANY FURTHER.
WELL, IF YOUR BOSS AGREES, *I'D* LIKE YOU TO PURSUE IT FURTHER. DRAGAN?
WELL, I MEAN... THE CASE ALREADY WENT TO TRIAL AND WENNERSTRÖM IS A BIG DEAL... IT COULD BE VERY DANGEROUS.
MY CLIENT IS READY TO PAY WHAT IT TAKES, AND I'M SURE THAT, GIVEN MISS SALANDER'S TALENTS, THERE'S NOTHING TO WORRY ABOUT.
WELL, IF YOU INSIST... LISBETH, CAN YOU BE BACK ON IT TODAY?
IF YOU LIKE.
SO HE REALLY DOESN'T HAVE ANY SECRETS? HOW IS THAT POSSIBLE?
EVERYBODY HAS SECRETS. FOR INSTANCE, BLOMKVIST HAS BEEN HAVING AN AFFAIR FOR YEARS WITH HIS ASSOCIATE, ERIKA BERGER, WHO IS MARRIED TO LARS BECKMAN THE FAMOUS PAINTER.
THERE WE GO! WHY DIDN'T YOU MENTION THAT?
BECAUSE, WHILE THE AFFAIR COST BLOMKVIST HIS MARRIAGE TO MONICA ABRAHAMSSON, ERIKA BERGER'S HUSBAND, WHO IS OBVIOUSLY AWARE OF IT, SEEMS TO BE OK WITH THEIR RELATIONSHIP.

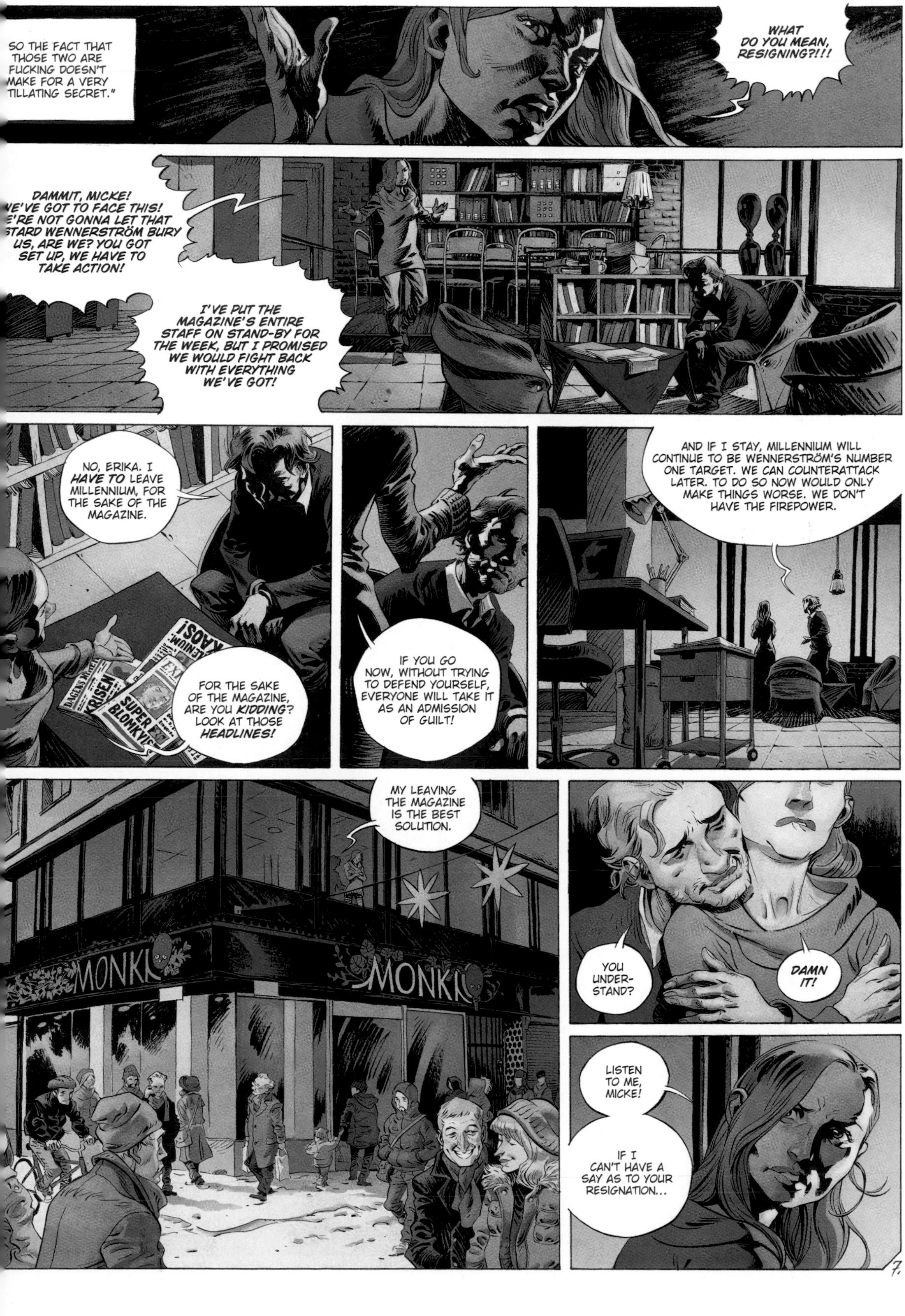
SO THE FACT THAT THOSE TWO ARE FUCKING DOESN'T MAKE FOR A VERY TILLATING SECRET."
WHAT DO YOU MEAN, RESIGNING?!!!
DAMMIT, MICKE! VE'VE GOT TO FACE THIS! E'RE NOT GONNA LET THAT STARD WENNERSTRÖM BURY US, ARE WE? YOU GOT SET UP, WE HAVE TO TAKE ACTION!
I'VE PUT THE MAGAZINE'S ENTIRE STAFF ON STAND-BY FOR THE WEEK, BUT I PROMISED WE WOULD FIGHT BACK WITH EVERYTHING WE'VE GOT!
NO, ERIKA. I HAVE TO LEAVE MILLENNIUM, FOR THE SAKE OF THE MAGAZINE.
FOR THE SAKE OF THE MAGAZINE, ARE YOU KIDDING? LOOK AT THOSE HEADLINES!
KRISEN
SUPER
BLOMKVIS
KAOS!
IF YOU GO NOW, WITHOUT TRYING TO DEFEND YOURSELF, EVERYONE WILL TAKE IT AS AN ADMISSION OF GUILT!
AND IF I STAY, MILLENNIUM WILL CONTINUE TO BE WENNERSTRÖM'S NUMBER ONE TARGET. WE CAN COUNTERATTACK LATER. TO DO SO NOW WOULD ONLY MAKE THINGS WORSE. WE DON'T HAVE THE FIREPOWER.
MY LEAVING THE MAGAZINE IS THE BEST SOLUTION.
MONKI
MONKI
YOU UNDER-STAND?
DAMN IT!
LISTEN TO ME, MICKE!
IF I CAN'T HAVE A SAY AS TO YOUR RESIGNATION...

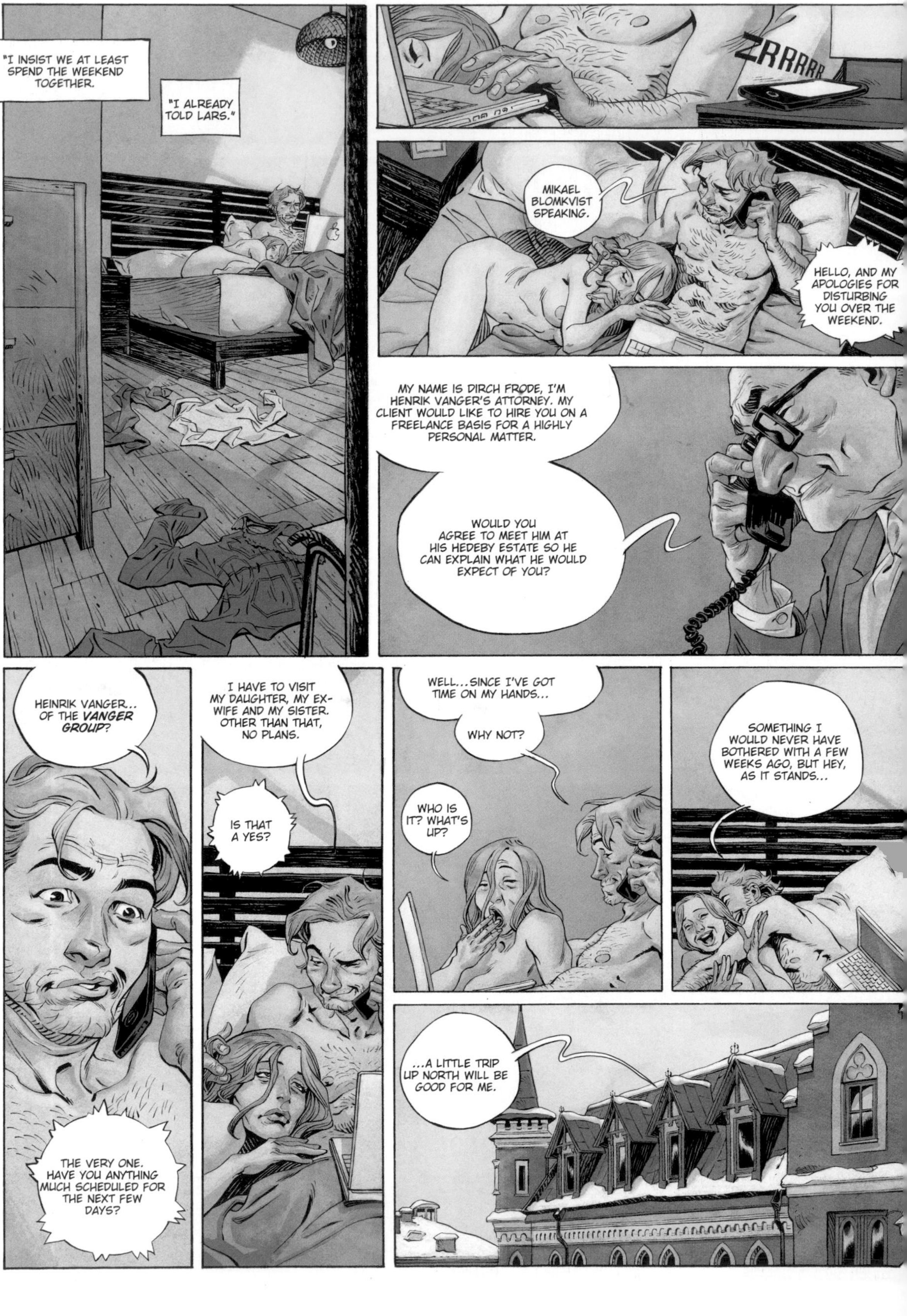
"I INSIST WE AT LEAST SPEND THE WEEKEND TOGETHER.
"I ALREADY TOLD LARS."
ZRRRRR
MIKAEL BLOMKVIST SPEAKING.
HELLO, AND MY APOLOGIES FOR DISTURBING YOU OVER THE WEEKEND.
MY NAME IS DIRCH FRODE, I'M HENRIK VANGER'S ATTORNEY. MY CLIENT WOULD LIKE TO HIRE YOU ON A FREELANCE BASIS FOR A HIGHLY PERSONAL MATTER.
WOULD YOU AGREE TO MEET HIM AT HIS HEDEBY ESTATE SO HE CAN EXPLAIN WHAT HE WOULD EXPECT OF YOU?
HEINRIK VANGER... OF THE ***VANGER GROUP***?
THE VERY ONE. HAVE YOU ANYTHING MUCH SCHEDULED FOR THE NEXT FEW DAYS?
I HAVE TO VISIT MY DAUGHTER, MY EX-WIFE AND MY SISTER. OTHER THAN THAT, NO PLANS.
IS THAT A YES?
WELL... SINCE I'VE GOT TIME ON MY HANDS...
WHY NOT?
WHO IS IT? WHAT'S UP?
SOMETHING I WOULD NEVER HAVE BOTHERED WITH A FEW WEEKS AGO, BUT HEY, AS IT STANDS...
...A LITTLE TRIP UP NORTH WILL BE GOOD FOR ME.

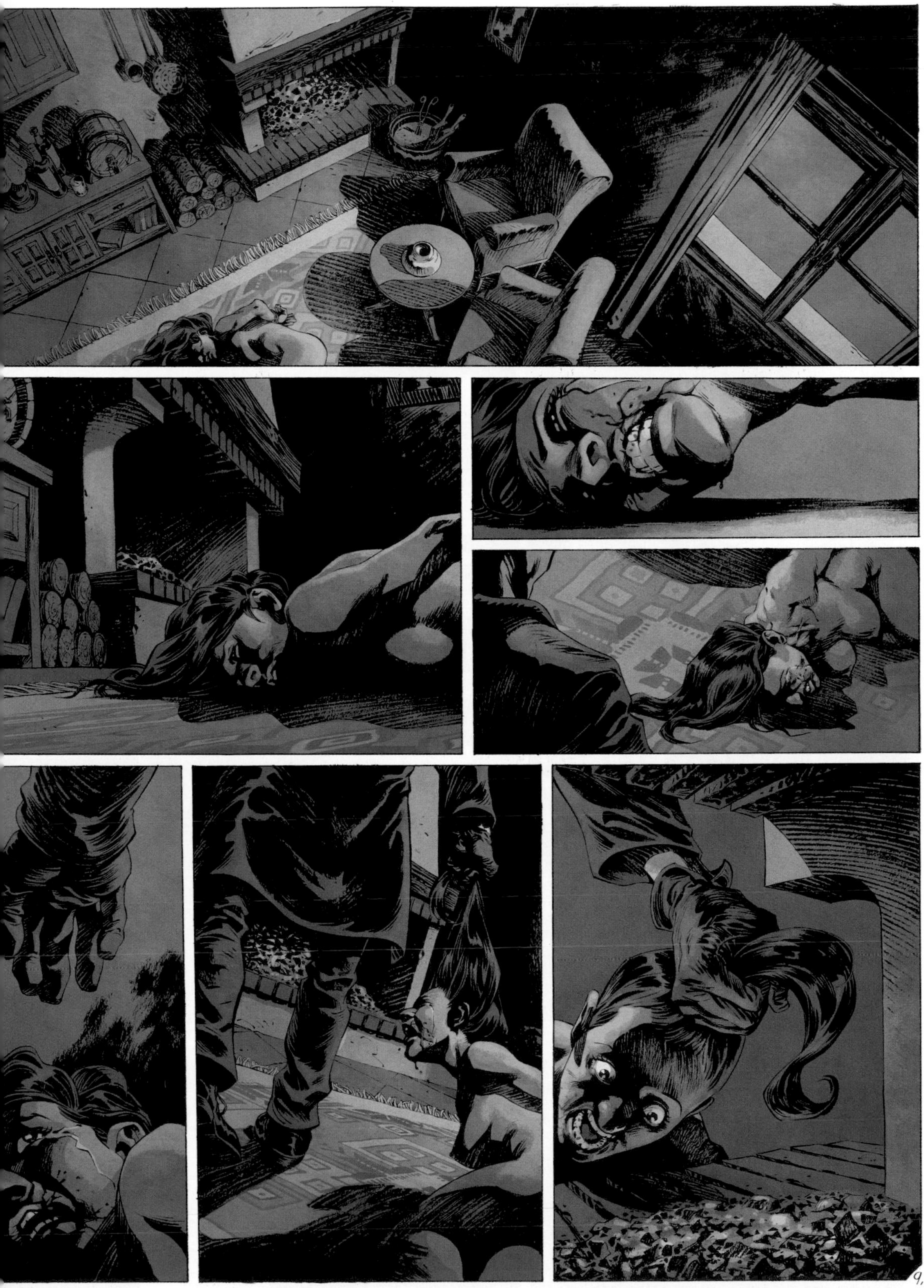

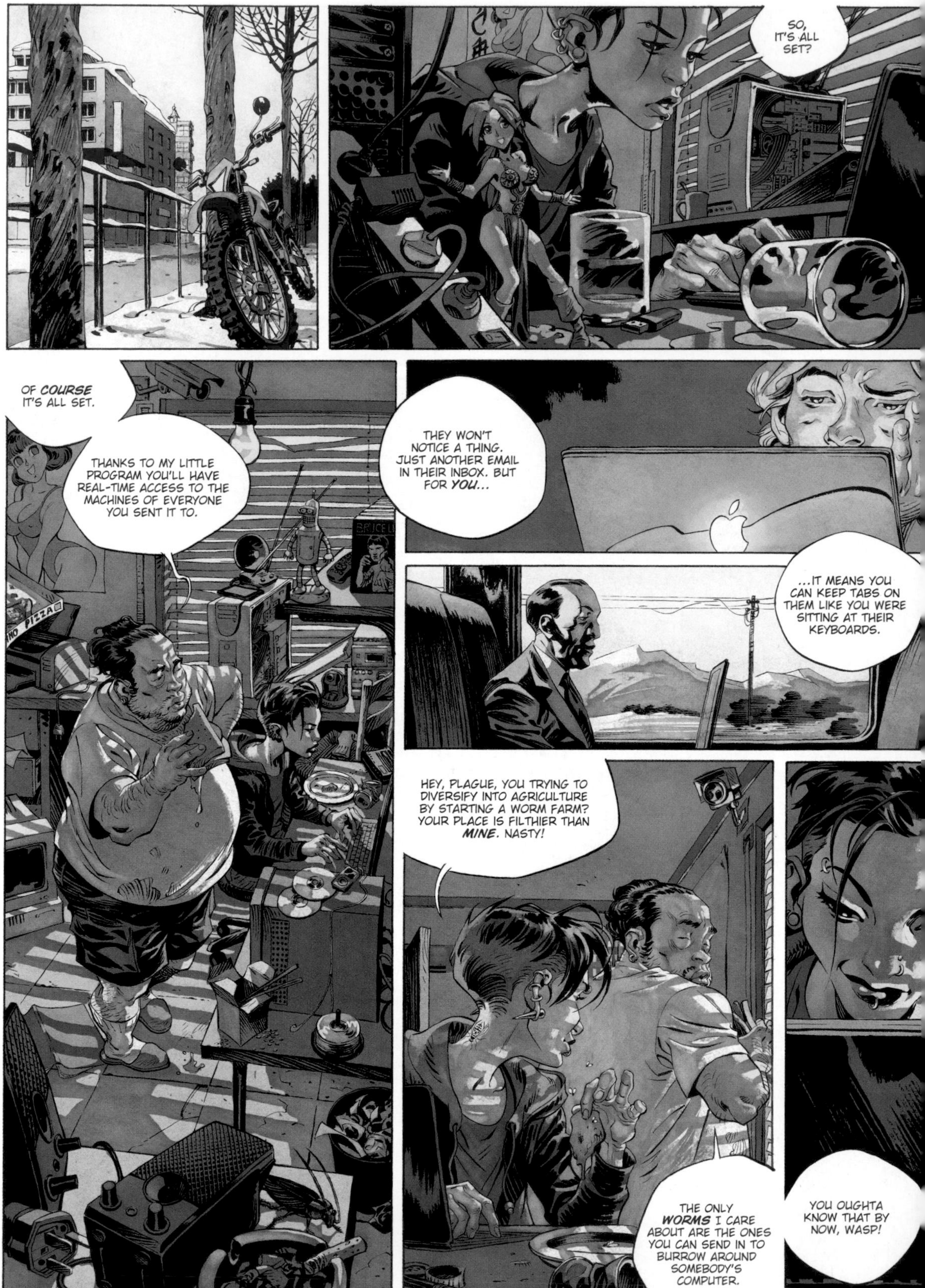
SO, IT'S ALL SET?
OF COURSE IT'S ALL SET.
THANKS TO MY LITTLE PROGRAM YOU'LL HAVE REAL-TIME ACCESS TO THE MACHINES OF EVERYONE YOU SENT IT TO.
THEY WON'T NOTICE A THING. JUST ANOTHER EMAIL IN THEIR INBOX. BUT FOR YOU...
...IT MEANS YOU CAN KEEP TABS ON THEM LIKE YOU WERE SITTING AT THEIR KEYBOARDS.
HEY, PLAGUE, YOU TRYING TO DIVERSIFY INTO AGRICULTURE BY STARTING A WORM FARM? YOUR PLACE IS FILTHIER THAN MINE. NASTY!
THE ONLY WORMS I CARE ABOUT ARE THE ONES YOU CAN SEND IN TO BURROW AROUND SOMEBODY'S COMPUTER.
YOU OUGHTA KNOW THAT BY NOW, WASP!

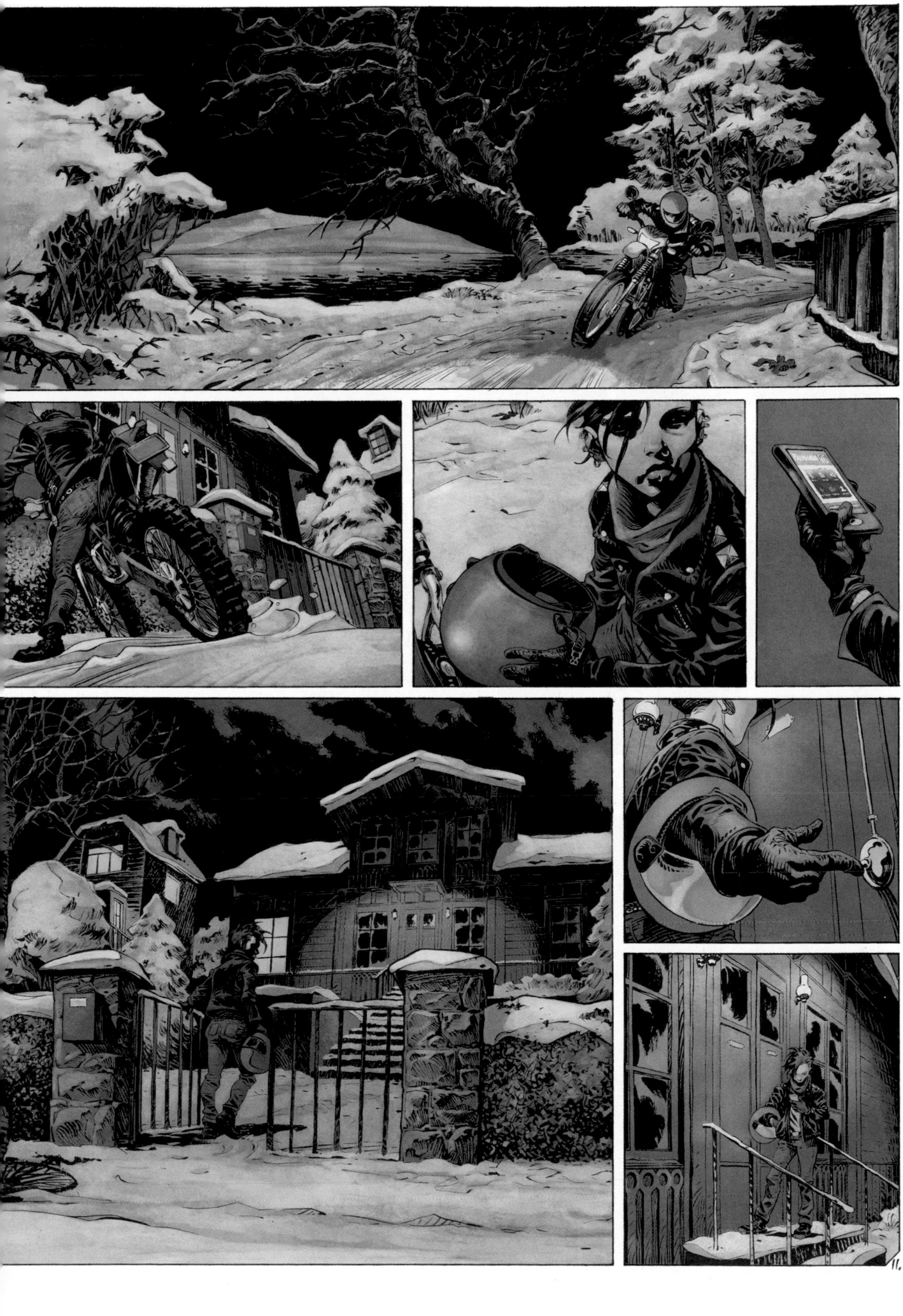

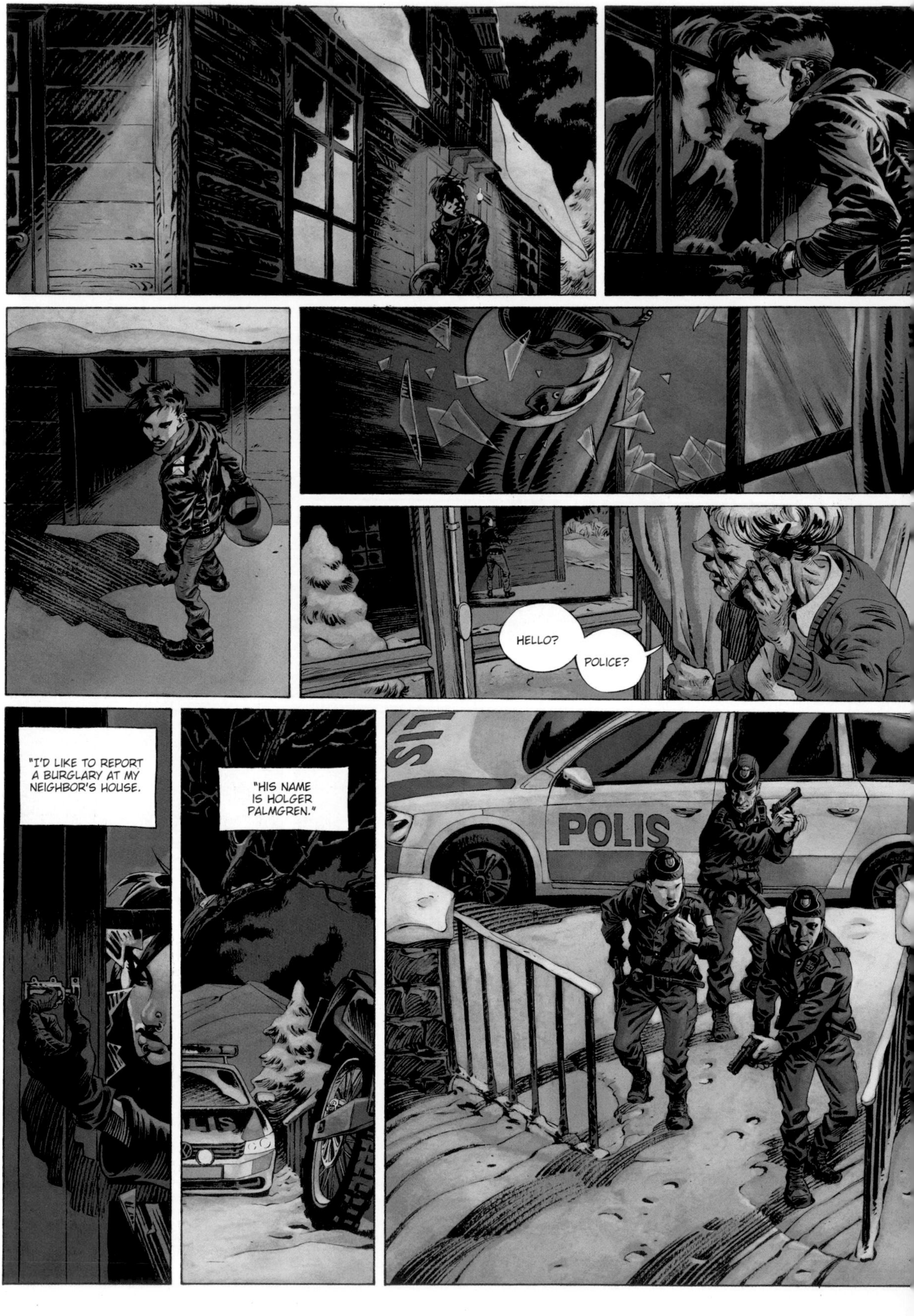
HELLO?
POLICE?
"I'D LIKE TO REPORT A BURGLARY AT MY NEIGHBOR'S HOUSE.
"HIS NAME IS HOLGER PALMGREN."
POLIS

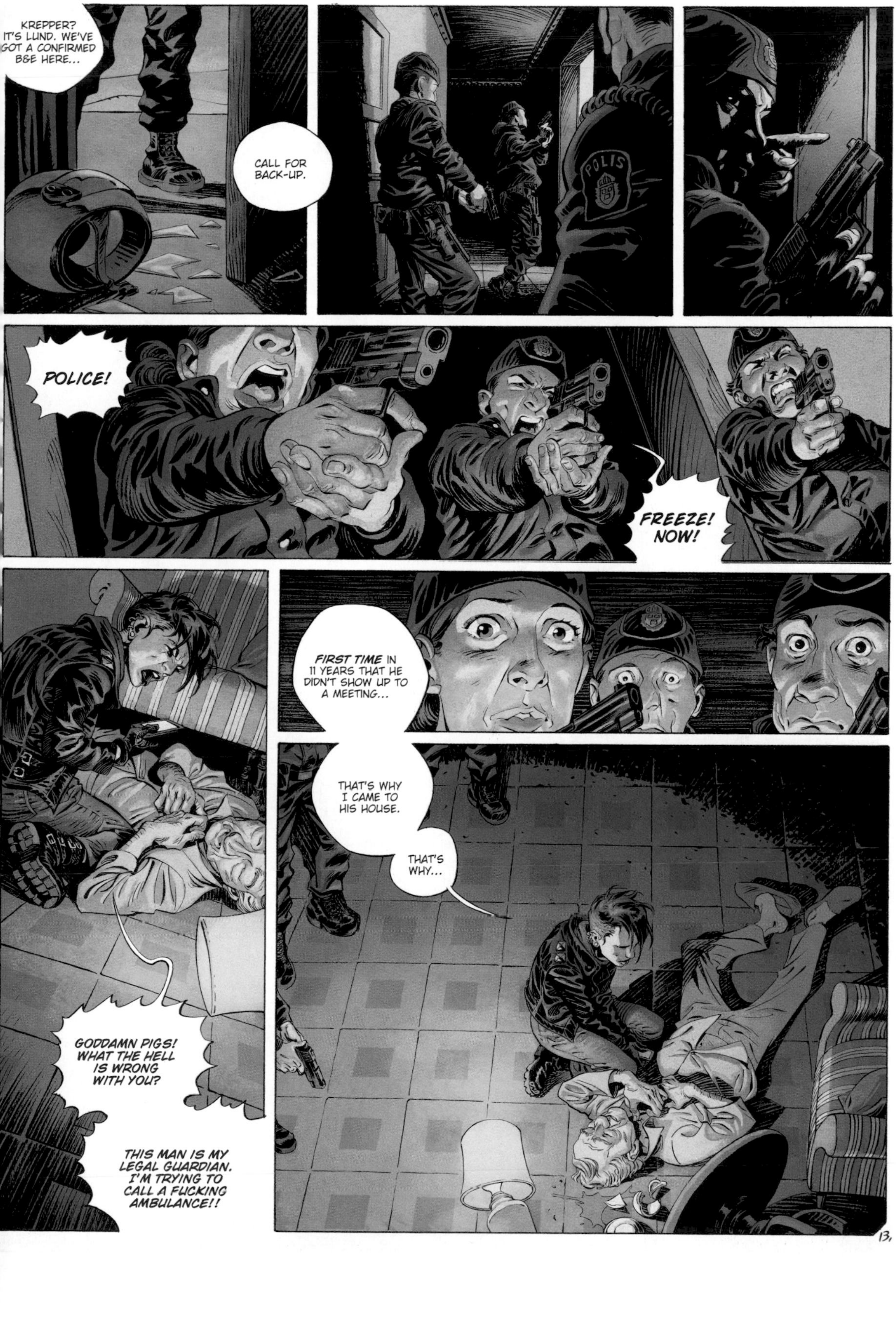
KREPPER? IT'S LUND. WE'VE GOT A CONFIRMED B&E HERE...
CALL FOR BACK-UP.
POLICE!
FREEZE! NOW!
FIRST TIME IN 11 YEARS THAT HE DIDN'T SHOW UP TO A MEETING...
THAT'S WHY I CAME TO HIS HOUSE.
THAT'S WHY...
GODDAMN PIGS! WHAT THE HELL IS WRONG WITH YOU?
THIS MAN IS MY LEGAL GUARDIAN. I'M TRYING TO CALL A FUCKING AMBULANCE!!

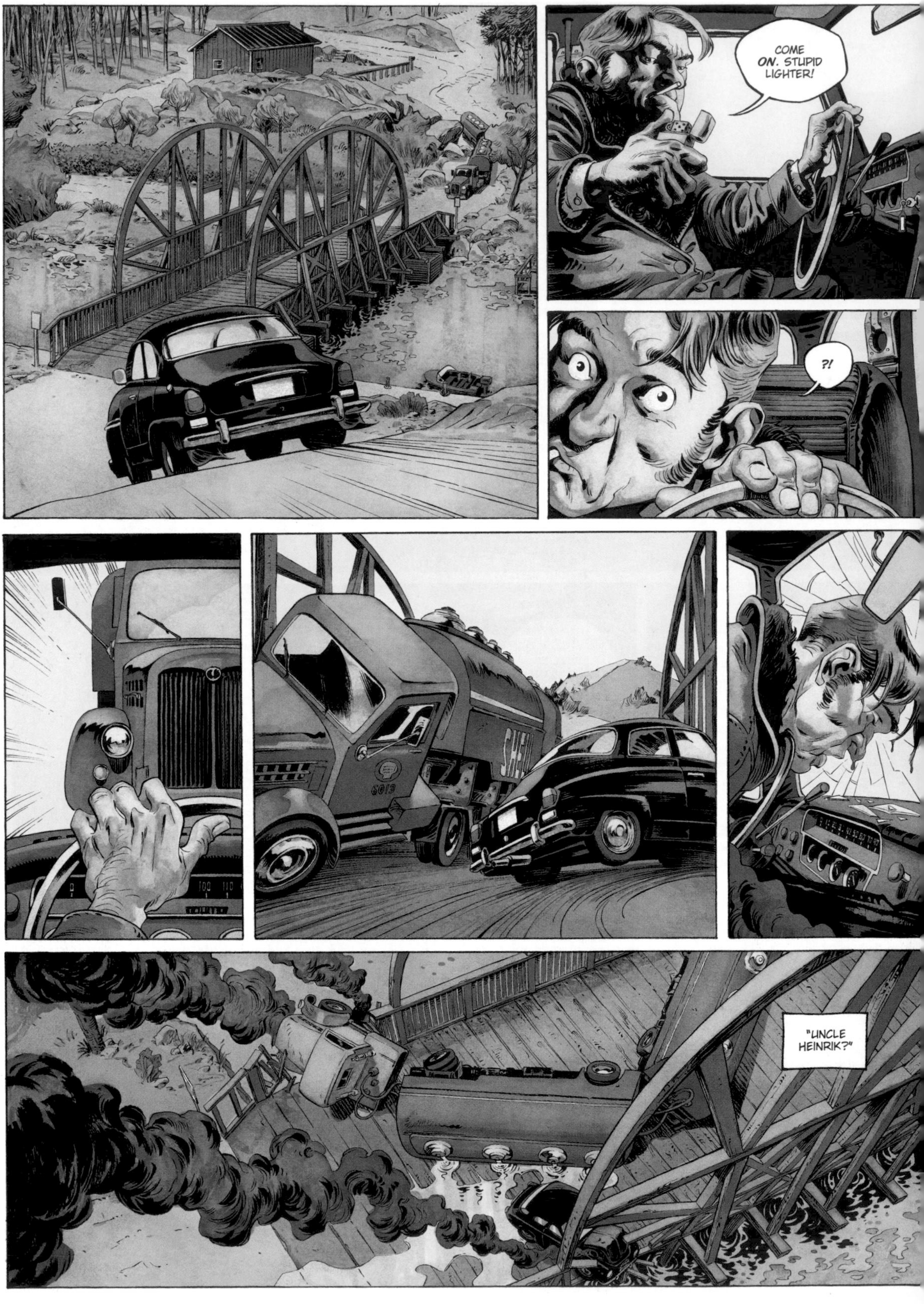
COME ON. STUPID LIGHTER!
?!
"UNCLE HEINRIK?"

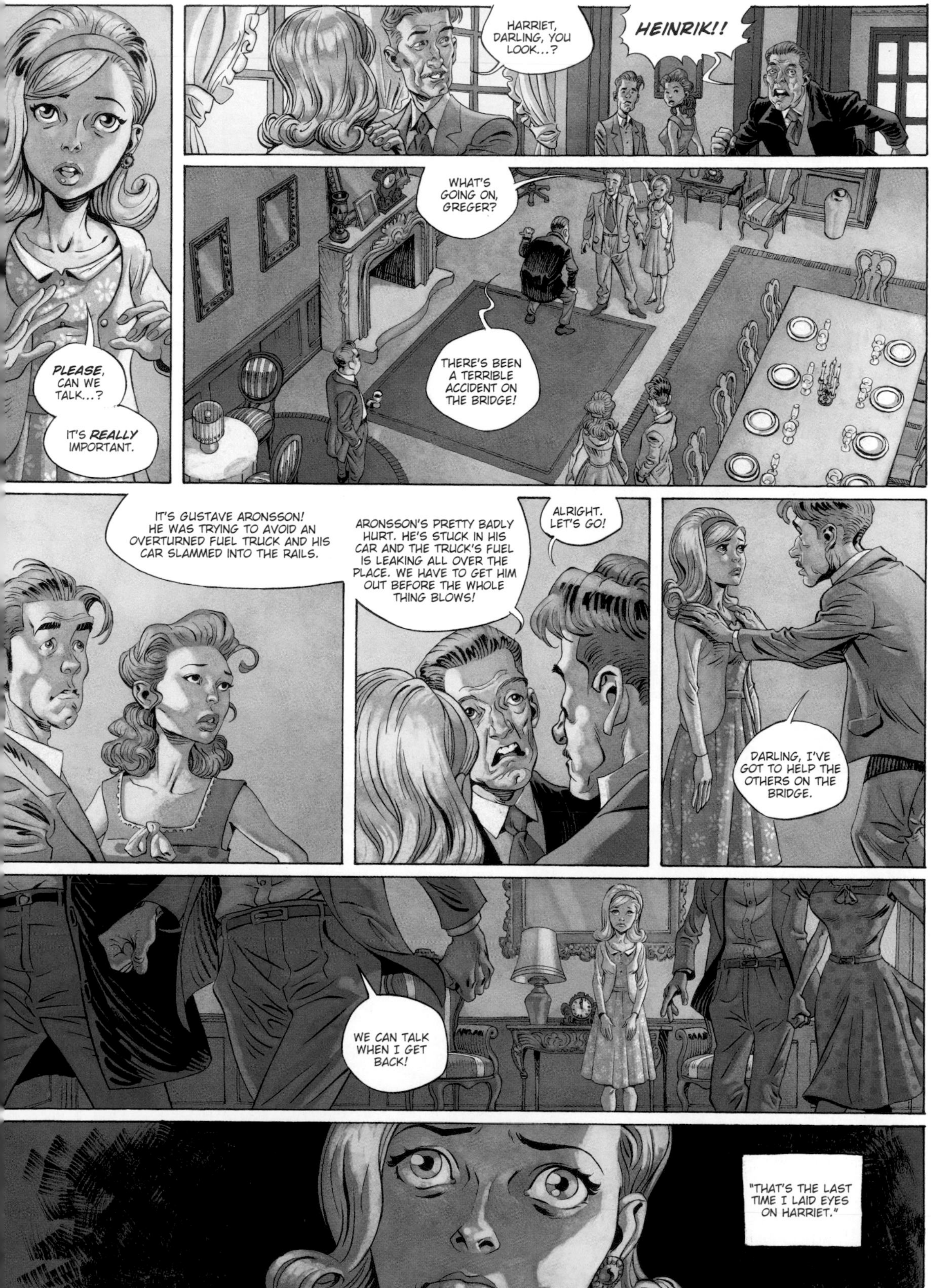
PLEASE, CAN WE TALK...?
IT'S REALLY IMPORTANT.
HARRIET, DARLING, YOU LOOK...?
HEINRIK!!
WHAT'S GOING ON, GREGER?
THERE'S BEEN A TERRIBLE ACCIDENT ON THE BRIDGE!
IT'S GUSTAVE ARONSSON! HE WAS TRYING TO AVOID AN OVERTURNED FUEL TRUCK AND HIS CAR SLAMMED INTO THE RAILS.
ARONSSON'S PRETTY BADLY HURT. HE'S STUCK IN HIS CAR AND THE TRUCK'S FUEL IS LEAKING ALL OVER THE PLACE. WE HAVE TO GET HIM OUT BEFORE THE WHOLE THING BLOWS!
ALRIGHT. LET'S GO!
DARLING, I'VE GOT TO HELP THE OTHERS ON THE BRIDGE.
WE CAN TALK WHEN I GET BACK!
"THAT'S THE LAST TIME I LAID EYES ON HARRIET."

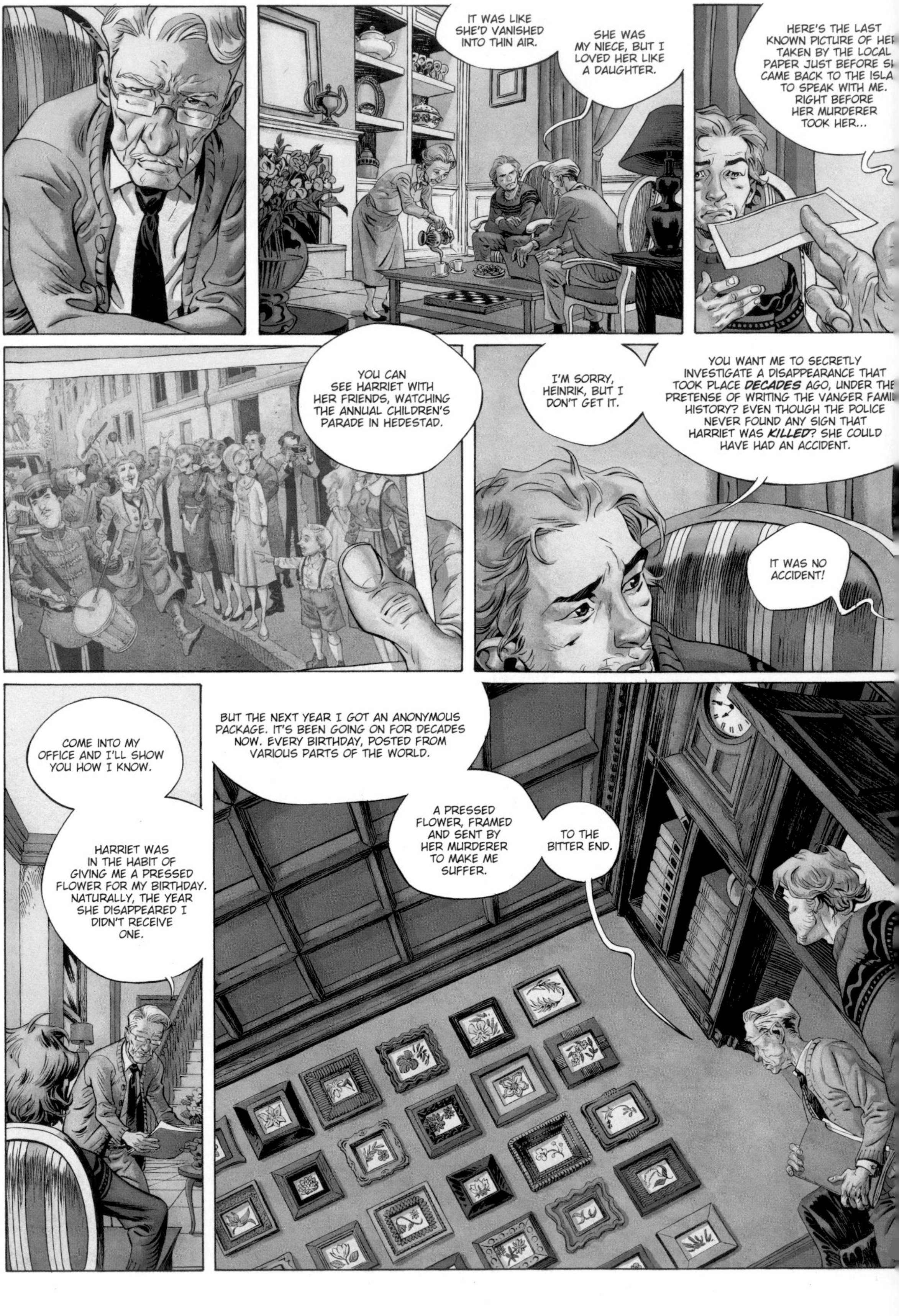
IT WAS LIKE SHE'D VANISHED INTO THIN AIR.
SHE WAS MY NIECE, BUT I LOVED HER LIKE A DAUGHTER.
HERE'S THE LAST KNOWN PICTURE OF HE[R] TAKEN BY THE LOCAL PAPER JUST BEFORE S[HE] CAME BACK TO THE ISLA[ND] TO SPEAK WITH ME. RIGHT BEFORE HER MURDERER TOOK HER...
YOU CAN SEE HARRIET WITH HER FRIENDS, WATCHING THE ANNUAL CHILDREN'S PARADE IN HEDESTAD.
I'M SORRY, HEINRIK, BUT I DON'T GET IT.
YOU WANT ME TO SECRETLY INVESTIGATE A DISAPPEARANCE THAT TOOK PLACE ***DECADES*** AGO, UNDER THE PRETENSE OF WRITING THE VANGER FAMI[LY] HISTORY? EVEN THOUGH THE POLICE NEVER FOUND ANY SIGN THAT HARRIET WAS ***KILLED***? SHE COULD HAVE HAD AN ACCIDENT.
IT WAS NO ACCIDENT!
COME INTO MY OFFICE AND I'LL SHOW YOU HOW I KNOW.
HARRIET WAS IN THE HABIT OF GIVING ME A PRESSED FLOWER FOR MY BIRTHDAY. NATURALLY, THE YEAR SHE DISAPPEARED I DIDN'T RECEIVE ONE.
BUT THE NEXT YEAR I GOT AN ANONYMOUS PACKAGE. IT'S BEEN GOING ON FOR DECADES NOW. EVERY BIRTHDAY, POSTED FROM VARIOUS PARTS OF THE WORLD.
A PRESSED FLOWER, FRAMED AND SENT BY HER MURDERER TO MAKE ME SUFFER.
TO THE BITTER END.

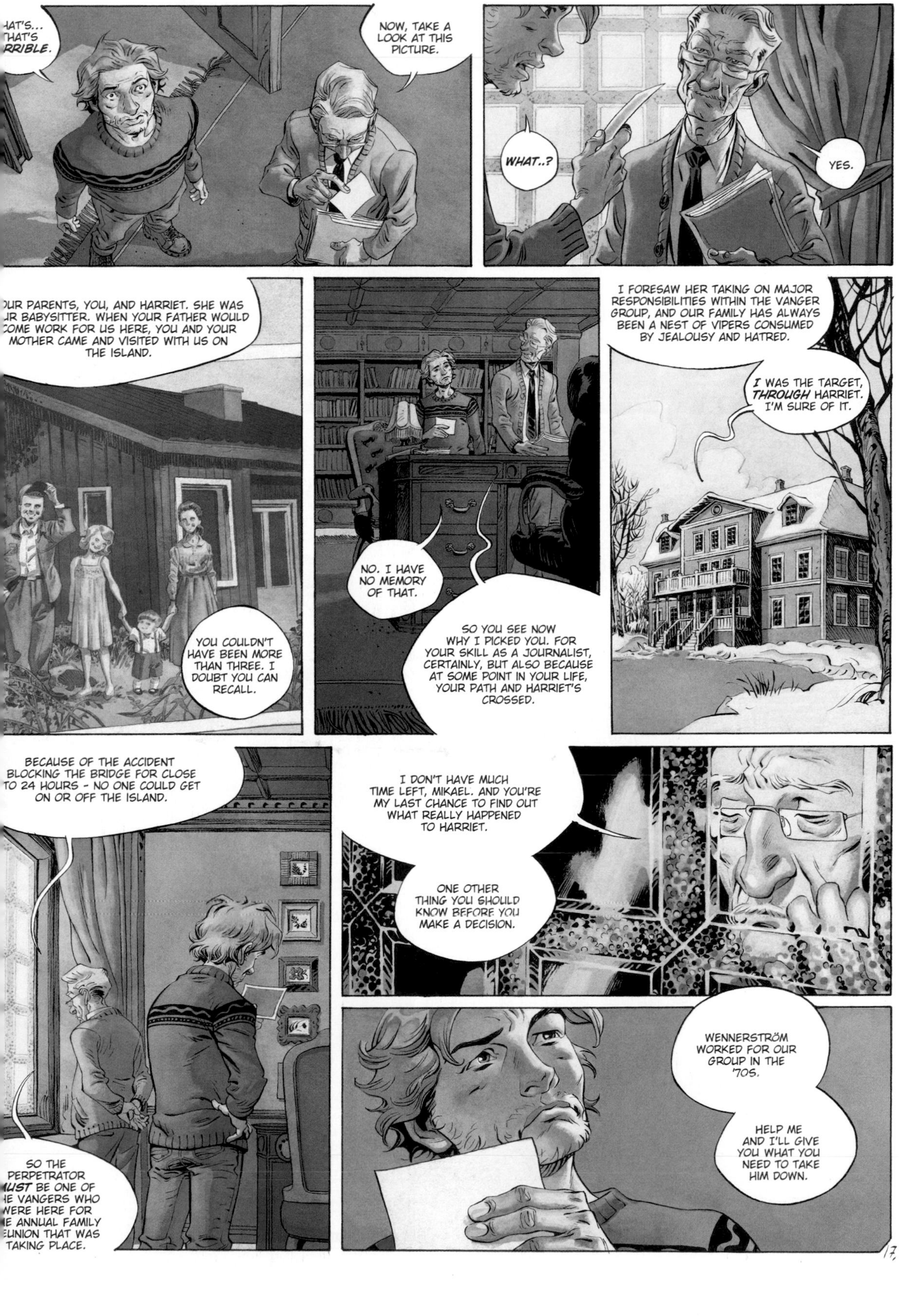
HAT'S... THAT'S RRIBLE.
NOW, TAKE A LOOK AT THIS PICTURE.
WHAT..?
YES.
OUR PARENTS, YOU, AND HARRIET. SHE WAS UR BABYSITTER. WHEN YOUR FATHER WOULD COME WORK FOR US HERE, YOU AND YOUR MOTHER CAME AND VISITED WITH US ON THE ISLAND.
YOU COULDN'T HAVE BEEN MORE THAN THREE. I DOUBT YOU CAN RECALL.
NO. I HAVE NO MEMORY OF THAT.
SO YOU SEE NOW WHY I PICKED YOU. FOR YOUR SKILL AS A JOURNALIST, CERTAINLY, BUT ALSO BECAUSE AT SOME POINT IN YOUR LIFE, YOUR PATH AND HARRIET'S CROSSED.
I FORESAW HER TAKING ON MAJOR RESPONSIBILITIES WITHIN THE VANGER GROUP, AND OUR FAMILY HAS ALWAYS BEEN A NEST OF VIPERS CONSUMED BY JEALOUSY AND HATRED.
I WAS THE TARGET, THROUGH HARRIET. I'M SURE OF IT.
BECAUSE OF THE ACCIDENT BLOCKING THE BRIDGE FOR CLOSE TO 24 HOURS - NO ONE COULD GET ON OR OFF THE ISLAND.
SO THE PERPETRATOR UST BE ONE OF E VANGERS WHO WERE HERE FOR E ANNUAL FAMILY EUNION THAT WAS TAKING PLACE.
I DON'T HAVE MUCH TIME LEFT, MIKAEL. AND YOU'RE MY LAST CHANCE TO FIND OUT WHAT REALLY HAPPENED TO HARRIET.
ONE OTHER THING YOU SHOULD KNOW BEFORE YOU MAKE A DECISION.
WENNERSTRÖM WORKED FOR OUR GROUP IN THE '70S.
HELP ME AND I'LL GIVE YOU WHAT YOU NEED TO TAKE HIM DOWN.

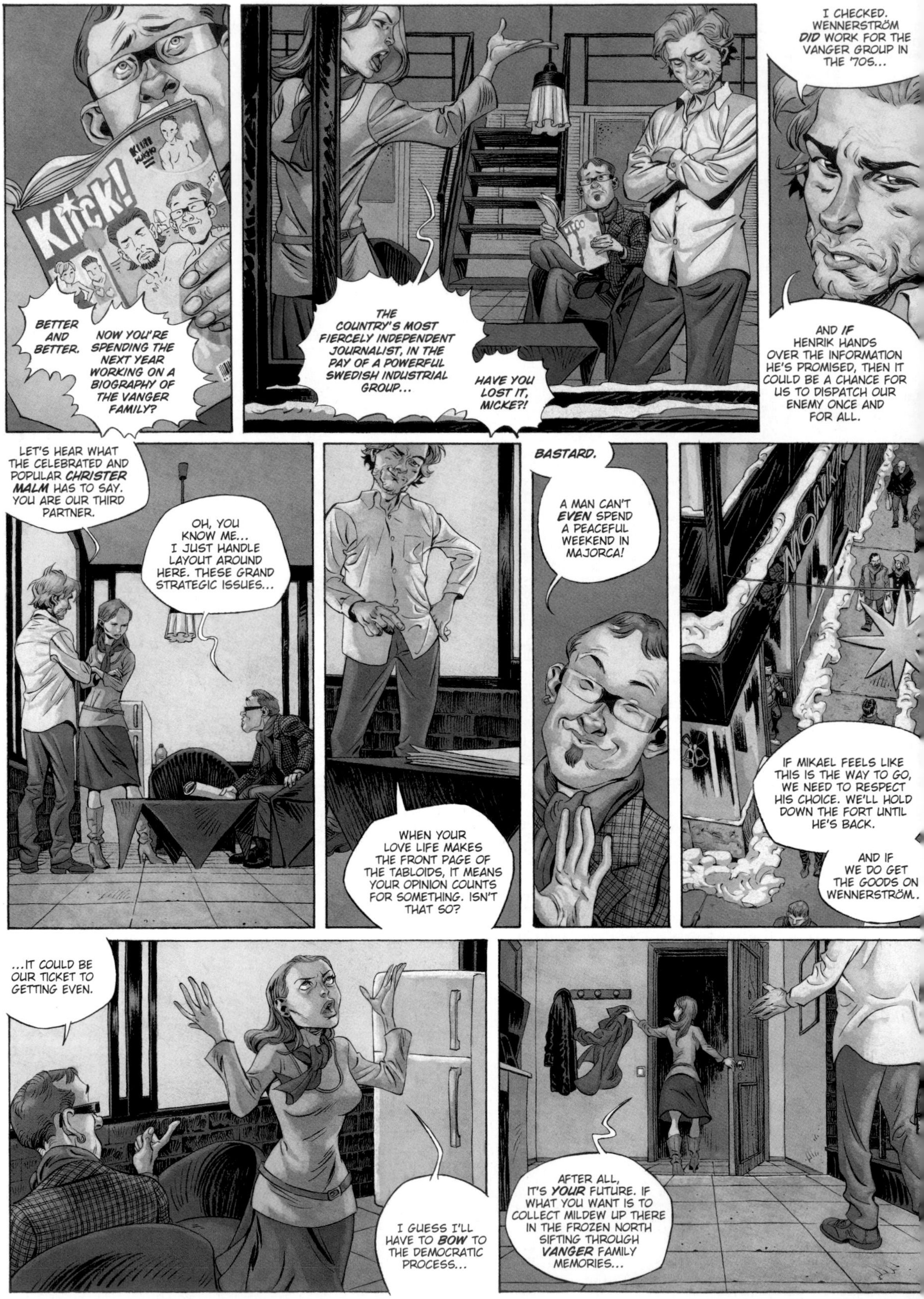
KICK!
BETTER AND BETTER.
NOW YOU'RE SPENDING THE NEXT YEAR WORKING ON A BIOGRAPHY OF THE VANGER FAMILY?
THE COUNTRY'S MOST FIERCELY INDEPENDENT JOURNALIST, IN THE PAY OF A POWERFUL SWEDISH INDUSTRIAL GROUP...
HAVE YOU LOST IT, MICKE?!
I CHECKED. WENNERSTRÖM DID WORK FOR THE VANGER GROUP IN THE '70S...
AND IF HENRIK HANDS OVER THE INFORMATION HE'S PROMISED, THEN IT COULD BE A CHANCE FOR US TO DISPATCH OUR ENEMY ONCE AND FOR ALL.
LET'S HEAR WHAT THE CELEBRATED AND POPULAR CHRISTER MALM HAS TO SAY. YOU ARE OUR THIRD PARTNER.
OH, YOU KNOW ME... I JUST HANDLE LAYOUT AROUND HERE. THESE GRAND STRATEGIC ISSUES...
WHEN YOUR LOVE LIFE MAKES THE FRONT PAGE OF THE TABLOIDS, IT MEANS YOUR OPINION COUNTS FOR SOMETHING. ISN'T THAT SO?
BASTARD.
A MAN CAN'T EVEN SPEND A PEACEFUL WEEKEND IN MAJORCA!
IF MIKAEL FEELS LIKE THIS IS THE WAY TO GO, WE NEED TO RESPECT HIS CHOICE. WE'LL HOLD DOWN THE FORT UNTIL HE'S BACK.
AND IF WE DO GET THE GOODS ON WENNERSTRÖM...
...IT COULD BE OUR TICKET TO GETTING EVEN.
I GUESS I'LL HAVE TO BOW TO THE DEMOCRATIC PROCESS...
AFTER ALL, IT'S YOUR FUTURE. IF WHAT YOU WANT IS TO COLLECT MILDEW UP THERE IN THE FROZEN NORTH SIFTING THROUGH VANGER FAMILY MEMORIES...

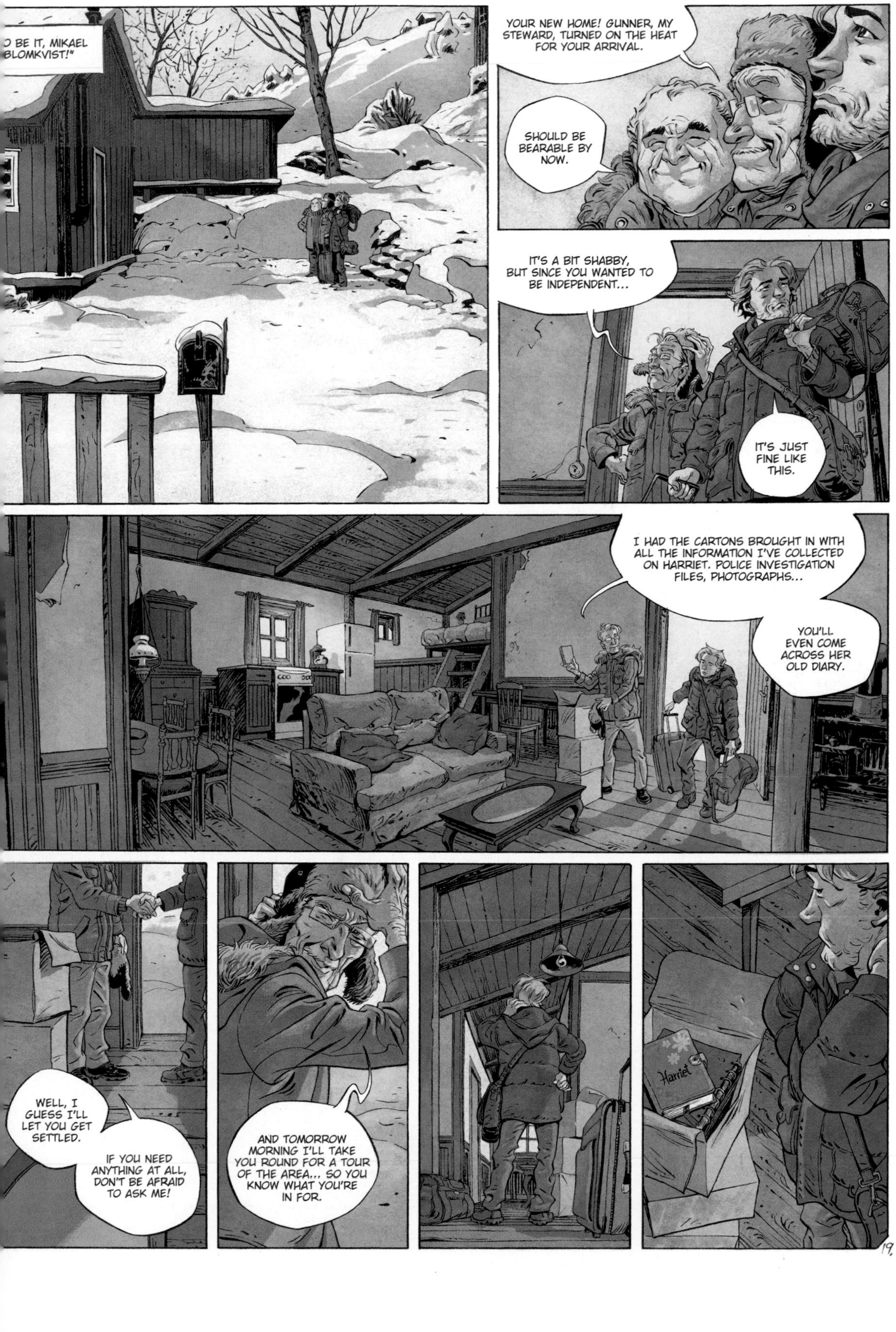
O BE IT, MIKAEL BLOMKVIST!"
YOUR NEW HOME! GUNNER, MY STEWARD, TURNED ON THE HEAT FOR YOUR ARRIVAL.
SHOULD BE BEARABLE BY NOW.
IT'S A BIT SHABBY, BUT SINCE YOU WANTED TO BE INDEPENDENT...
IT'S JUST FINE LIKE THIS.
I HAD THE CARTONS BROUGHT IN WITH ALL THE INFORMATION I'VE COLLECTED ON HARRIET. POLICE INVESTIGATION FILES, PHOTOGRAPHS...
YOU'LL EVEN COME ACROSS HER OLD DIARY.
WELL, I GUESS I'LL LET YOU GET SETTLED.
IF YOU NEED ANYTHING AT ALL, DON'T BE AFRAID TO ASK ME!
AND TOMORROW MORNING I'LL TAKE YOU ROUND FOR A TOUR OF THE AREA... SO YOU KNOW WHAT YOU'RE IN FOR.
Harriet

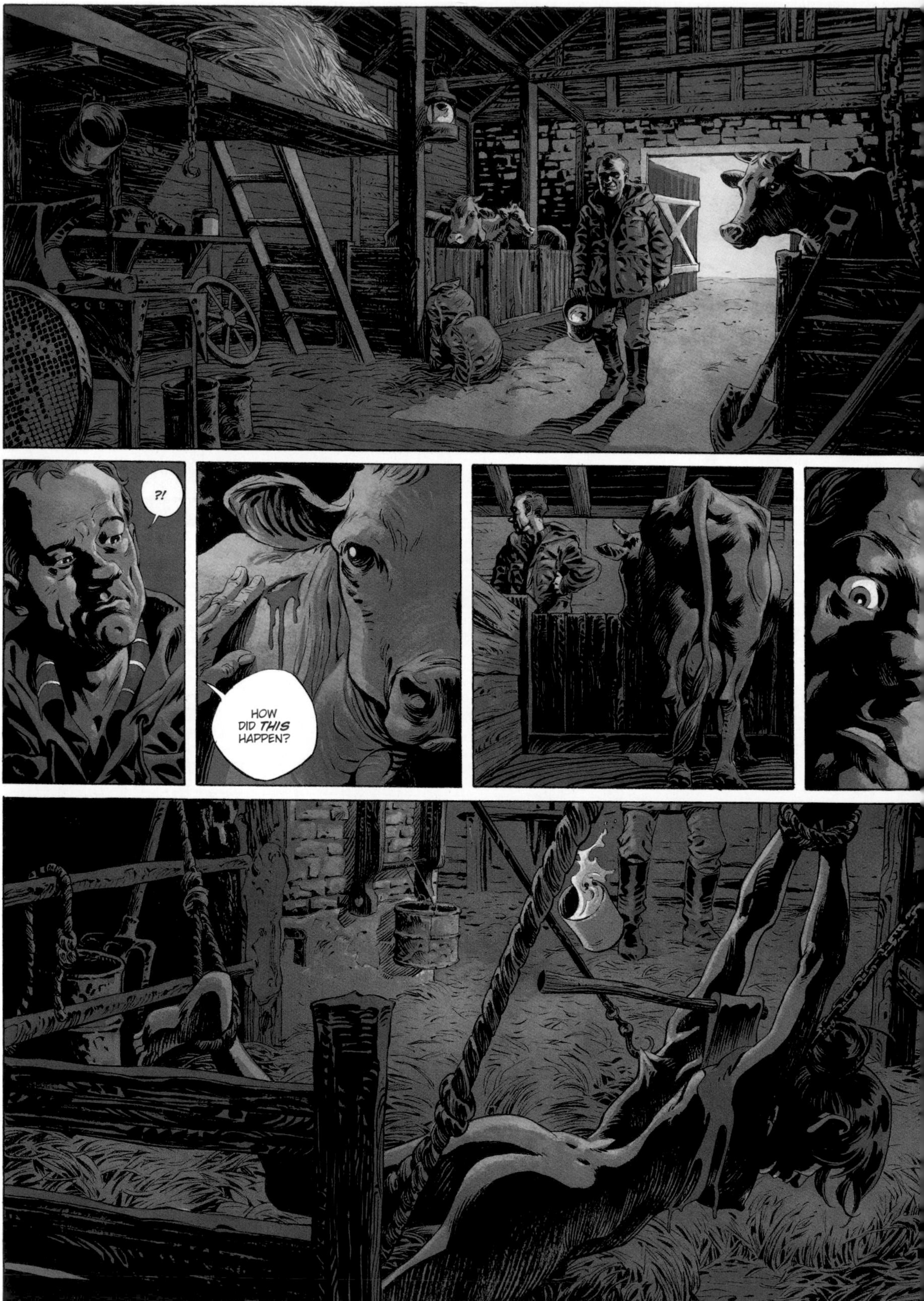

?!
HOW DID THIS HAPPEN?

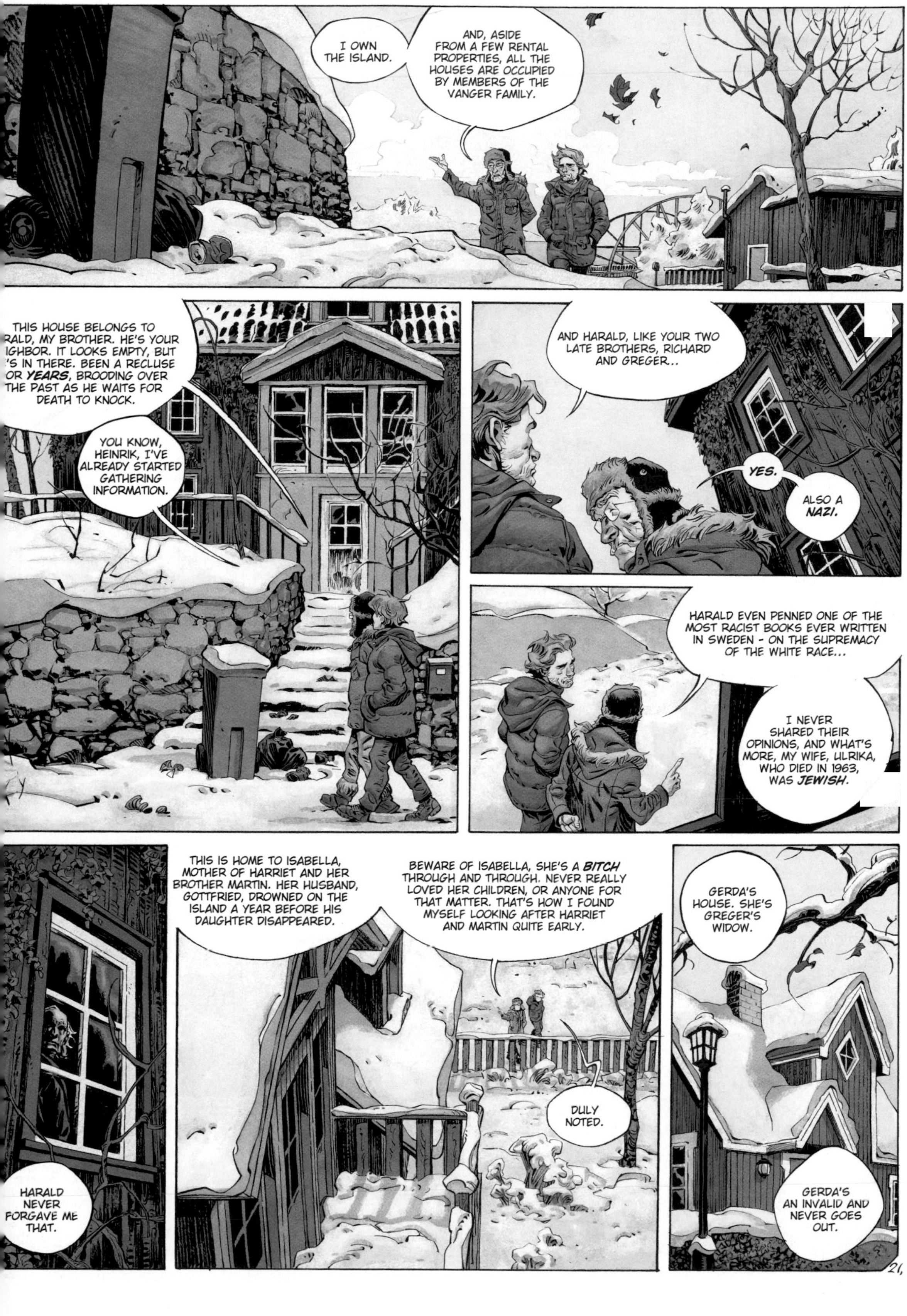
I OWN THE ISLAND.
AND, ASIDE FROM A FEW RENTAL PROPERTIES, ALL THE HOUSES ARE OCCUPIED BY MEMBERS OF THE VANGER FAMILY.
THIS HOUSE BELONGS TO RALD, MY BROTHER. HE'S YOUR IGHBOR. IT LOOKS EMPTY, BUT 'S IN THERE. BEEN A RECLUSE OR *YEARS*, BROODING OVER THE PAST AS HE WAITS FOR DEATH TO KNOCK.
YOU KNOW, HEINRIK, I'VE ALREADY STARTED GATHERING INFORMATION.
AND HARALD, LIKE YOUR TWO LATE BROTHERS, RICHARD AND GREGER...
YES.
ALSO A *NAZI.*
HARALD EVEN PENNED ONE OF THE MOST RACIST BOOKS EVER WRITTEN IN SWEDEN - ON THE SUPREMACY OF THE WHITE RACE...
I NEVER SHARED THEIR OPINIONS, AND WHAT'S MORE, MY WIFE, ULRIKA, WHO DIED IN 1963, WAS *JEWISH*.
HARALD NEVER FORGAVE ME THAT.
THIS IS HOME TO ISABELLA, MOTHER OF HARRIET AND HER BROTHER MARTIN. HER HUSBAND, GOTTFRIED, DROWNED ON THE ISLAND A YEAR BEFORE HIS DAUGHTER DISAPPEARED.
BEWARE OF ISABELLA, SHE'S A *BITCH* THROUGH AND THROUGH. NEVER REALLY LOVED HER CHILDREN, OR ANYONE FOR THAT MATTER. THAT'S HOW I FOUND MYSELF LOOKING AFTER HARRIET AND MARTIN QUITE EARLY.
DULY NOTED.
GERDA'S HOUSE. SHE'S GREGER'S WIDOW.
GERDA'S AN INVALID AND NEVER GOES OUT.

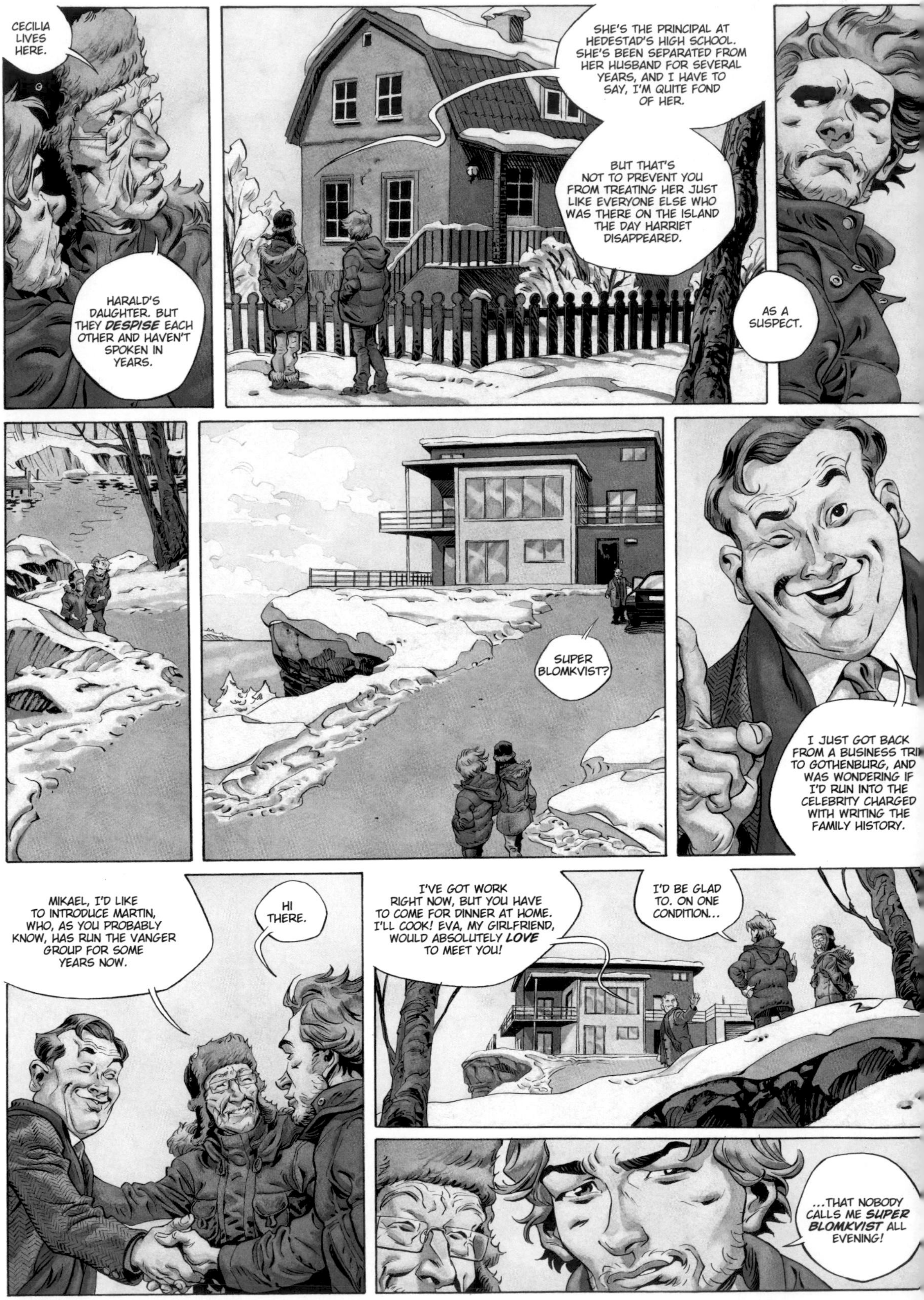

CECILIA LIVES HERE.
HARALD'S DAUGHTER. BUT THEY *DESPISE* EACH OTHER AND HAVEN'T SPOKEN IN YEARS.
SHE'S THE PRINCIPAL AT HEDESTAD'S HIGH SCHOOL. SHE'S BEEN SEPARATED FROM HER HUSBAND FOR SEVERAL YEARS, AND I HAVE TO SAY, I'M QUITE FOND OF HER.
BUT THAT'S NOT TO PREVENT YOU FROM TREATING HER JUST LIKE EVERYONE ELSE WHO WAS THERE ON THE ISLAND THE DAY HARRIET DISAPPEARED.
AS A SUSPECT.
SUPER BLOMKVIST?
I JUST GOT BACK FROM A BUSINESS TRI TO GOTHENBURG, AND WAS WONDERING IF I'D RUN INTO THE CELEBRITY CHARGED WITH WRITING THE FAMILY HISTORY.
MIKAEL, I'D LIKE TO INTRODUCE MARTIN, WHO, AS YOU PROBABLY KNOW, HAS RUN THE VANGER GROUP FOR SOME YEARS NOW.
HI THERE.
I'VE GOT WORK RIGHT NOW, BUT YOU HAVE TO COME FOR DINNER AT HOME. I'LL COOK! EVA, MY GIRLFRIEND, WOULD ABSOLUTELY *LOVE* TO MEET YOU!
I'D BE GLAD TO. ON ONE CONDITION...
...THAT NOBODY CALLS ME *SUPER BLOMKVIST* ALL EVENING!

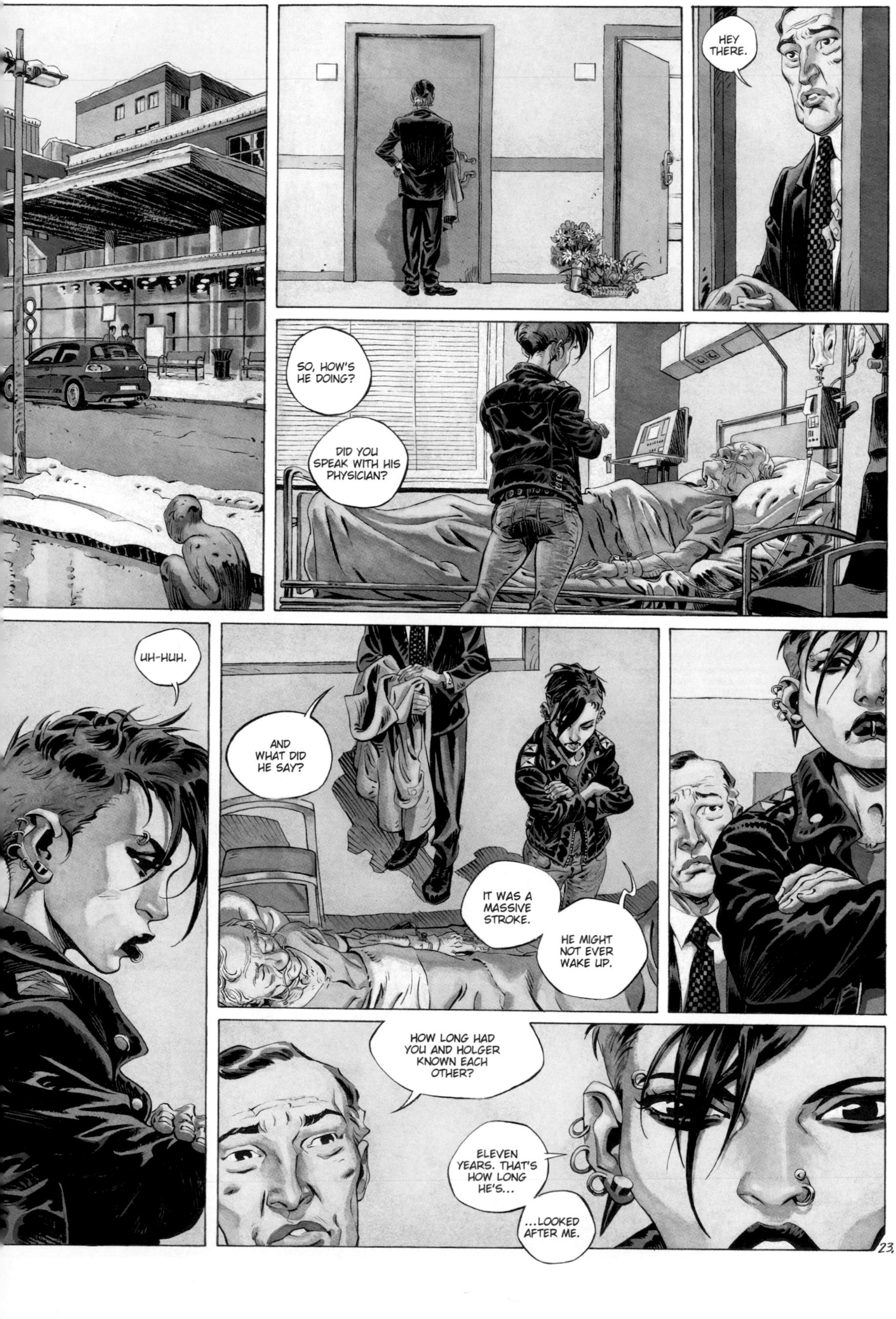
HEY THERE.
SO, HOW'S HE DOING?
DID YOU SPEAK WITH HIS PHYSICIAN?
UH-HUH.
AND WHAT DID HE SAY?
IT WAS A MASSIVE STROKE.
HE MIGHT NOT EVER WAKE UP.
HOW LONG HAD YOU AND HOLGER KNOWN EACH OTHER?
ELEVEN YEARS. THAT'S HOW LONG HE'S...
...LOOKED AFTER ME.

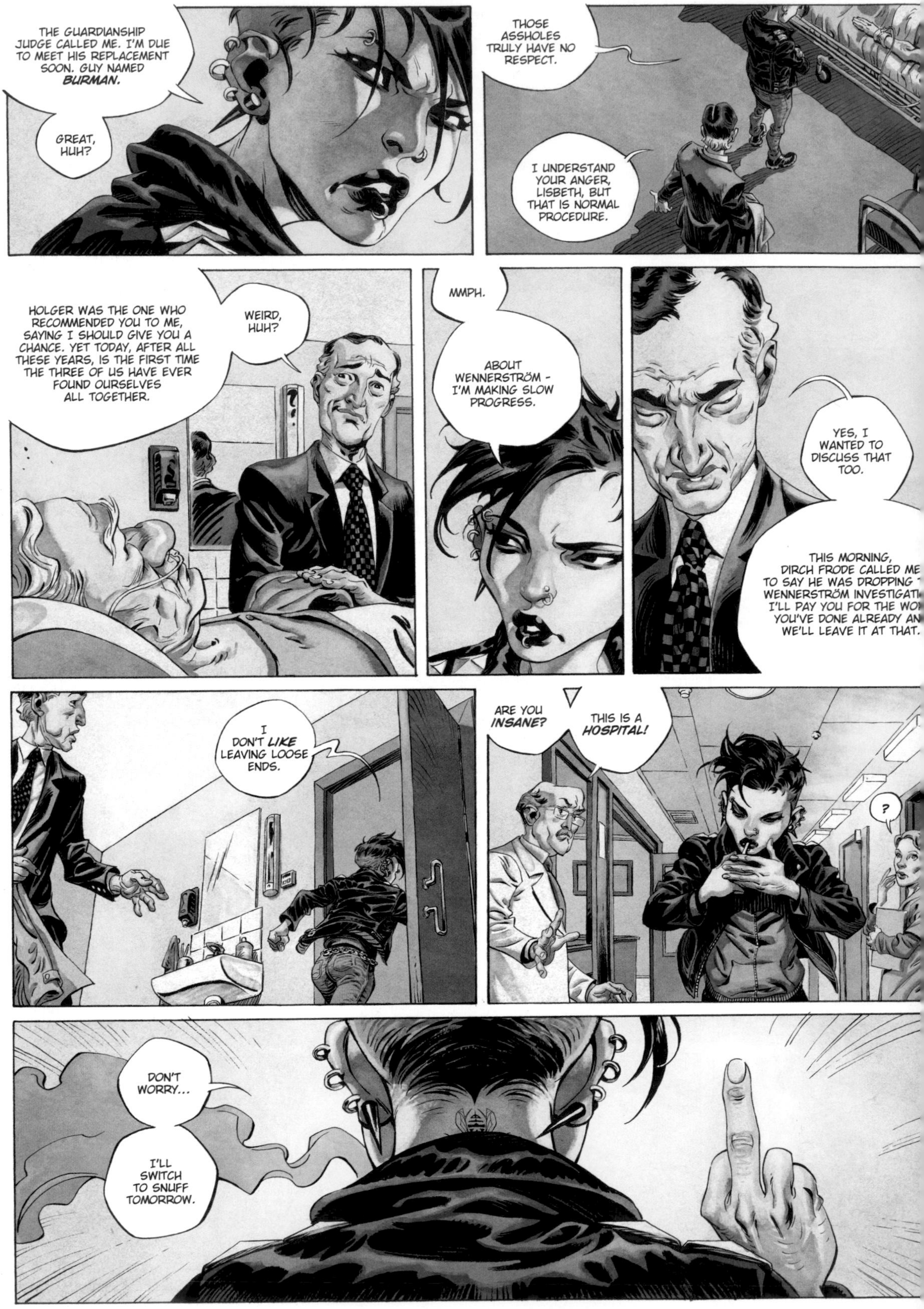
THE GUARDIANSHIP JUDGE CALLED ME. I'M DUE TO MEET HIS REPLACEMENT SOON. GUY NAMED BURMAN.
GREAT, HUH?
THOSE ASSHOLES TRULY HAVE NO RESPECT.
I UNDERSTAND YOUR ANGER, LISBETH, BUT THAT IS NORMAL PROCEDURE.
HOLGER WAS THE ONE WHO RECOMMENDED YOU TO ME, SAYING I SHOULD GIVE YOU A CHANCE. YET TODAY, AFTER ALL THESE YEARS, IS THE FIRST TIME THE THREE OF US HAVE EVER FOUND OURSELVES ALL TOGETHER.
WEIRD, HUH?
MMPH.
ABOUT WENNERSTRÖM - I'M MAKING SLOW PROGRESS.
YES, I WANTED TO DISCUSS THAT TOO.
THIS MORNING, DIRCH FRODE CALLED ME TO SAY HE WAS DROPPING T WENNERSTRÖM INVESTIGATI I'LL PAY YOU FOR THE WO YOU'VE DONE ALREADY AN WE'LL LEAVE IT AT THAT.
I DON'T LIKE LEAVING LOOSE ENDS.
ARE YOU INSANE?
THIS IS A HOSPITAL!
?
DON'T WORRY...
I'LL SWITCH TO SNUFF TOMORROW.

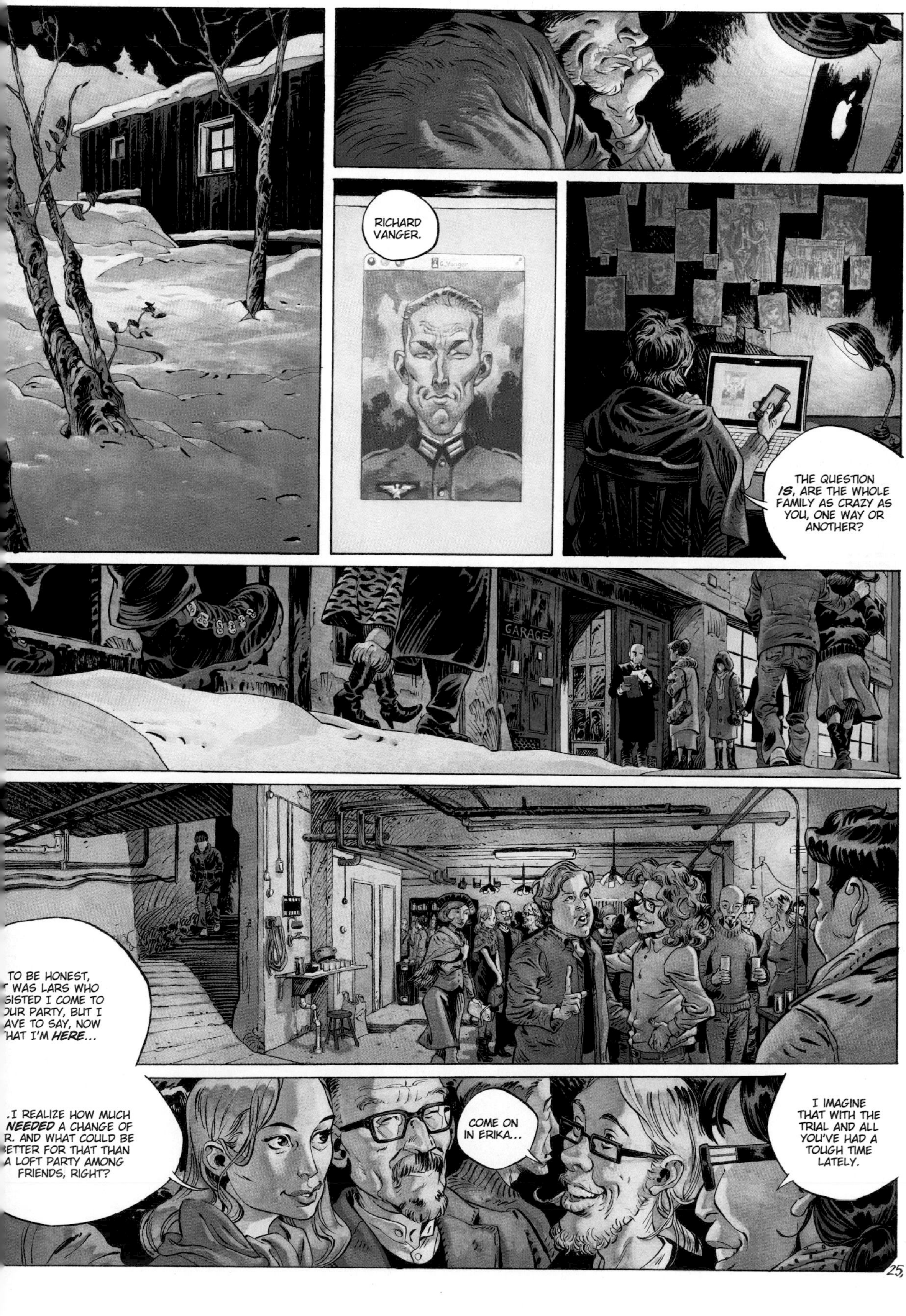
RICHARD VANGER.
G_Vanger
THE QUESTION IS, ARE THE WHOLE FAMILY AS CRAZY AS YOU, ONE WAY OR ANOTHER?
GARAGE
TO BE HONEST, T WAS LARS WHO SISTED I COME TO OUR PARTY, BUT I AVE TO SAY, NOW HAT I'M HERE...
.I REALIZE HOW MUCH NEEDED A CHANGE OF R. AND WHAT COULD BE BETTER FOR THAT THAN A LOFT PARTY AMONG FRIENDS, RIGHT?
COME ON IN ERIKA...
I IMAGINE THAT WITH THE TRIAL AND ALL YOU'VE HAD A TOUGH TIME LATELY.

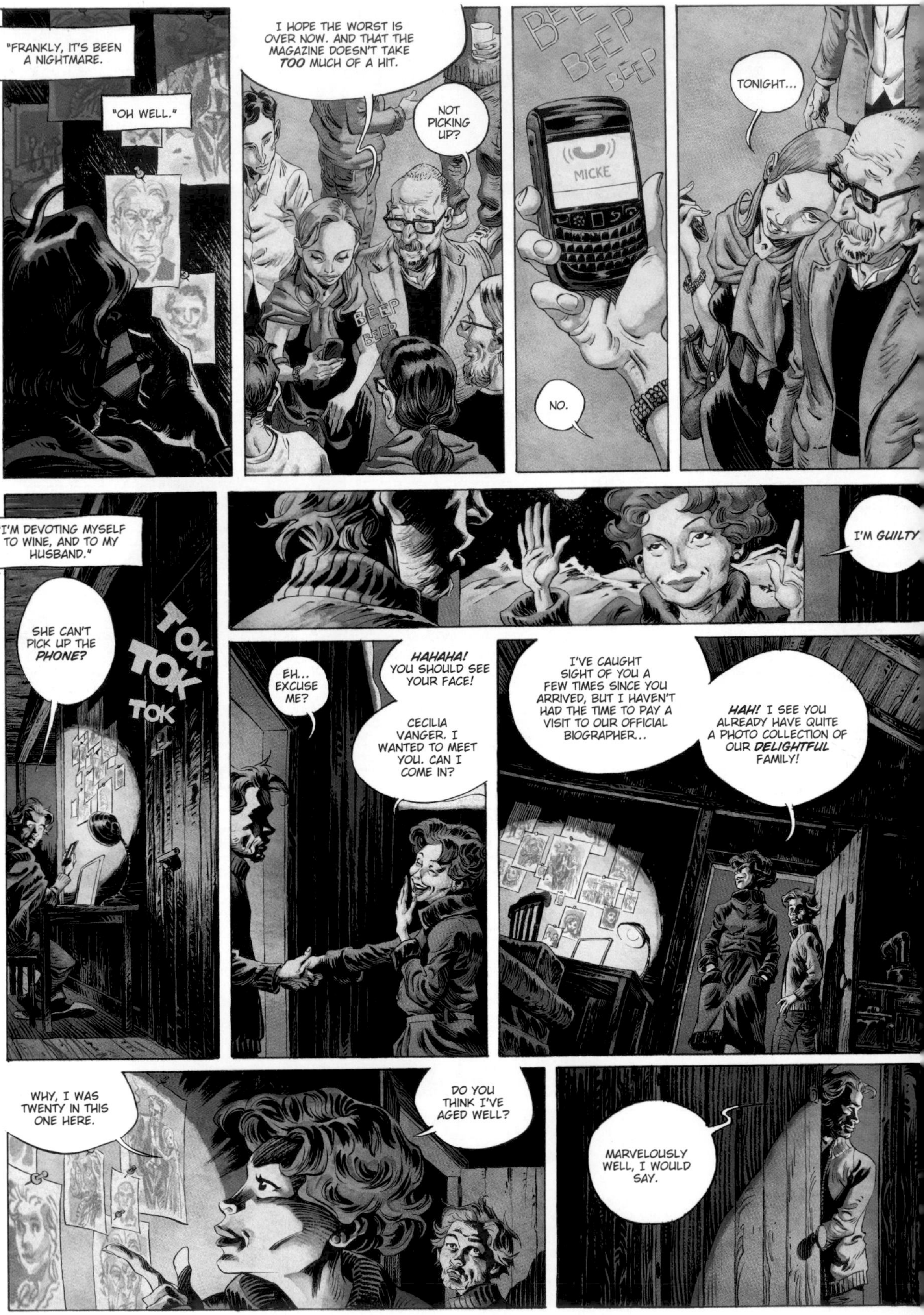
"FRANKLY, IT'S BEEN A NIGHTMARE.
"OH WELL."
I HOPE THE WORST IS OVER NOW. AND THAT THE MAGAZINE DOESN'T TAKE TOO MUCH OF A HIT.
NOT PICKING UP?
BEEP BEEP
BEEP BEEP BEEP
MICKE
NO.
TONIGHT...
"I'M DEVOTING MYSELF TO WINE, AND TO MY HUSBAND."
I'M GUILTY
SHE CAN'T PICK UP THE PHONE?
TOK TOK TOK
EH... EXCUSE ME?
HAHAHA! YOU SHOULD SEE YOUR FACE!
CECILIA VANGER. I WANTED TO MEET YOU. CAN I COME IN?
I'VE CAUGHT SIGHT OF YOU A FEW TIMES SINCE YOU ARRIVED, BUT I HAVEN'T HAD THE TIME TO PAY A VISIT TO OUR OFFICIAL BIOGRAPHER...
HAH! I SEE YOU ALREADY HAVE QUITE A PHOTO COLLECTION OF OUR DELIGHTFUL FAMILY!
WHY, I WAS TWENTY IN THIS ONE HERE.
DO YOU THINK I'VE AGED WELL?
MARVELOUSLY WELL, I WOULD SAY.

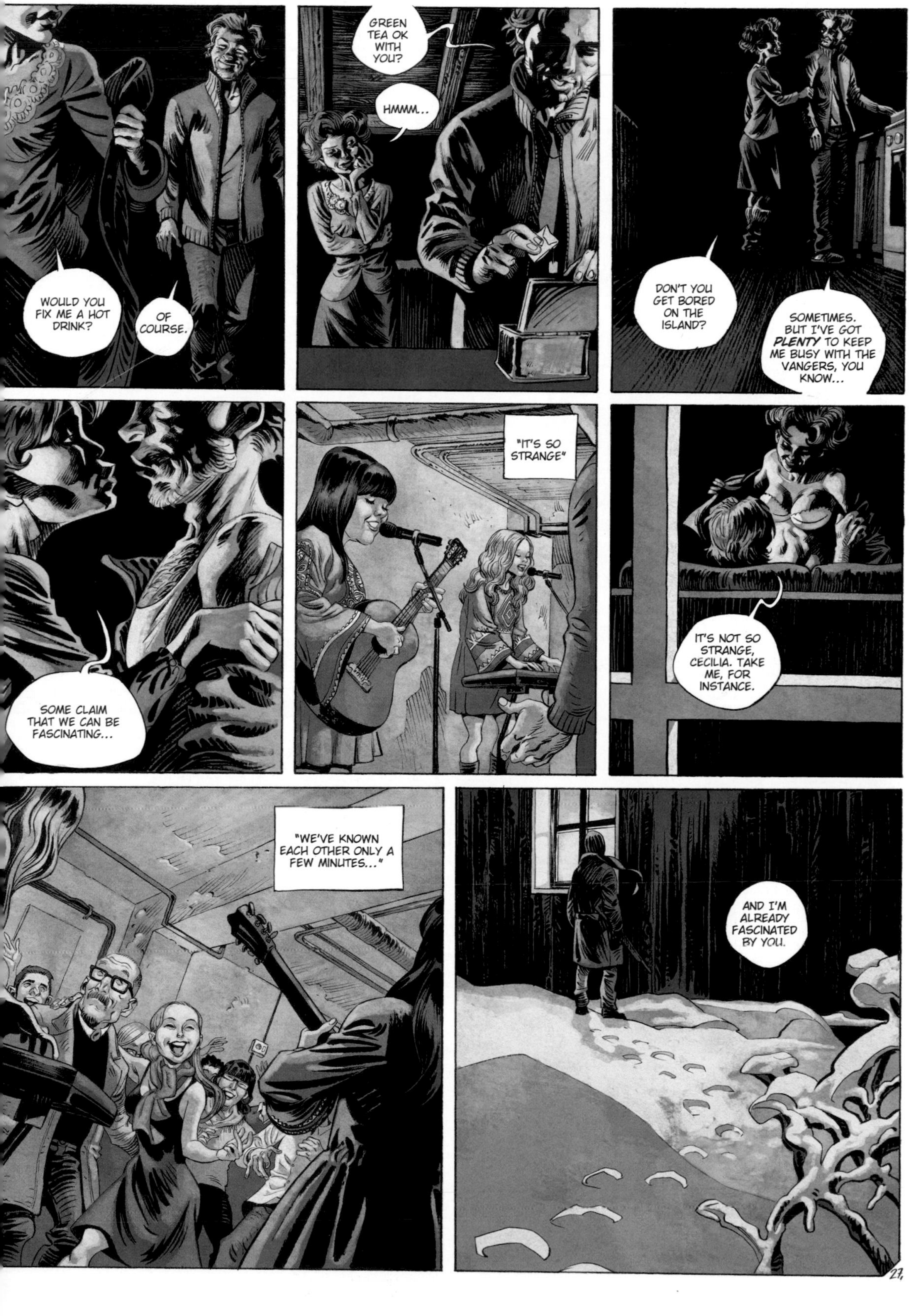
WOULD YOU FIX ME A HOT DRINK?
OF COURSE.
GREEN TEA OK WITH YOU?
HMMM...
DON'T YOU GET BORED ON THE ISLAND?
SOMETIMES. BUT I'VE GOT PLENTY TO KEEP ME BUSY WITH THE VANGERS, YOU KNOW...
SOME CLAIM THAT WE CAN BE FASCINATING...
"IT'S SO STRANGE"
IT'S NOT SO STRANGE, CECILIA. TAKE ME, FOR INSTANCE.
"WE'VE KNOWN EACH OTHER ONLY A FEW MINUTES..."
AND I'M ALREADY FASCINATED BY YOU.

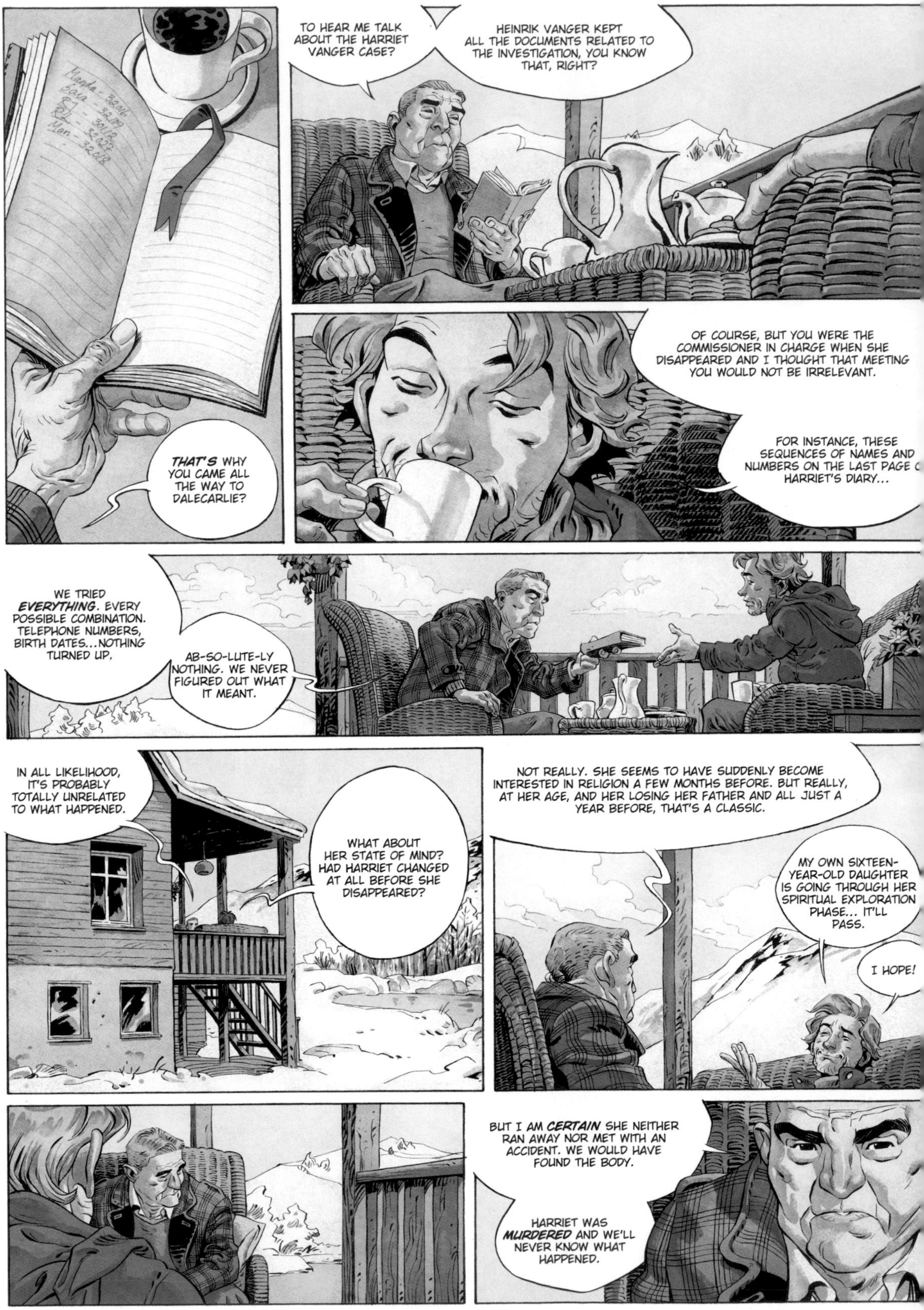
THAT'S WHY YOU CAME ALL THE WAY TO DALECARLIE?
TO HEAR ME TALK ABOUT THE HARRIET VANGER CASE?
HEINRIK VANGER KEPT ALL THE DOCUMENTS RELATED TO THE INVESTIGATION, YOU KNOW THAT, RIGHT?
OF COURSE, BUT YOU WERE THE COMMISSIONER IN CHARGE WHEN SHE DISAPPEARED AND I THOUGHT THAT MEETING YOU WOULD NOT BE IRRELEVANT.
FOR INSTANCE, THESE SEQUENCES OF NAMES AND NUMBERS ON THE LAST PAGE OF HARRIET'S DIARY...
WE TRIED EVERYTHING. EVERY POSSIBLE COMBINATION. TELEPHONE NUMBERS, BIRTH DATES... NOTHING TURNED UP.
AB-SO-LUTE-LY NOTHING. WE NEVER FIGURED OUT WHAT IT MEANT.
IN ALL LIKELIHOOD, IT'S PROBABLY TOTALLY UNRELATED TO WHAT HAPPENED.
WHAT ABOUT HER STATE OF MIND? HAD HARRIET CHANGED AT ALL BEFORE SHE DISAPPEARED?
NOT REALLY. SHE SEEMS TO HAVE SUDDENLY BECOME INTERESTED IN RELIGION A FEW MONTHS BEFORE. BUT REALLY, AT HER AGE, AND HER LOSING HER FATHER AND ALL JUST A YEAR BEFORE, THAT'S A CLASSIC.
MY OWN SIXTEEN-YEAR-OLD DAUGHTER IS GOING THROUGH HER SPIRITUAL EXPLORATION PHASE... IT'LL PASS.
I HOPE!
BUT I AM CERTAIN SHE NEITHER RAN AWAY NOR MET WITH AN ACCIDENT. WE WOULD HAVE FOUND THE BODY.
HARRIET WAS MURDERED AND WE'LL NEVER KNOW WHAT HAPPENED.

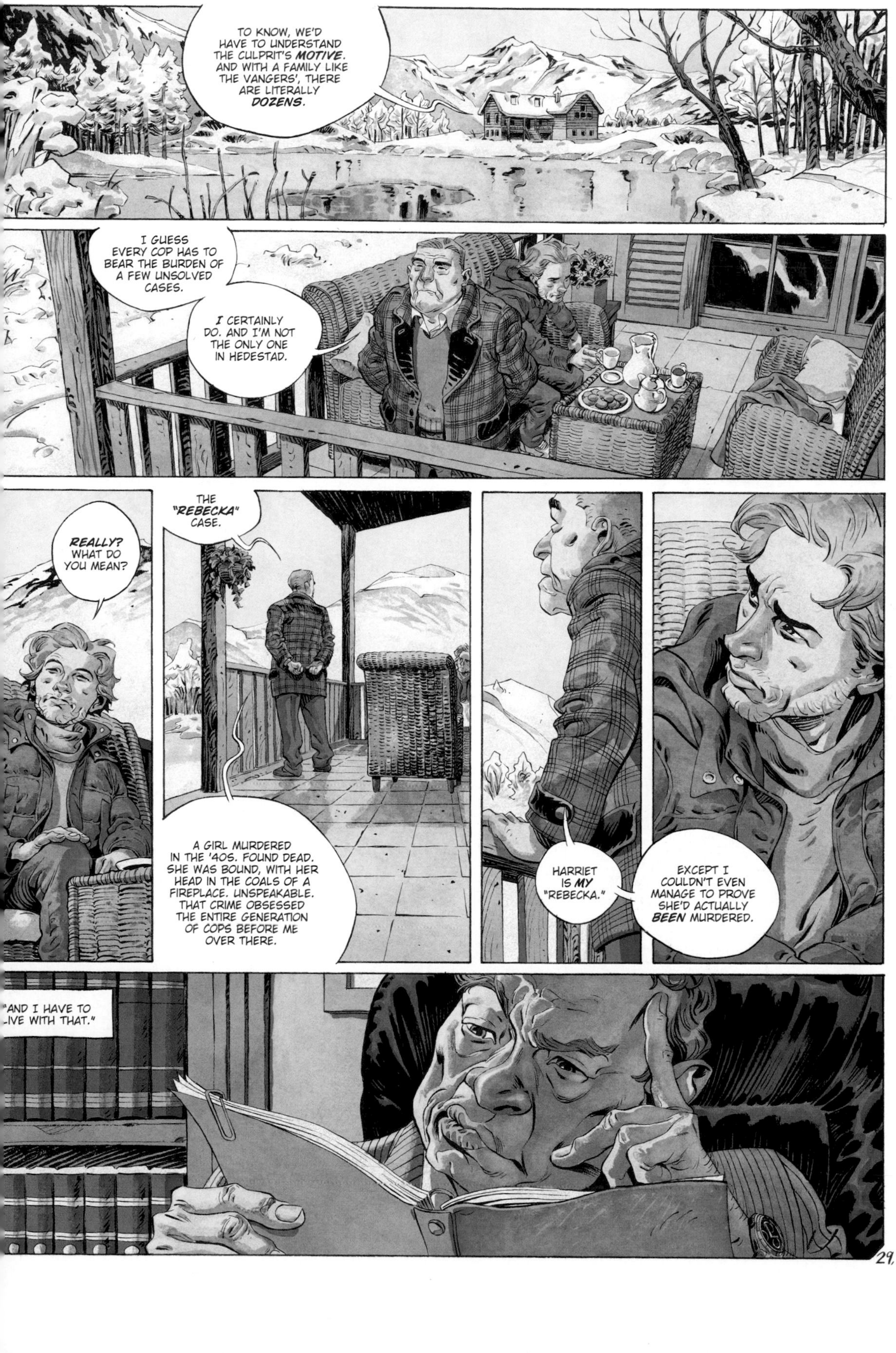
TO KNOW, WE'D HAVE TO UNDERSTAND THE CULPRIT'S *MOTIVE*. AND WITH A FAMILY LIKE THE VANGERS', THERE ARE LITERALLY *DOZENS*.
I GUESS EVERY COP HAS TO BEAR THE BURDEN OF A FEW UNSOLVED CASES.
I CERTAINLY DO. AND I'M NOT THE ONLY ONE IN HEDESTAD.
REALLY? WHAT DO YOU MEAN?
THE *"REBECKA"* CASE.
A GIRL MURDERED IN THE '40S. FOUND DEAD. SHE WAS BOUND, WITH HER HEAD IN THE COALS OF A FIREPLACE. UNSPEAKABLE. THAT CRIME OBSESSED THE ENTIRE GENERATION OF COPS BEFORE ME OVER THERE.
HARRIET IS *MY* "REBECKA."
EXCEPT I COULDN'T EVEN MANAGE TO PROVE SHE'D ACTUALLY *BEEN* MURDERED.
"AND I HAVE TO LIVE WITH THAT."

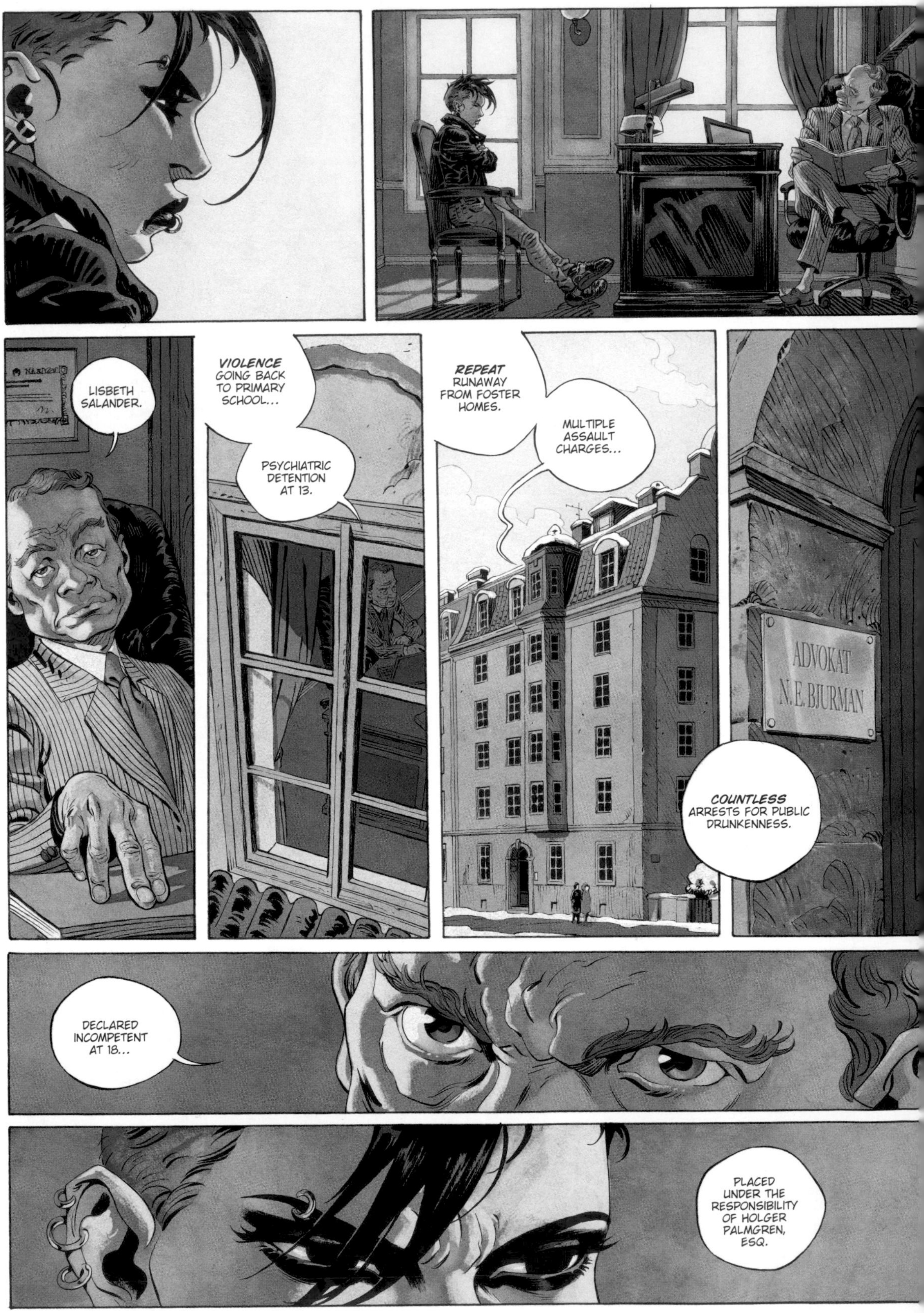
LISBETH SALANDER.
VIOLENCE GOING BACK TO PRIMARY SCHOOL...
PSYCHIATRIC DETENTION AT 13.
REPEAT RUNAWAY FROM FOSTER HOMES.
MULTIPLE ASSAULT CHARGES...
ADVOKAT N.E. BJURMAN
COUNTLESS ARRESTS FOR PUBLIC DRUNKENNESS.
DECLARED INCOMPETENT AT 18...
PLACED UNDER THE RESPONSIBILITY OF HOLGER PALMGREN, ESQ.

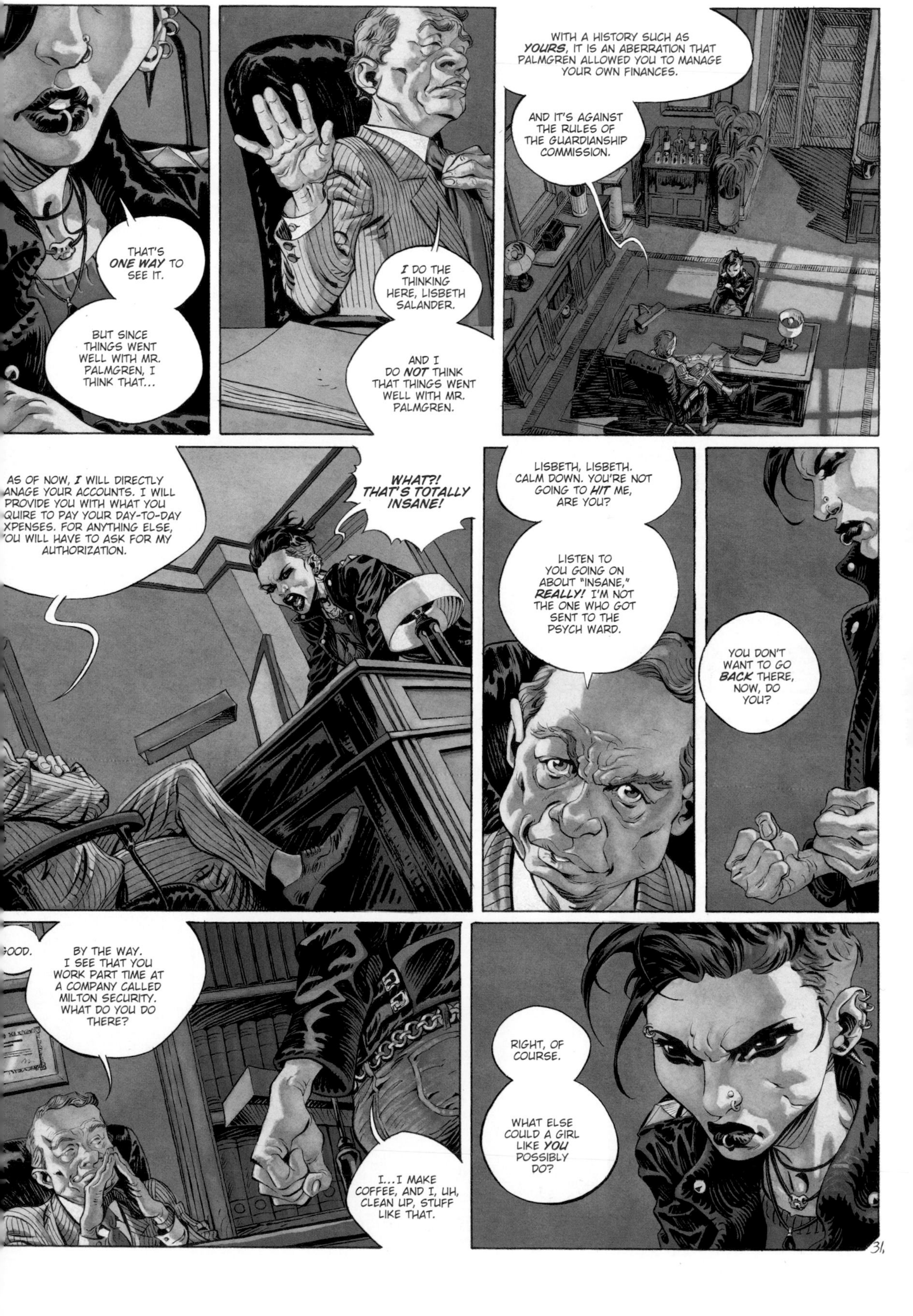
THAT'S ONE WAY TO SEE IT.
BUT SINCE THINGS WENT WELL WITH MR. PALMGREN, I THINK THAT...
I DO THE THINKING HERE, LISBETH SALANDER.
AND I DO NOT THINK THAT THINGS WENT WELL WITH MR. PALMGREN.
WITH A HISTORY SUCH AS YOURS, IT IS AN ABERRATION THAT PALMGREN ALLOWED YOU TO MANAGE YOUR OWN FINANCES.
AND IT'S AGAINST THE RULES OF THE GUARDIANSHIP COMMISSION.
AS OF NOW, I WILL DIRECTLY ANAGE YOUR ACCOUNTS. I WILL PROVIDE YOU WITH WHAT YOU QUIRE TO PAY YOUR DAY-TO-DAY XPENSES. FOR ANYTHING ELSE, OU WILL HAVE TO ASK FOR MY AUTHORIZATION.
WHAT?! THAT'S TOTALLY INSANE!
LISBETH, LISBETH. CALM DOWN. YOU'RE NOT GOING TO HIT ME, ARE YOU?
LISTEN TO YOU GOING ON ABOUT "INSANE," REALLY! I'M NOT THE ONE WHO GOT SENT TO THE PSYCH WARD.
YOU DON'T WANT TO GO BACK THERE, NOW, DO YOU?
OOD.
BY THE WAY. I SEE THAT YOU WORK PART TIME AT A COMPANY CALLED MILTON SECURITY. WHAT DO YOU DO THERE?
I...I MAKE COFFEE, AND I, UH, CLEAN UP, STUFF LIKE THAT.
RIGHT, OF COURSE.
WHAT ELSE COULD A GIRL LIKE YOU POSSIBLY DO?

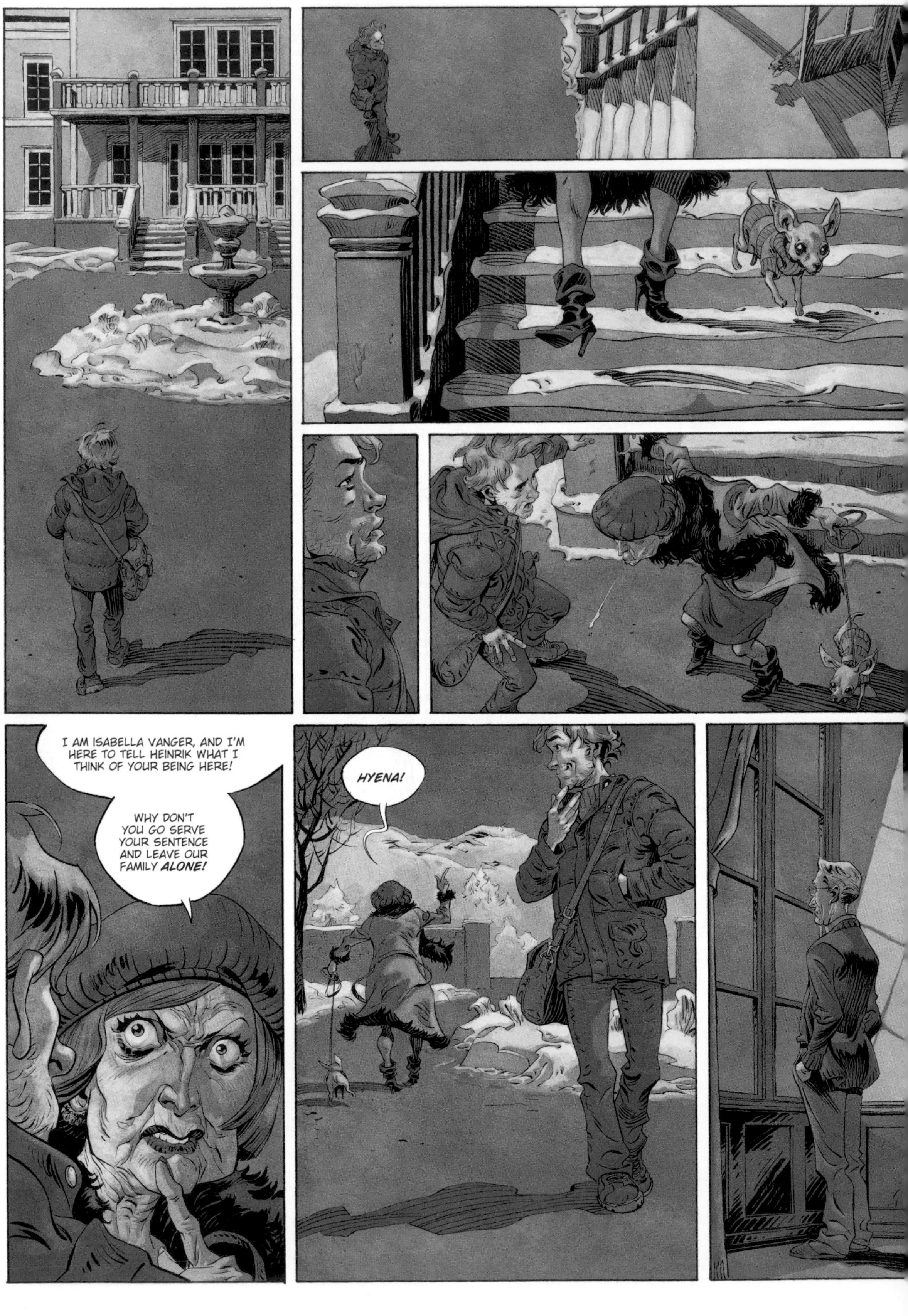
I AM ISABELLA VANGER, AND I'M HERE TO TELL HEINRIK WHAT I THINK OF YOUR BEING HERE!
WHY DON'T YOU GO SERVE YOUR SENTENCE AND LEAVE OUR FAMILY ALONE!
HYENA!

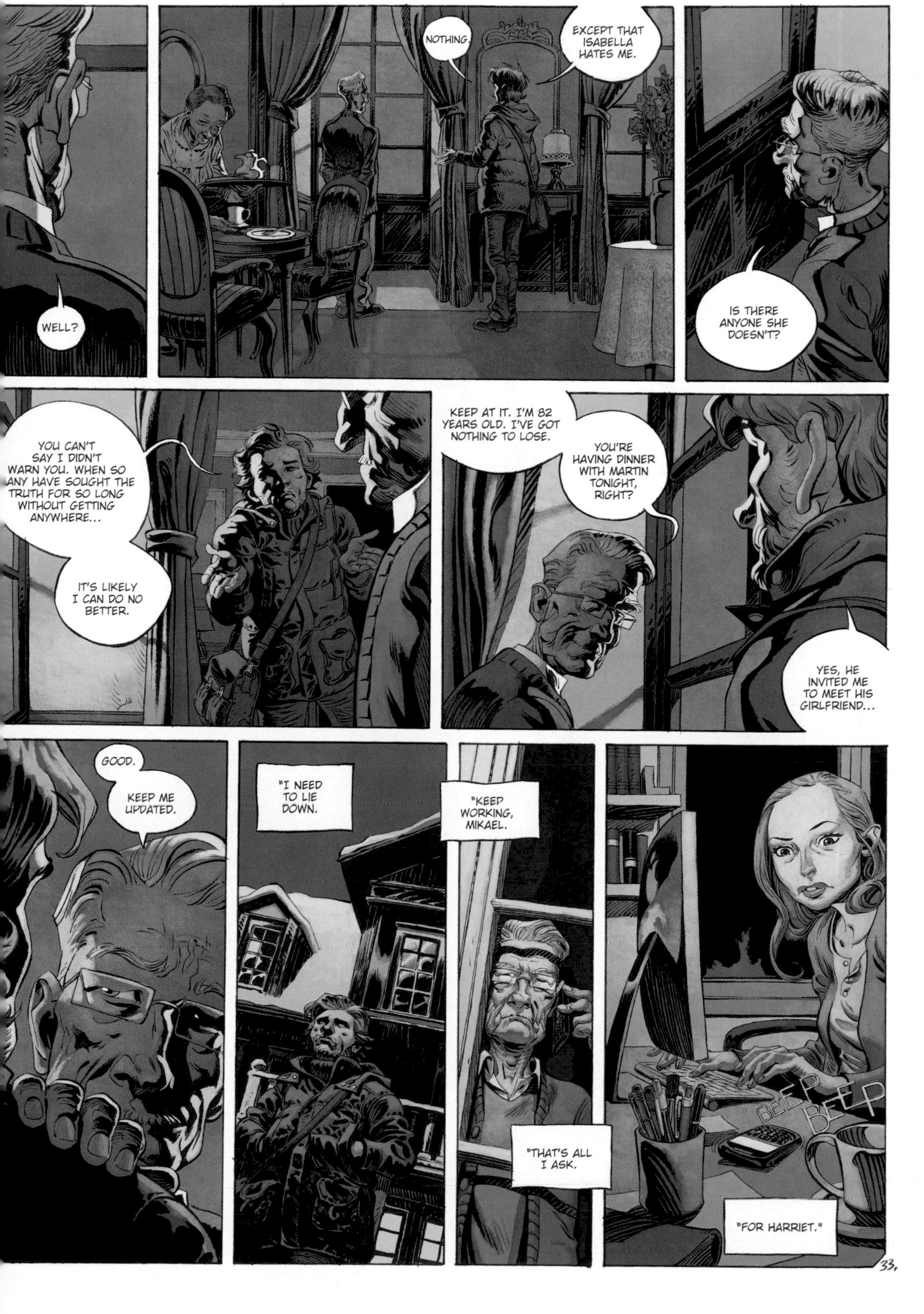
WELL?
NOTHING.
EXCEPT THAT ISABELLA HATES ME.
IS THERE ANYONE SHE DOESN'T?
YOU CAN'T SAY I DIDN'T WARN YOU. WHEN SO ANY HAVE SOUGHT THE TRUTH FOR SO LONG WITHOUT GETTING ANYWHERE...
IT'S LIKELY I CAN DO NO BETTER.
KEEP AT IT. I'M 82 YEARS OLD. I'VE GOT NOTHING TO LOSE.
YOU'RE HAVING DINNER WITH MARTIN TONIGHT, RIGHT?
YES, HE INVITED ME TO MEET HIS GIRLFRIEND...
GOOD.
KEEP ME UPDATED.
"I NEED TO LIE DOWN.
"KEEP WORKING, MIKAEL.
"THAT'S ALL I ASK.
BEEP BEEP
"FOR HARRIET."

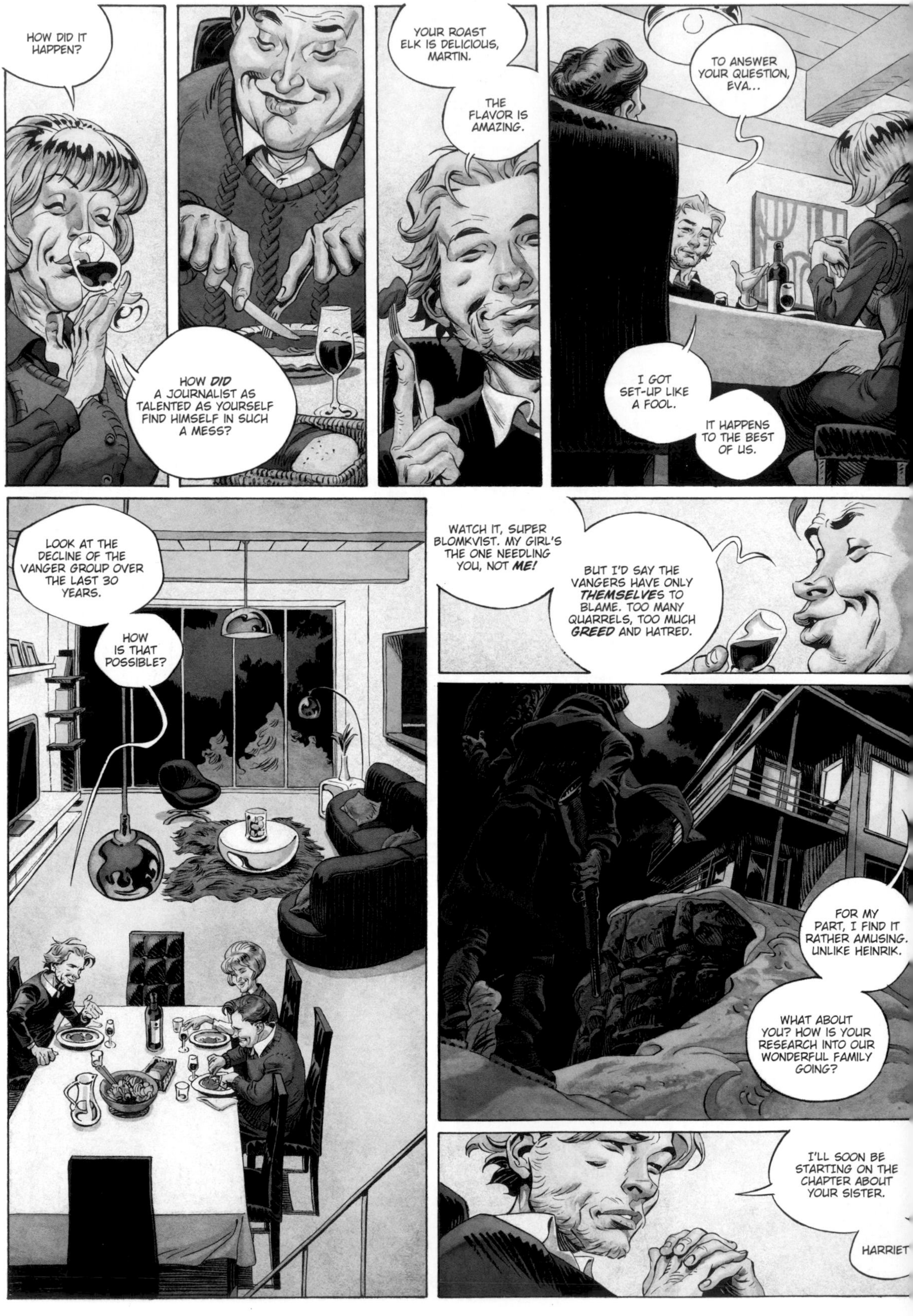

HOW DID IT HAPPEN?
HOW DID A JOURNALIST AS TALENTED AS YOURSELF FIND HIMSELF IN SUCH A MESS?
YOUR ROAST ELK IS DELICIOUS, MARTIN.
THE FLAVOR IS AMAZING.
TO ANSWER YOUR QUESTION, EVA...
I GOT SET-UP LIKE A FOOL.
IT HAPPENS TO THE BEST OF US.
LOOK AT THE DECLINE OF THE VANGER GROUP OVER THE LAST 30 YEARS.
HOW IS THAT POSSIBLE?
WATCH IT, SUPER BLOMKVIST. MY GIRL'S THE ONE NEEDLING YOU, NOT ME!
BUT I'D SAY THE VANGERS HAVE ONLY THEMSELVES TO BLAME. TOO MANY QUARRELS, TOO MUCH GREED AND HATRED.
FOR MY PART, I FIND IT RATHER AMUSING. UNLIKE HEINRIK.
WHAT ABOUT YOU? HOW IS YOUR RESEARCH INTO OUR WONDERFUL FAMILY GOING?
I'LL SOON BE STARTING ON THE CHAPTER ABOUT YOUR SISTER.
HARRIET

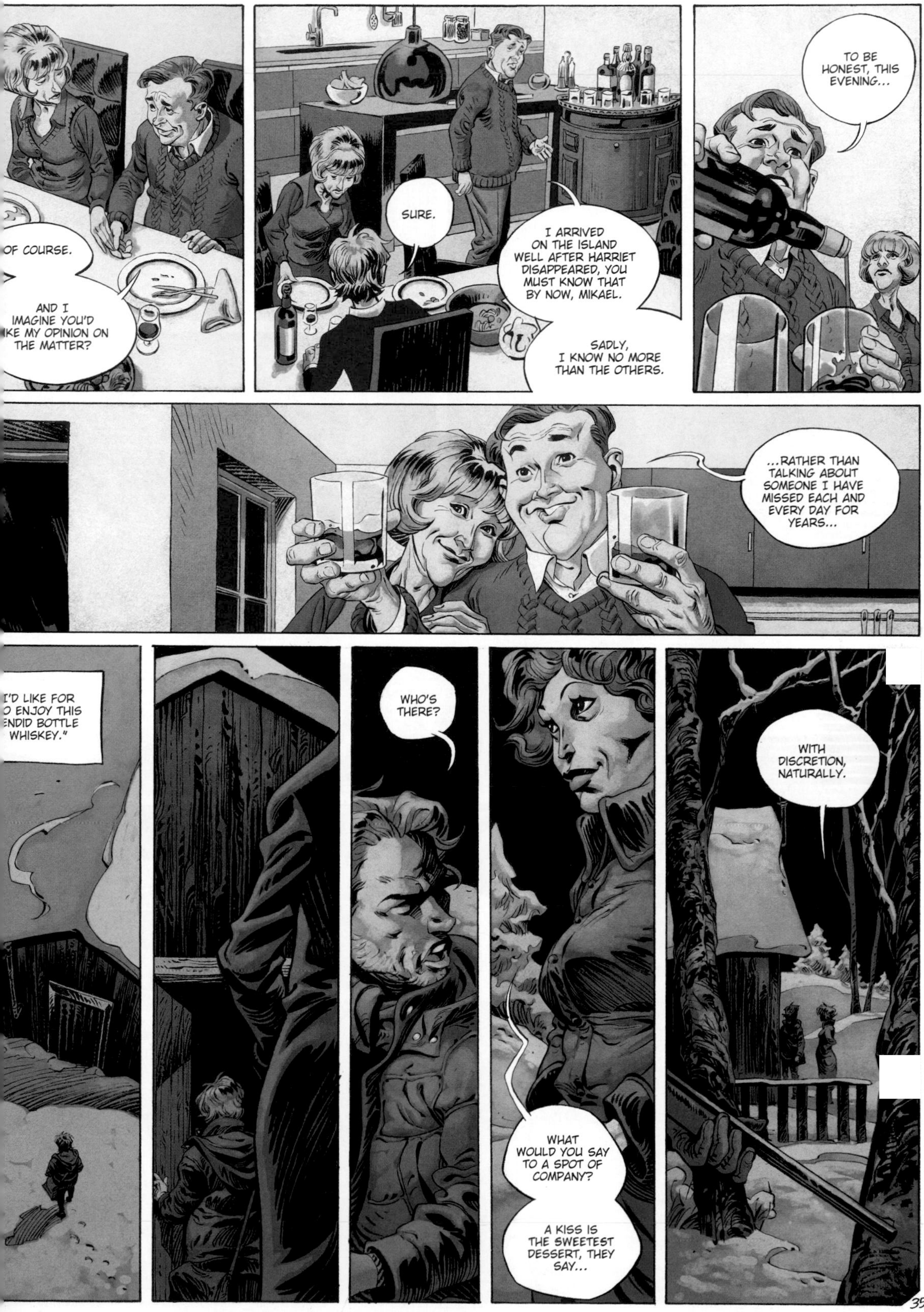
OF COURSE.
AND I IMAGINE YOU'D KE MY OPINION ON THE MATTER?
SURE.
I ARRIVED ON THE ISLAND WELL AFTER HARRIET DISAPPEARED, YOU MUST KNOW THAT BY NOW, MIKAEL.
SADLY, I KNOW NO MORE THAN THE OTHERS.
TO BE HONEST, THIS EVENING...
...RATHER THAN TALKING ABOUT SOMEONE I HAVE MISSED EACH AND EVERY DAY FOR YEARS...
I'D LIKE FOR O ENJOY THIS ENDID BOTTLE WHISKEY."
WHO'S THERE?
WHAT WOULD YOU SAY TO A SPOT OF COMPANY?
A KISS IS THE SWEETEST DESSERT, THEY SAY...
WITH DISCRETION, NATURALLY.

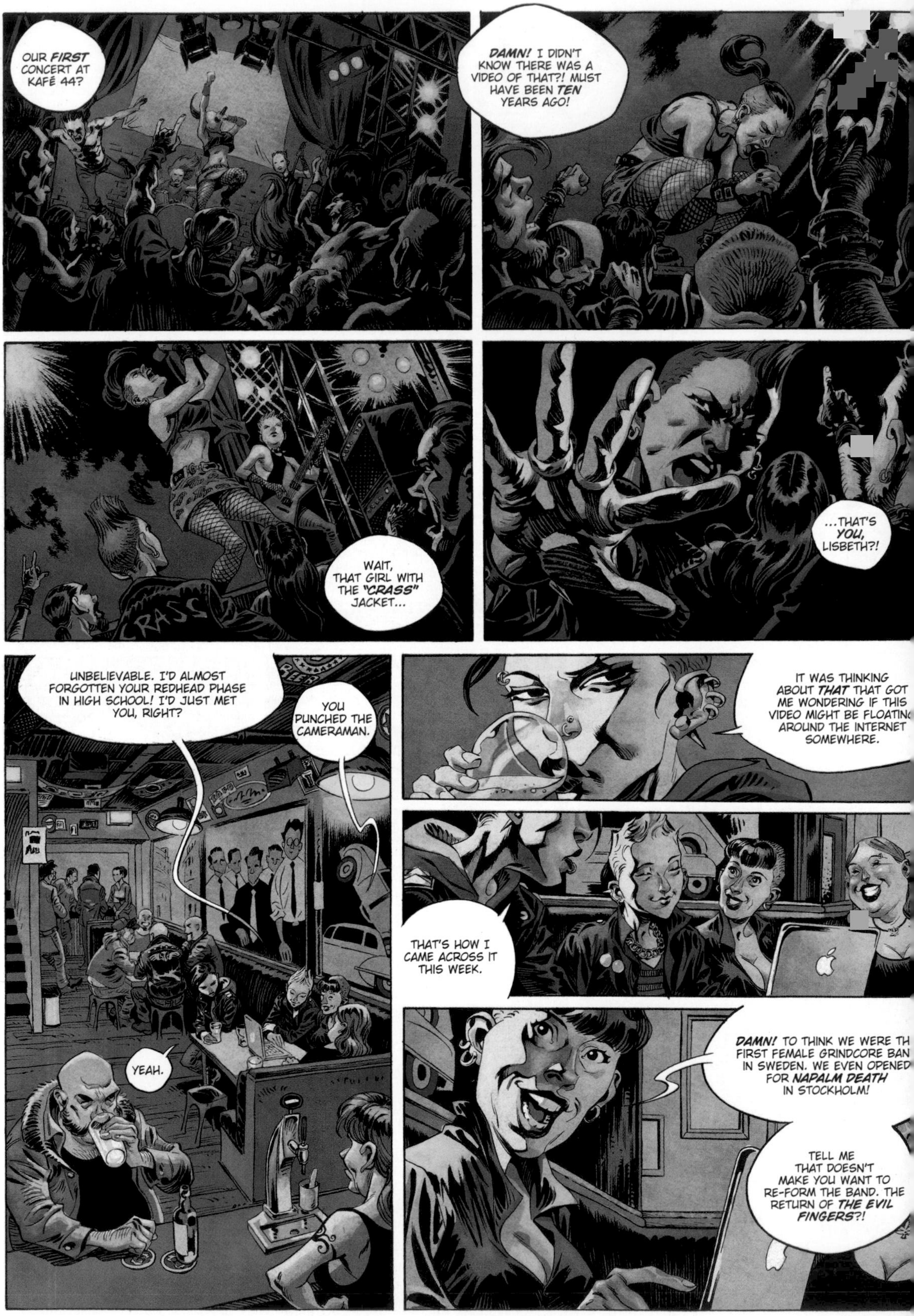
OUR FIRST CONCERT AT KAFÉ 44?
DAMN! I DIDN'T KNOW THERE WAS A VIDEO OF THAT?! MUST HAVE BEEN TEN YEARS AGO!
WAIT, THAT GIRL WITH THE "CRASS" JACKET...
CRASS
...THAT'S YOU, LISBETH?!
UNBELIEVABLE. I'D ALMOST FORGOTTEN YOUR REDHEAD PHASE IN HIGH SCHOOL! I'D JUST MET YOU, RIGHT?
YOU PUNCHED THE CAMERAMAN.
YEAH.
IT WAS THINKING ABOUT THAT THAT GOT ME WONDERING IF THIS VIDEO MIGHT BE FLOATIN AROUND THE INTERNET SOMEWHERE.
THAT'S HOW I CAME ACROSS IT THIS WEEK.
DAMN! TO THINK WE WERE TH FIRST FEMALE GRINDCORE BAN IN SWEDEN. WE EVEN OPENED FOR NAPALM DEATH IN STOCKHOLM!
TELL ME THAT DOESN'T MAKE YOU WANT TO RE-FORM THE BAND. THE RETURN OF THE EVIL FINGERS?!

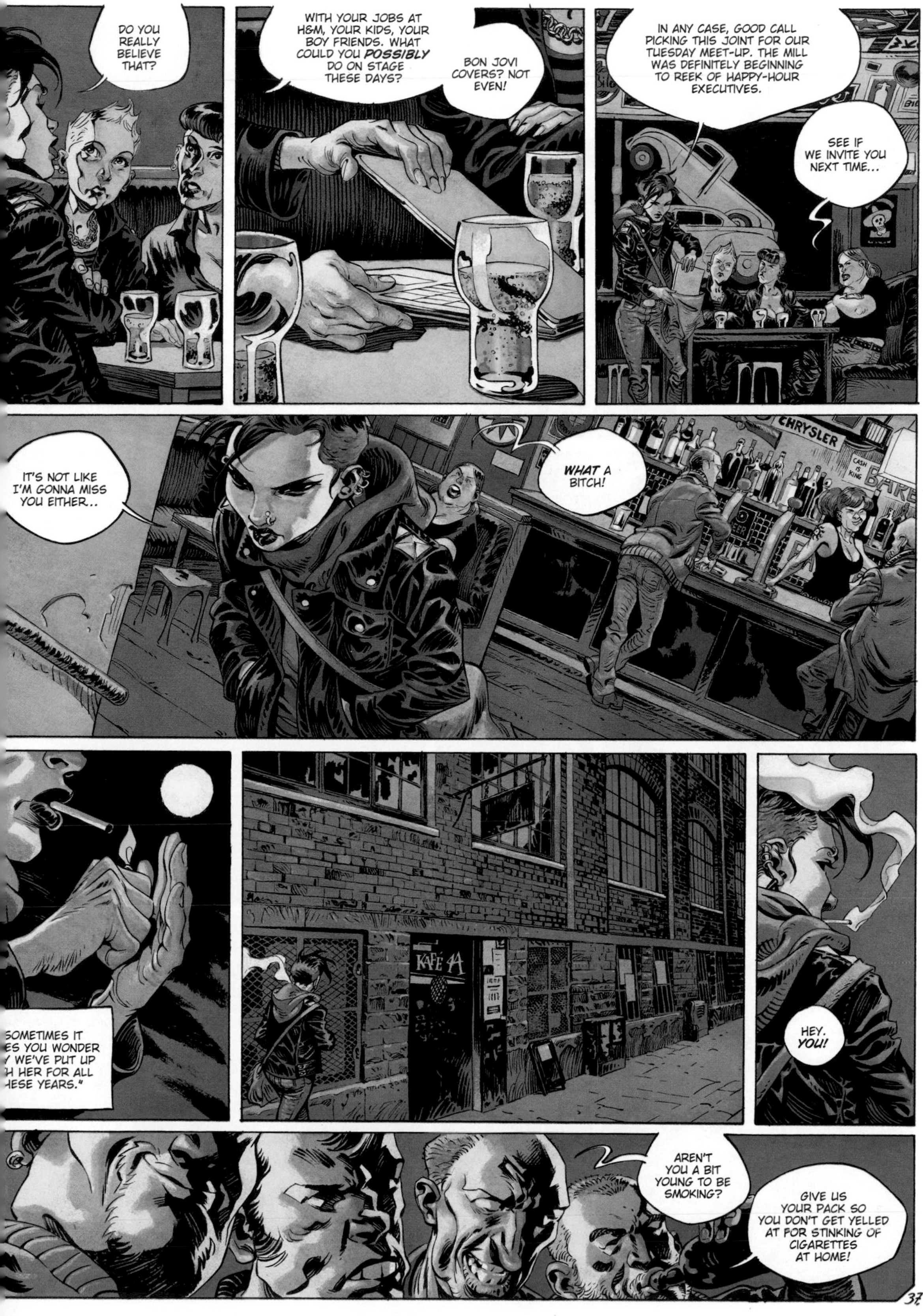
DO YOU REALLY BELIEVE THAT?
WITH YOUR JOBS AT H&M, YOUR KIDS, YOUR BOY FRIENDS. WHAT COULD YOU POSSIBLY DO ON STAGE THESE DAYS?
BON JOVI COVERS? NOT EVEN!
IN ANY CASE, GOOD CALL PICKING THIS JOINT FOR OUR TUESDAY MEET-UP. THE MILL WAS DEFINITELY BEGINNING TO REEK OF HAPPY-HOUR EXECUTIVES.
SEE IF WE INVITE YOU NEXT TIME...
IT'S NOT LIKE I'M GONNA MISS YOU EITHER..
WHAT A BITCH!
CHRYSLER
CASH IS KING
SOMETIMES IT
ES YOU WONDER
Y WE'VE PUT UP
H HER FOR ALL
HESE YEARS."
KAFÉ 44
HEY. YOU!
AREN'T YOU A BIT YOUNG TO BE SMOKING?
GIVE US YOUR PACK SO YOU DON'T GET YELLED AT FOR STINKING OF CIGARETTES AT HOME!

GO FUCK YOURSELVES.

THE TWO-BIT WHORE'S TALKIN' BACK? YOU'RE *GONNA* GIVE US THAT PACK AND SAY YOU'RE SORRY!

ON YOUR KNEES!

YEAH! RIGHT! ON YOUR KNEES!

AHHHH!

WHAT'S SHE DOING?

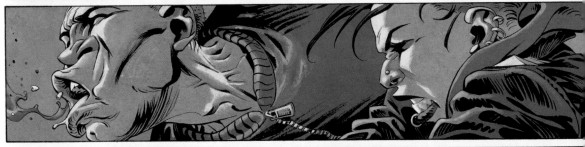

HANS?!

BITCH!

CRACK!

FUUUCK

FORGET HER. GET BACK HERE AND HELP ME. I GOTTA GET TO THE ER!

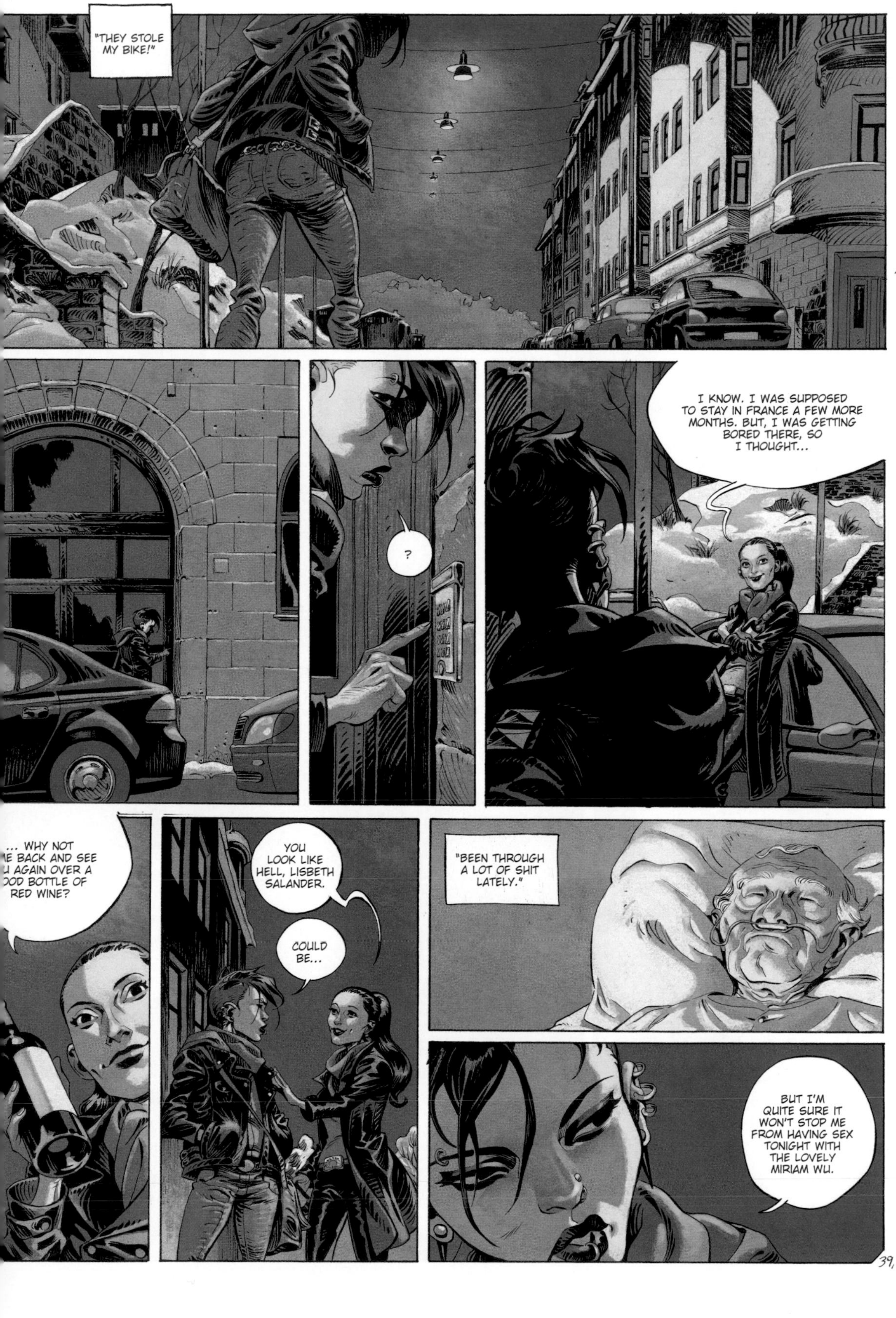

"THEY STOLE MY BIKE!"
?
I KNOW. I WAS SUPPOSED TO STAY IN FRANCE A FEW MORE MONTHS. BUT, I WAS GETTING BORED THERE, SO I THOUGHT...
... WHY NOT
ME BACK AND SEE
U AGAIN OVER A
OOD BOTTLE OF
RED WINE?
YOU LOOK LIKE HELL, LISBETH SALANDER.
COULD BE...
"BEEN THROUGH A LOT OF SHIT LATELY."
BUT I'M QUITE SURE IT WON'T STOP ME FROM HAVING SEX TONIGHT WITH THE LOVELY MIRIAM WU.

AND HERE IS YOUR TEA...

I'M SURE. BUT, TELL ME, IF I UNDERSTAND THINGS CORRECTLY - HEINRIK BROUGHT YOU HERE TO INVESTIGATE HARRIET.

SO, WHY HAVEN'T YOU ASKED ME ANYTHING ABOUT HER? IS IT BECAUSE I'M A SUSPECT?

JUST A COUPLE OF EVENINGS TOGETHER AND YOU ALREADY KNOW MY POST-COITAL PREFERENCES. *VERY GOOD*, MIKAEL, VERY GOOD INDEED!

I'VE BEEN TOLD I'M A QUICK STUDY.

ON THE OTHER HAND, YOU'RE SLEEPING WITH ME, SO PRUDENCE CAN'T BE YOUR STRONG SUIT.

MAKES ONE WONDER IF I WASN'T A WOM THAT DRAGGED DOWN IN THE WENNERSTRÖ CASE.

IN WENNERSTRÖM'S CASE IT WAS MORE BIG CAPITAL THAT TRIPPED ME UP.

BUT SINCE YOU'RE SO PERCEPTIVE, WHAT DO *YOU* THINK OF HARRIET'S DISAPPEARANCE?

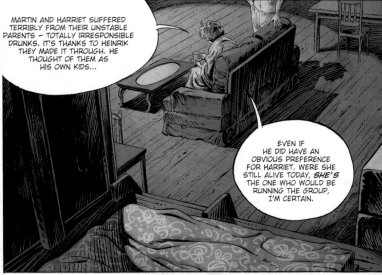

MARTIN AND HARRIET SUFFERED TERRIBLY FROM THEIR UNSTABLE PARENTS - TOTALLY IRRESPONSIBLE DRUNKS. IT'S THANKS TO HEINRIK THEY MADE IT THROUGH. HE THOUGHT OF THEM AS HIS OWN KIDS...

EVEN IF HE DID HAVE AN OBVIOUS PREFERENCE FOR HARRIET. WERE SHE STILL ALIVE TODAY, *SHE'S* THE ONE WHO WOULD BE RUNNING THE GROUP, I'M CERTAIN.

AS FOR THE REST OF IT, I DON'T KNOW MUCH WORTH NOTING. HARRIET TURNED INWARD THE YEAR AFTER HER FATHER DIED. HE DROWNED ON THE ISLAND, DEAD DRUNK OF COURSE. AND THEN...SHE JUST DISAPPEARED.

MY SISTER, ANITA WAS MUCH CLOSER TO HARRIET THAN I WAS, BUT I'M QUITE SURE SHE CAN TELL YOU NO MORE THAN I ABOUT IT.

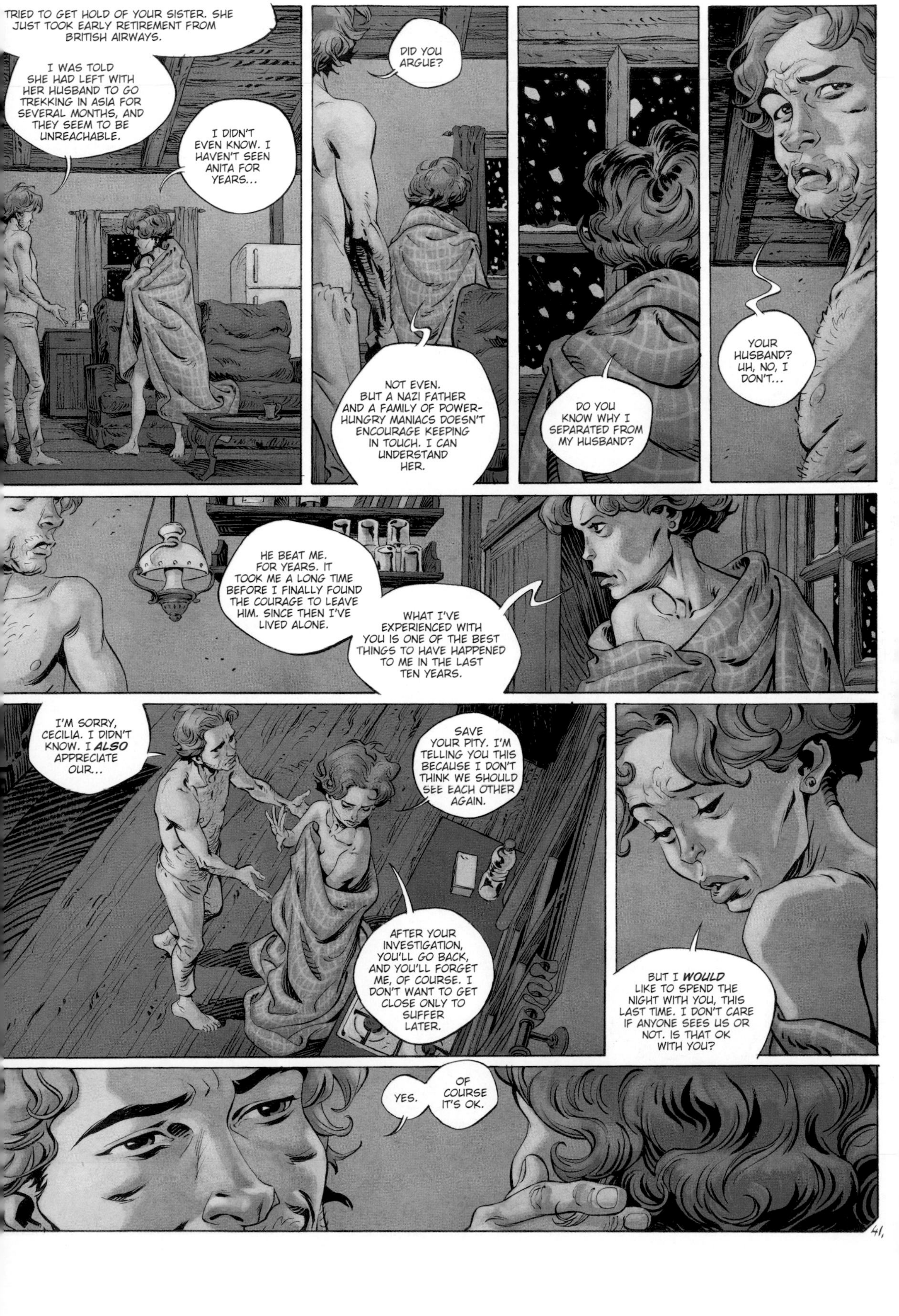
TRIED TO GET HOLD OF YOUR SISTER. SHE JUST TOOK EARLY RETIREMENT FROM BRITISH AIRWAYS.
I WAS TOLD SHE HAD LEFT WITH HER HUSBAND TO GO TREKKING IN ASIA FOR SEVERAL MONTHS, AND THEY SEEM TO BE UNREACHABLE.
I DIDN'T EVEN KNOW. I HAVEN'T SEEN ANITA FOR YEARS...
DID YOU ARGUE?
NOT EVEN. BUT A NAZI FATHER AND A FAMILY OF POWER-HUNGRY MANIACS DOESN'T ENCOURAGE KEEPING IN TOUCH. I CAN UNDERSTAND HER.
DO YOU KNOW WHY I SEPARATED FROM MY HUSBAND?
YOUR HUSBAND? UH, NO, I DON'T...
HE BEAT ME. FOR YEARS. IT TOOK ME A LONG TIME BEFORE I FINALLY FOUND THE COURAGE TO LEAVE HIM. SINCE THEN I'VE LIVED ALONE.
WHAT I'VE EXPERIENCED WITH YOU IS ONE OF THE BEST THINGS TO HAVE HAPPENED TO ME IN THE LAST TEN YEARS.
I'M SORRY, CECILIA. I DIDN'T KNOW. I ***ALSO*** APPRECIATE OUR...
SAVE YOUR PITY. I'M TELLING YOU THIS BECAUSE I DON'T THINK WE SHOULD SEE EACH OTHER AGAIN.
AFTER YOUR INVESTIGATION, YOU'LL GO BACK, AND YOU'LL FORGET ME, OF COURSE. I DON'T WANT TO GET CLOSE ONLY TO SUFFER LATER.
BUT I ***WOULD*** LIKE TO SPEND THE NIGHT WITH YOU, THIS LAST TIME. I DON'T CARE IF ANYONE SEES US OR NOT. IS THAT OK WITH YOU?
YES.
OF COURSE IT'S OK.

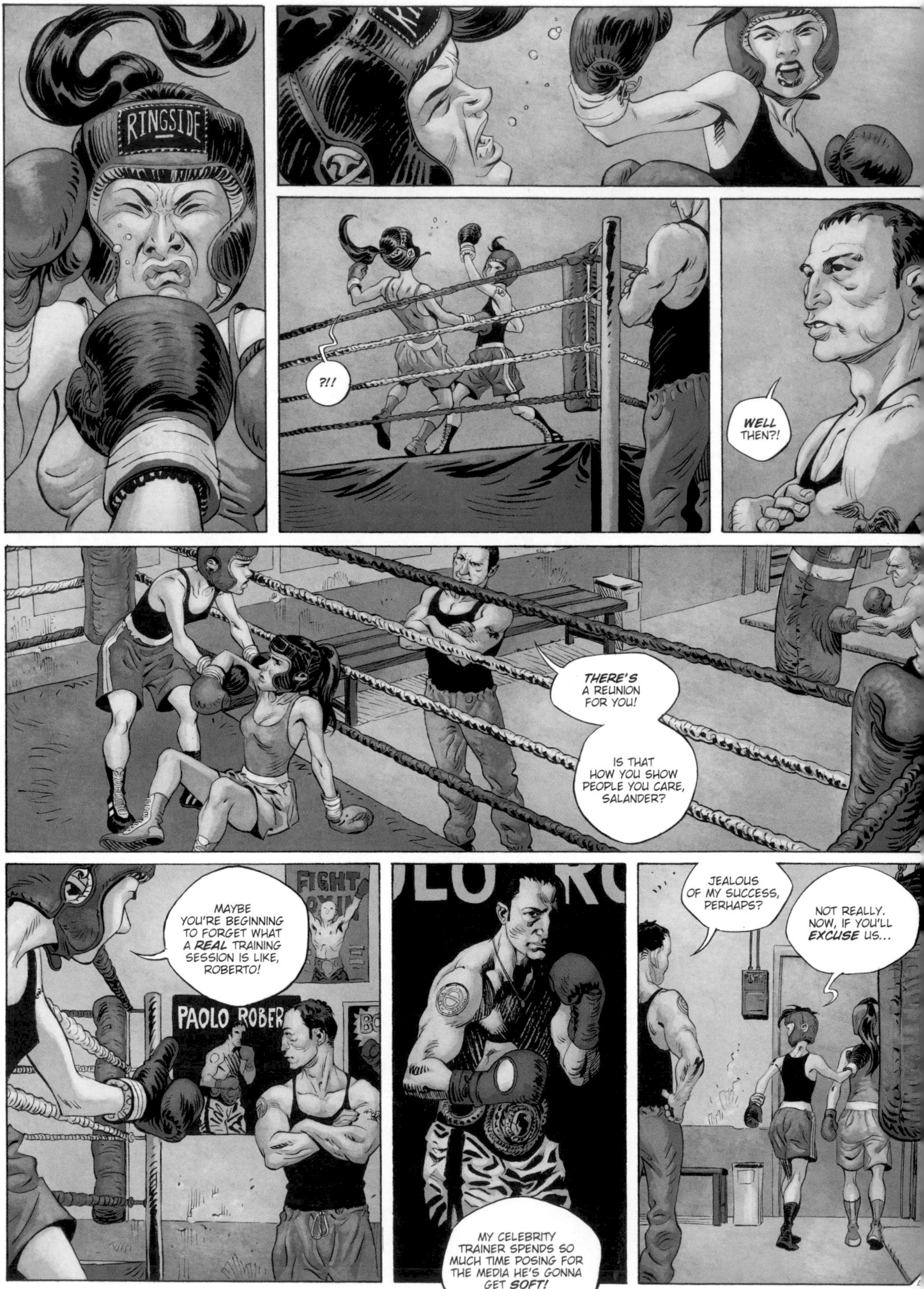

RINGSIDE
?!!
WELL THEN?!
THERE'S A REUNION FOR YOU!
IS THAT HOW YOU SHOW PEOPLE YOU CARE, SALANDER?
MAYBE YOU'RE BEGINNING TO FORGET WHAT A REAL TRAINING SESSION IS LIKE, ROBERTO!
PAOLO ROBER
MY CELEBRITY TRAINER SPENDS SO MUCH TIME POSING FOR THE MEDIA HE'S GONNA GET SOFT!
JEALOUS OF MY SUCCESS, PERHAPS?
NOT REALLY. NOW, IF YOU'LL EXCUSE US...

"...HAVE TO GO SHOWER."

YOU'RE *SUCH A* DOUCHEBAG!

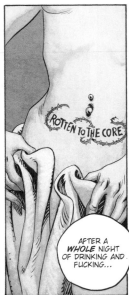

AFTER A *WHOLE* NIGHT OF DRINKING AND FUCKING...

YOU MAKE ME GO BOXING WITH YOU AT, LIKE, *DAWN...*

THEN YOU *PUMMEL* ME AS THOUGH YOUR LIFE DEPENDED ON IT!!

MAYBE IT DID.

COME ON. SPEND THE DAY WITH ME, AS PENANCE.

NO CAN DO. I HAVE AN IMPORTANT MEETING IN LESS THAN AN HOUR.

I'LL CALL YOU TOMORROW.

43

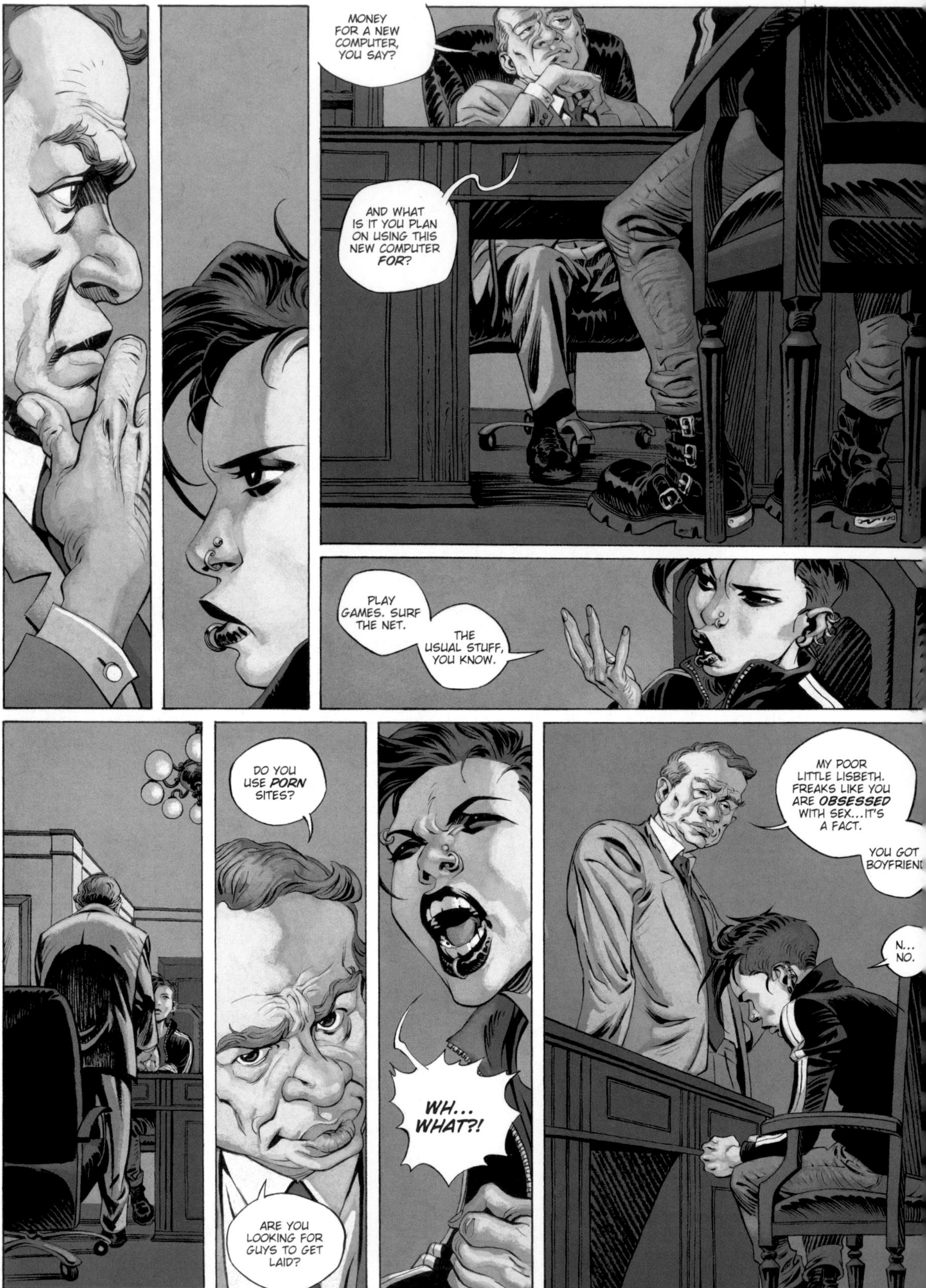
MONEY FOR A NEW COMPUTER, YOU SAY?
AND WHAT IS IT YOU PLAN ON USING THIS NEW COMPUTER *FOR*?
PLAY GAMES. SURF THE NET.
THE USUAL STUFF, YOU KNOW.
DO YOU USE *PORN* SITES?
ARE YOU LOOKING FOR GUYS TO GET LAID?
WH... WHAT?!
MY POOR LITTLE LISBETH. FREAKS LIKE YOU ARE *OBSESSED* WITH SEX... IT'S A FACT.
YOU GOT BOYFRIEND
N... NO.

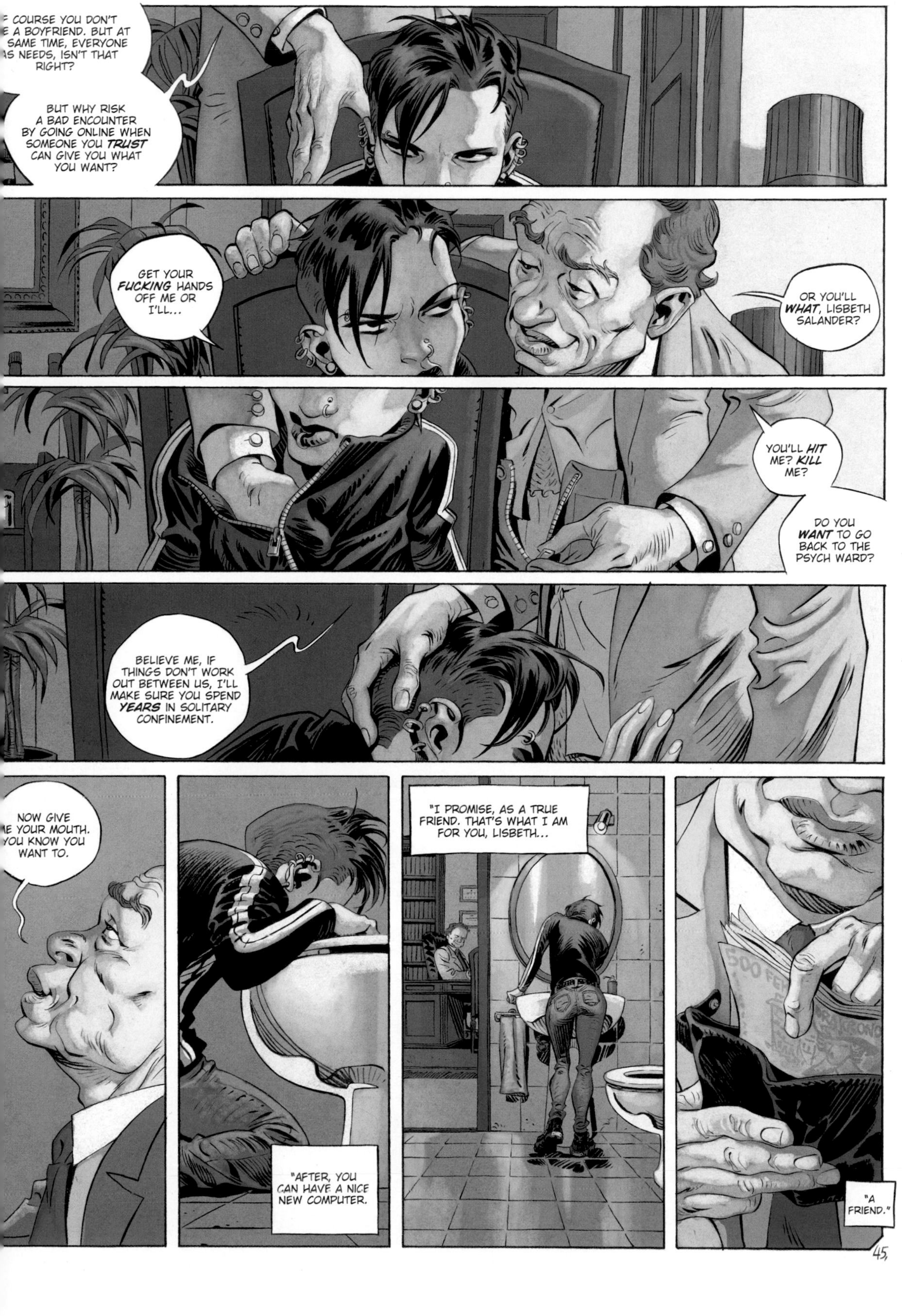
F COURSE YOU DON'T E A BOYFRIEND. BUT AT SAME TIME, EVERYONE AS NEEDS, ISN'T THAT RIGHT?
BUT WHY RISK A BAD ENCOUNTER BY GOING ONLINE WHEN SOMEONE YOU TRUST CAN GIVE YOU WHAT YOU WANT?
GET YOUR FUCKING HANDS OFF ME OR I'LL...
OR YOU'LL WHAT, LISBETH SALANDER?
YOU'LL HIT ME? KILL ME?
DO YOU WANT TO GO BACK TO THE PSYCH WARD?
BELIEVE ME, IF THINGS DON'T WORK OUT BETWEEN US, I'LL MAKE SURE YOU SPEND YEARS IN SOLITARY CONFINEMENT.
NOW GIVE E YOUR MOUTH. YOU KNOW YOU WANT TO.
"AFTER, YOU CAN HAVE A NICE NEW COMPUTER.
"I PROMISE, AS A TRUE FRIEND. THAT'S WHAT I AM FOR YOU, LISBETH...
"A FRIEND."

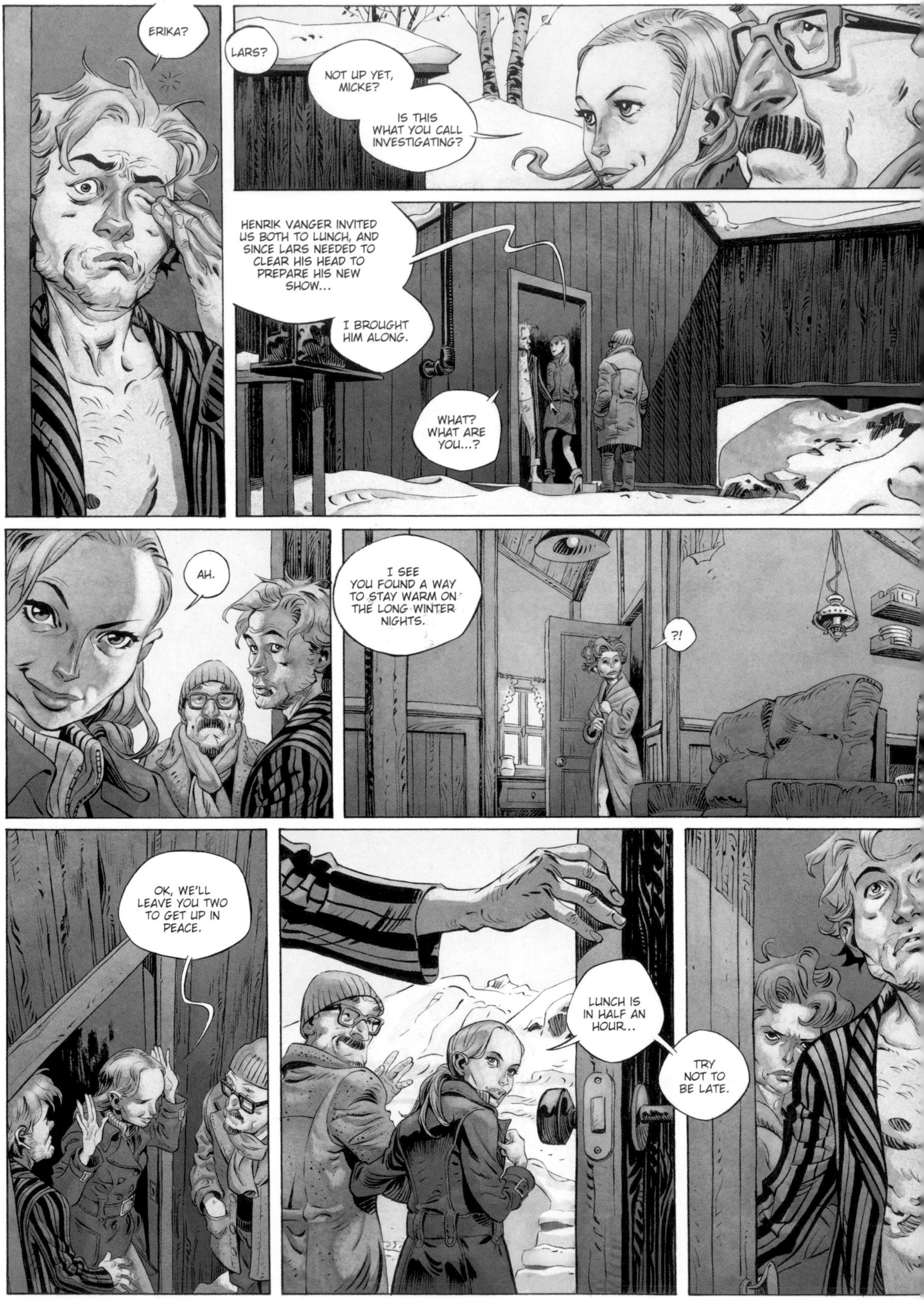
ERIKA?
LARS?
NOT UP YET, MICKE?
IS THIS WHAT YOU CALL INVESTIGATING?
HENRIK VANGER INVITED US BOTH TO LUNCH, AND SINCE LARS NEEDED TO CLEAR HIS HEAD TO PREPARE HIS NEW SHOW...
I BROUGHT HIM ALONG.
WHAT? WHAT ARE YOU...?
AH.
I SEE YOU FOUND A WAY TO STAY WARM ON THE LONG WINTER NIGHTS.
?!
OK, WE'LL LEAVE YOU TWO TO GET UP IN PEACE.
LUNCH IS IN HALF AN HOUR...
TRY NOT TO BE LATE.

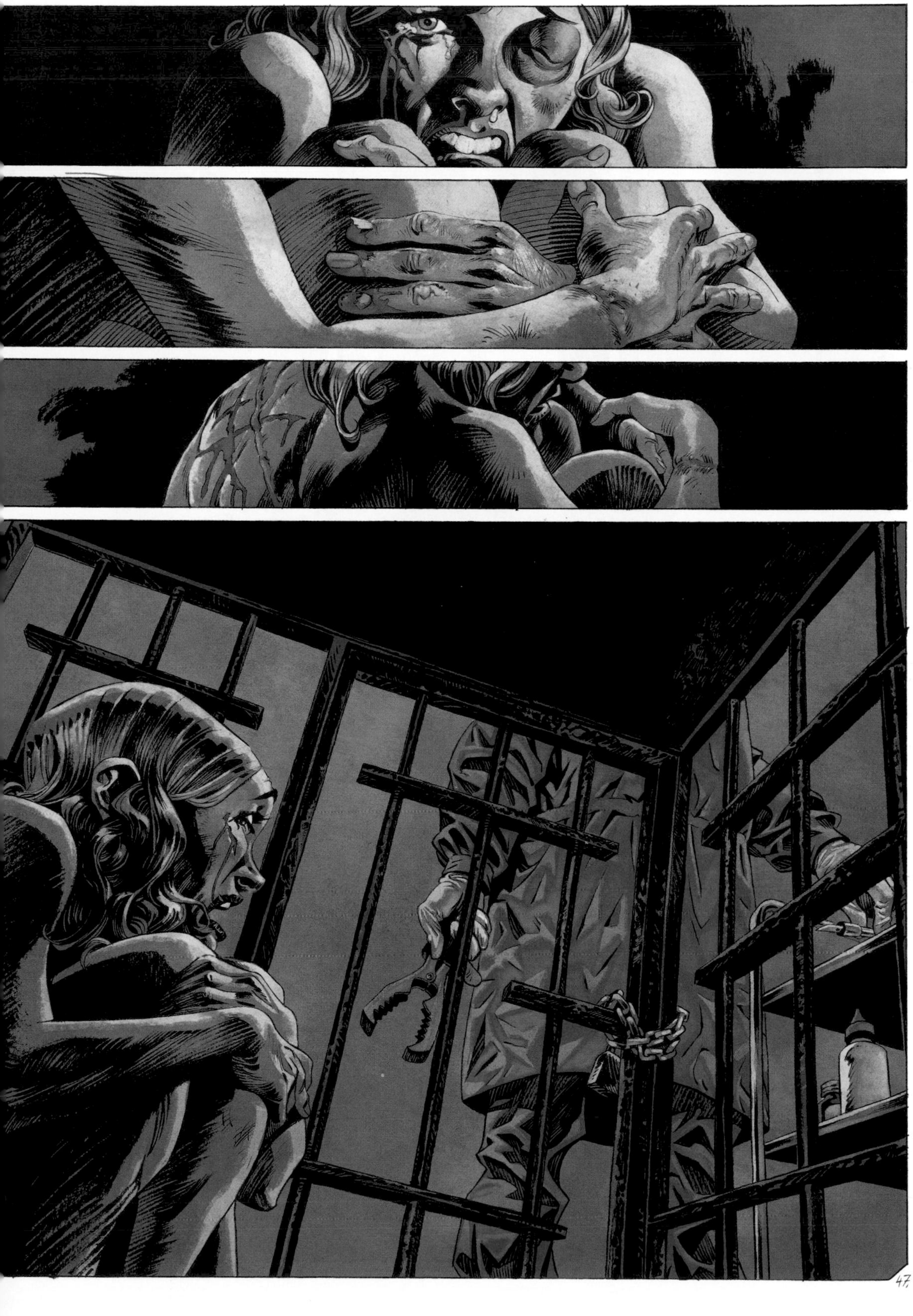

WHAT? YOU'RE NOW A *SHAREHOLDER* IN MILLENNIUM?

ERIKA? WHAT THE HELL IS THIS?!

ADVERTISERS WERE BEGINNING TO BAIL ON YOUR MAGAZINE. OUR GROUP'S INVESTMENT WILL NOT JUST KEEP YOU AFLOAT *FINANCIALLY*, IT WILL ALSO REASSURE SOME OF YOUR BUSINESS PARTNERS.

WE MAY BE LOSING STEAM, BUT WE'RE STILL QUITE POWERFUL IN SWEDEN.

ERIKA, WHY DIDN'T YOU *TELL* ME?

YOU RESIGNED FROM THE BOARD TO COME LOSE YOURSELF HERE. AT THE RATE THINGS WERE GOING THE MAGAZINE HAD SIX MONTHS LEFT.

SO WHY *WOULD* I SPEAK TO YOU ABOUT IT? YOU HAVE TO LIVE WITH YOUR CHOICES, MICKE.

WENNERSTRÖM MIGHT STEP UP HIS PRESSURE ON OTHER SKITTISH ADVERTISERS. HE'S THE VINDICTIVE TYPE, AS YOU WELL KNOW FROM EXPERIENCE.

LETTING THE VANGER GROUP TAKE A STAKE IN MILLENNIUM IS THE BEST WAY TO SHOW THAT THE MAGAZINE HAS *SUPPORT*.

IT SENDS A VERY STRONG MESSAGE TO EVERYONE.

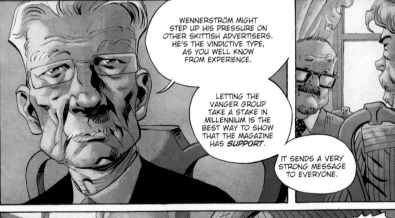

YOU'LL HAVE TO EXCUSE ME I'VE LOST MY APPETITE!

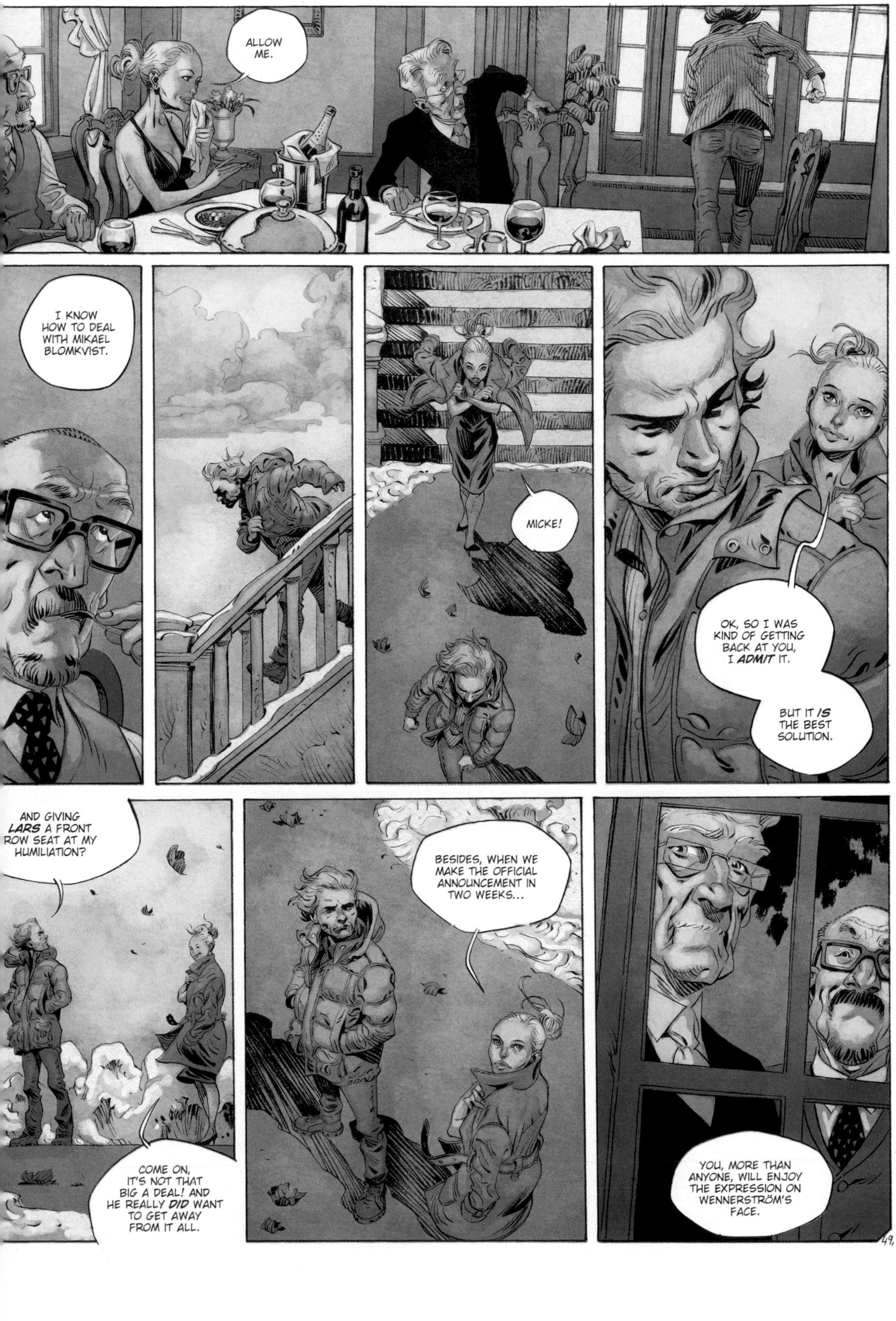
ALLOW ME.
I KNOW HOW TO DEAL WITH MIKAEL BLOMKVIST.
MICKE!
OK, SO I WAS KIND OF GETTING BACK AT YOU, I ADMIT IT.
BUT IT IS THE BEST SOLUTION.
AND GIVING LARS A FRONT ROW SEAT AT MY HUMILIATION?
COME ON, IT'S NOT THAT BIG A DEAL! AND HE REALLY DID WANT TO GET AWAY FROM IT ALL.
BESIDES, WHEN WE MAKE THE OFFICIAL ANNOUNCEMENT IN TWO WEEKS...
YOU, MORE THAN ANYONE, WILL ENJOY THE EXPRESSION ON WENNERSTRÖM'S FACE.

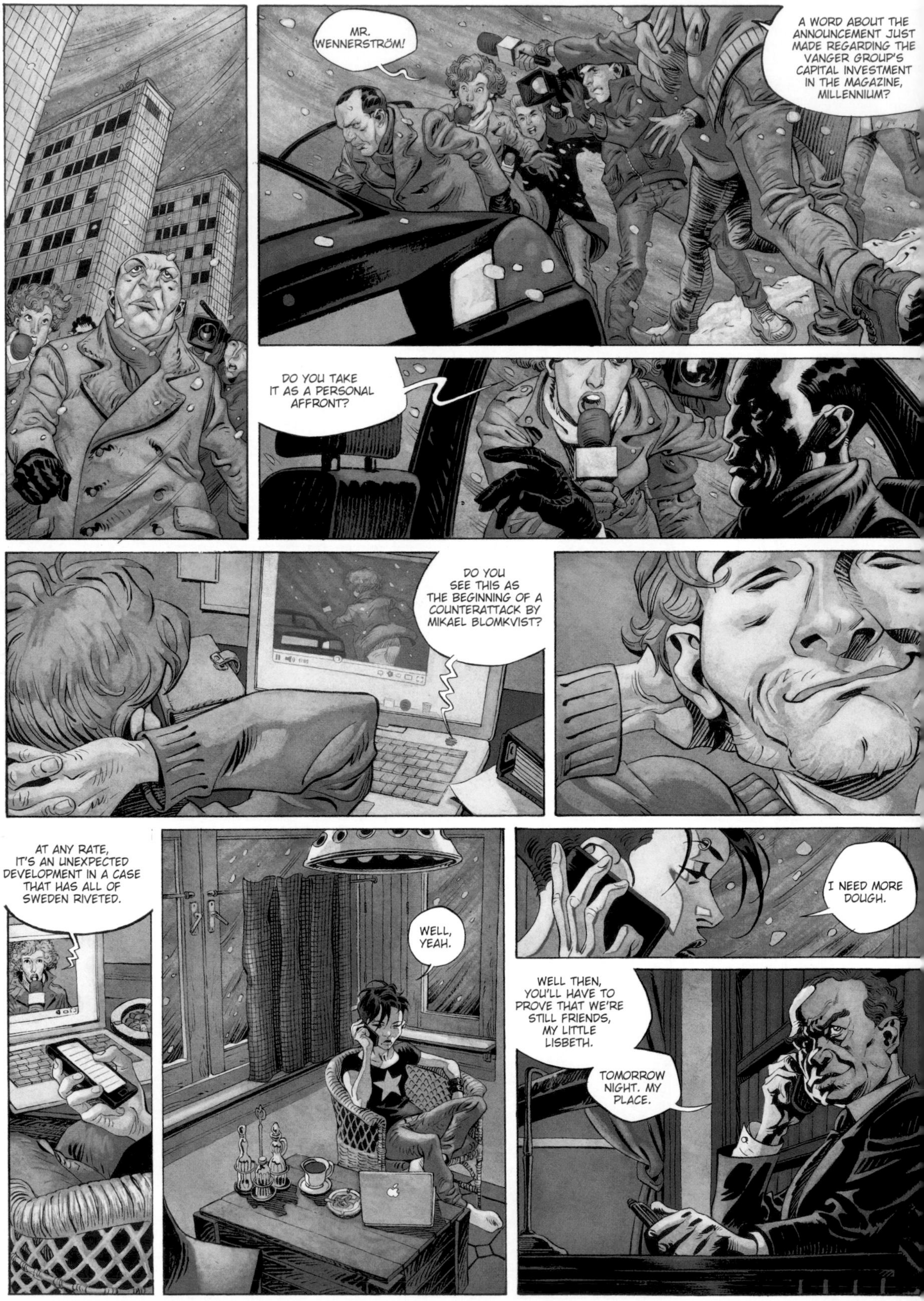
MR. WENNERSTRÖM!
A WORD ABOUT THE ANNOUNCEMENT JUST MADE REGARDING THE VANGER GROUP'S CAPITAL INVESTMENT IN THE MAGAZINE, MILLENNIUM?
DO YOU TAKE IT AS A PERSONAL AFFRONT?
DO YOU SEE THIS AS THE BEGINNING OF A COUNTERATTACK BY MIKAEL BLOMKVIST?
AT ANY RATE, IT'S AN UNEXPECTED DEVELOPMENT IN A CASE THAT HAS ALL OF SWEDEN RIVETED.
WELL, YEAH.
I NEED MORE DOUGH.
WELL THEN, YOU'LL HAVE TO PROVE THAT WE'RE STILL FRIENDS, MY LITTLE LISBETH.
TOMORROW NIGHT. MY PLACE.

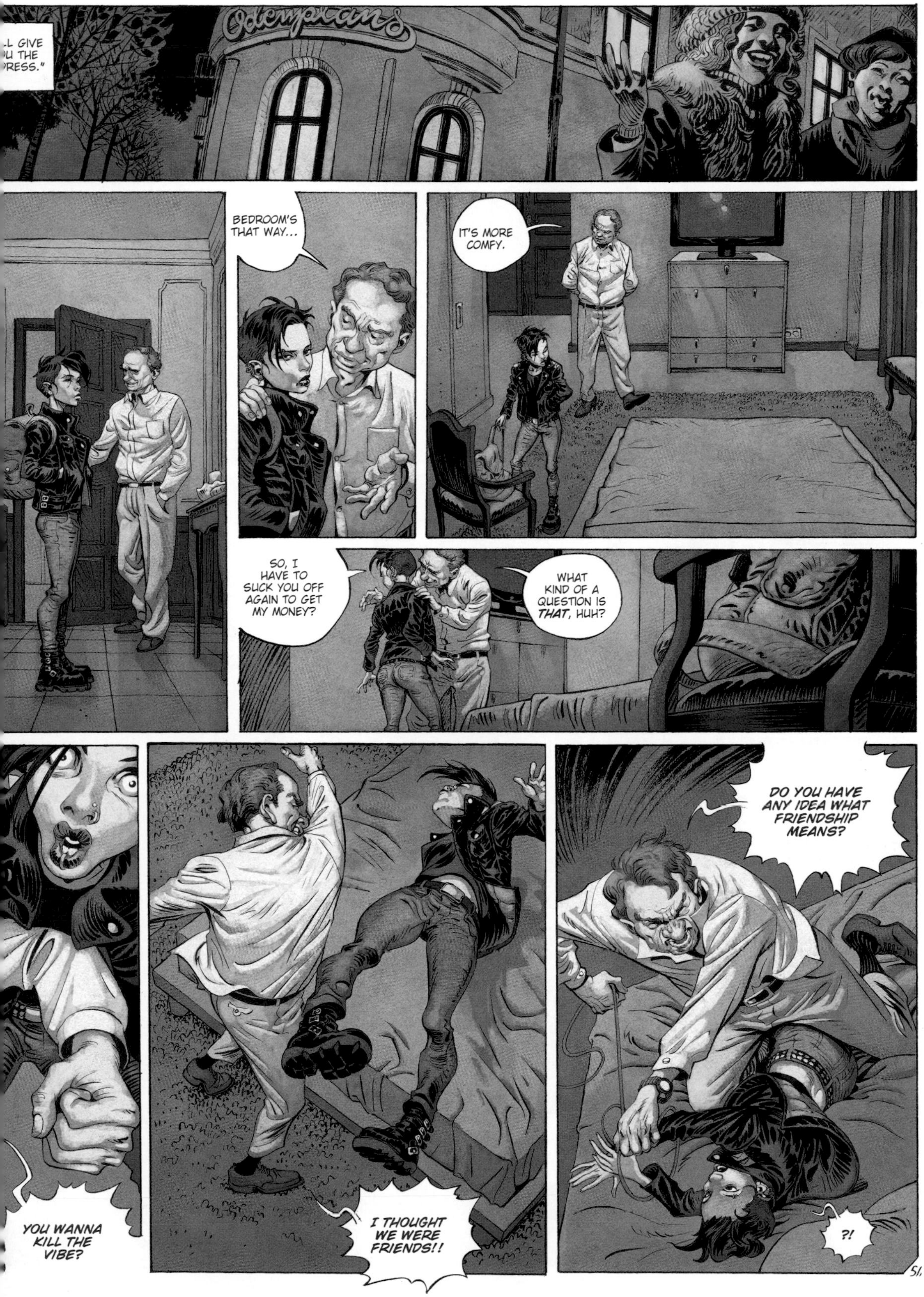

..L GIVE
..OU THE
..DRESS."
BEDROOM'S THAT WAY...
IT'S MORE COMFY.
SO, I HAVE TO SUCK YOU OFF AGAIN TO GET MY MONEY?
WHAT KIND OF A QUESTION IS THAT, HUH?
YOU WANNA KILL THE VIBE?
I THOUGHT WE WERE FRIENDS!!
DO YOU HAVE ANY IDEA WHAT FRIENDSHIP MEANS?
?!

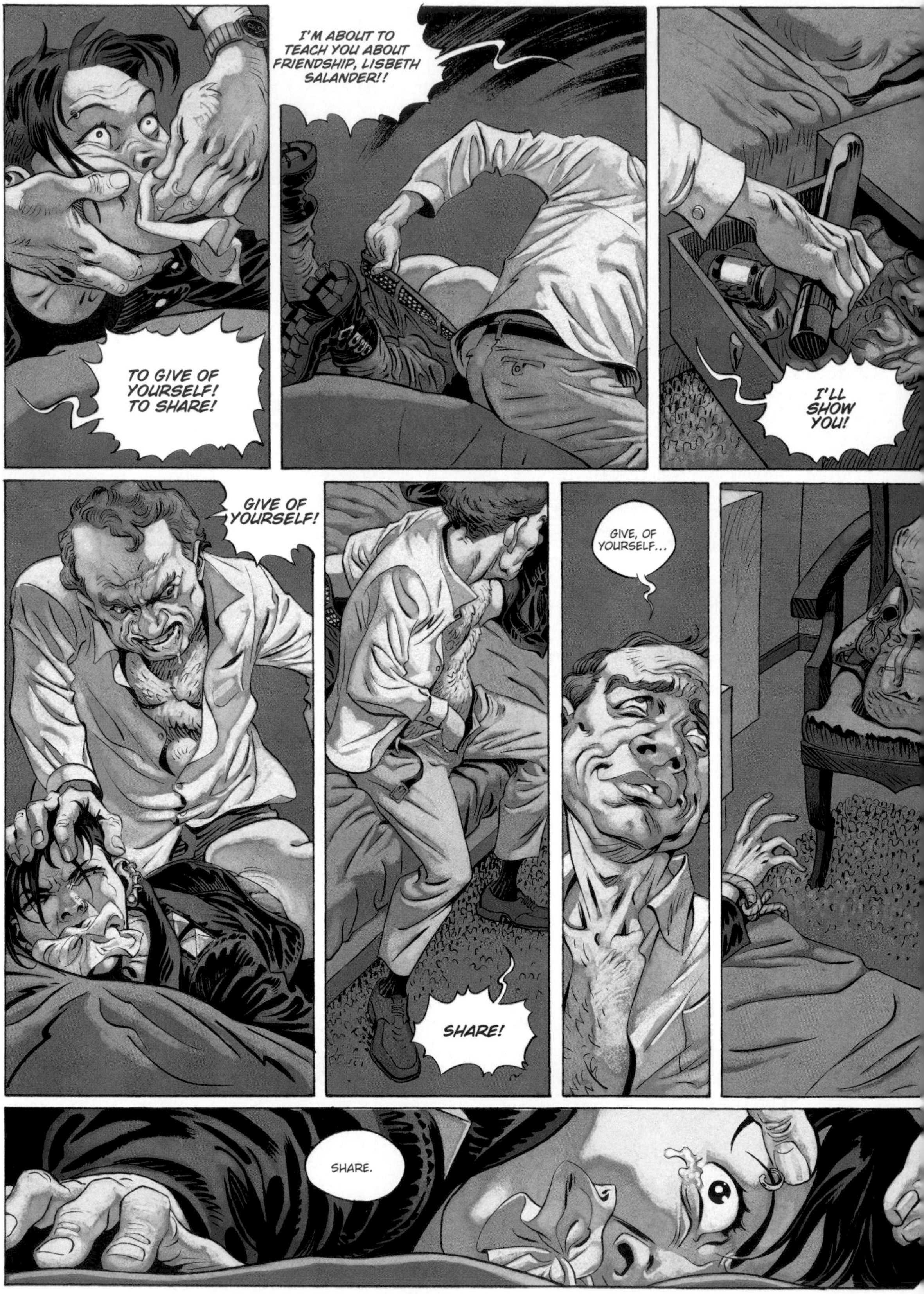
TO GIVE OF YOURSELF! TO SHARE!
I'M ABOUT TO TEACH YOU ABOUT FRIENDSHIP, LISBETH SALANDER!!
I'LL SHOW YOU!
GIVE OF YOURSELF!
SHARE!
GIVE, OF YOURSELF...
SHARE.

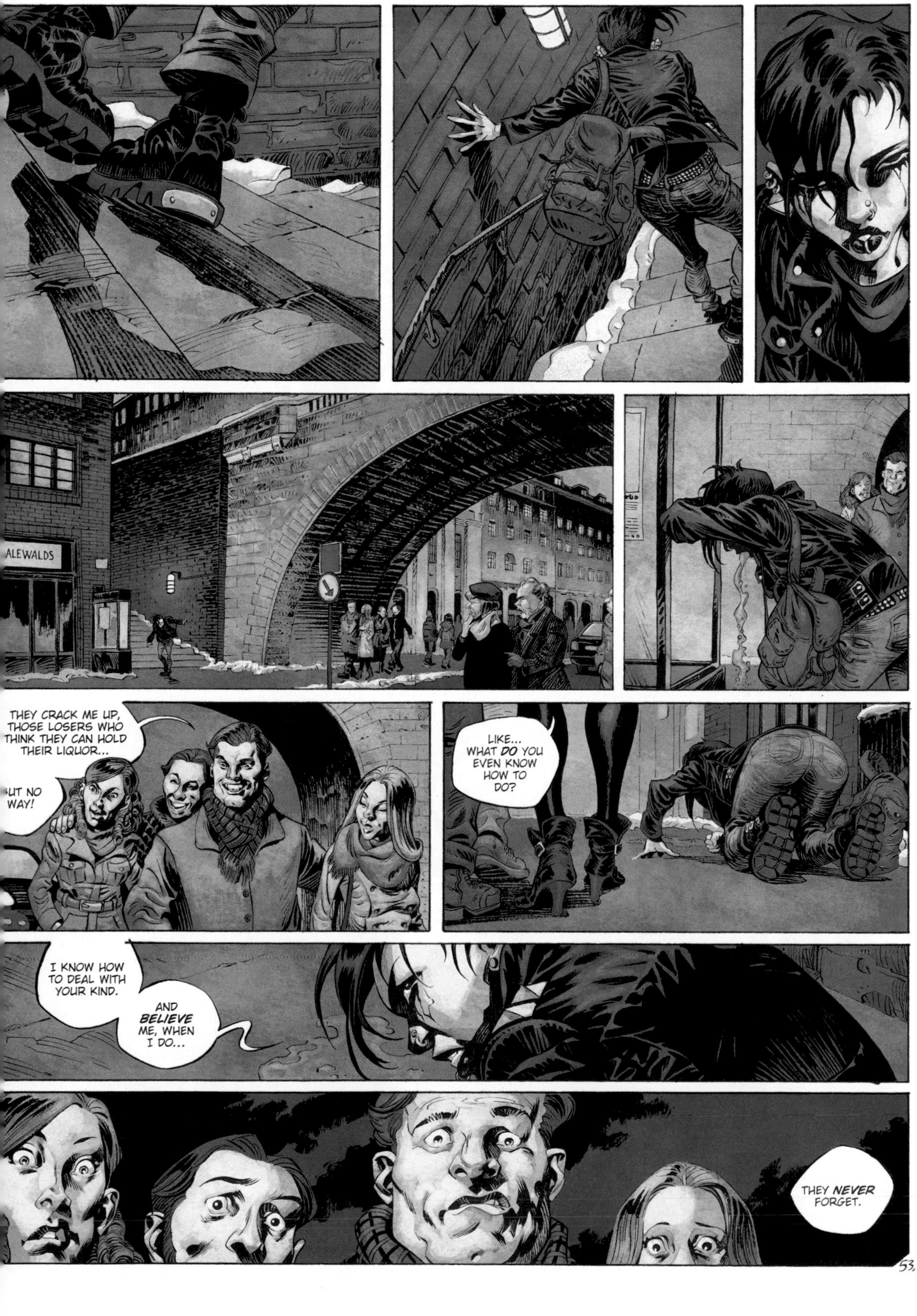

ALEWALDS
THEY CRACK ME UP, THOSE LOSERS WHO THINK THEY CAN HOLD THEIR LIQUOR...
UT NO WAY!
LIKE... WHAT *DO* YOU EVEN KNOW HOW TO DO?
I KNOW HOW TO DEAL WITH YOUR KIND.
AND *BELIEVE* ME, WHEN I DO...
THEY *NEVER* FORGET.

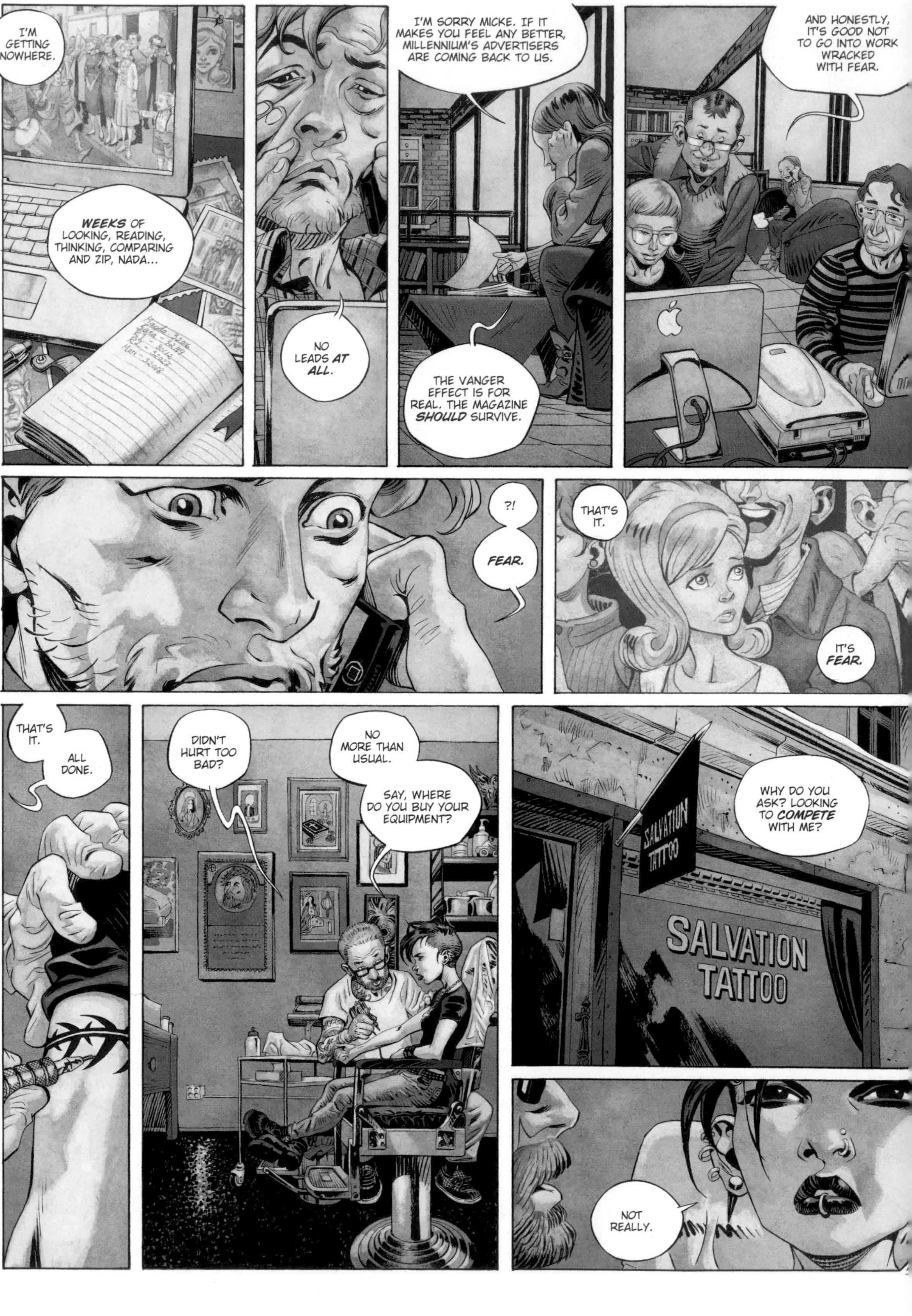
I'M GETTING NOWHERE.
WEEKS OF LOOKING, READING, THINKING, COMPARING AND ZIP, NADA...
NO LEADS AT ALL.
I'M SORRY MICKE. IF IT MAKES YOU FEEL ANY BETTER, MILLENNIUM'S ADVERTISERS ARE COMING BACK TO US.
THE VANGER EFFECT IS FOR REAL. THE MAGAZINE SHOULD SURVIVE.
AND HONESTLY, IT'S GOOD NOT TO GO INTO WORK WRACKED WITH FEAR.
?!
FEAR.
THAT'S IT.
IT'S FEAR.
THAT'S IT.
ALL DONE.
DIDN'T HURT TOO BAD?
NO MORE THAN USUAL.
SAY, WHERE DO YOU BUY YOUR EQUIPMENT?
SALVATION TATTOO
SALVATION TATTOO
WHY DO YOU ASK? LOOKING TO COMPETE WITH ME?
NOT REALLY.

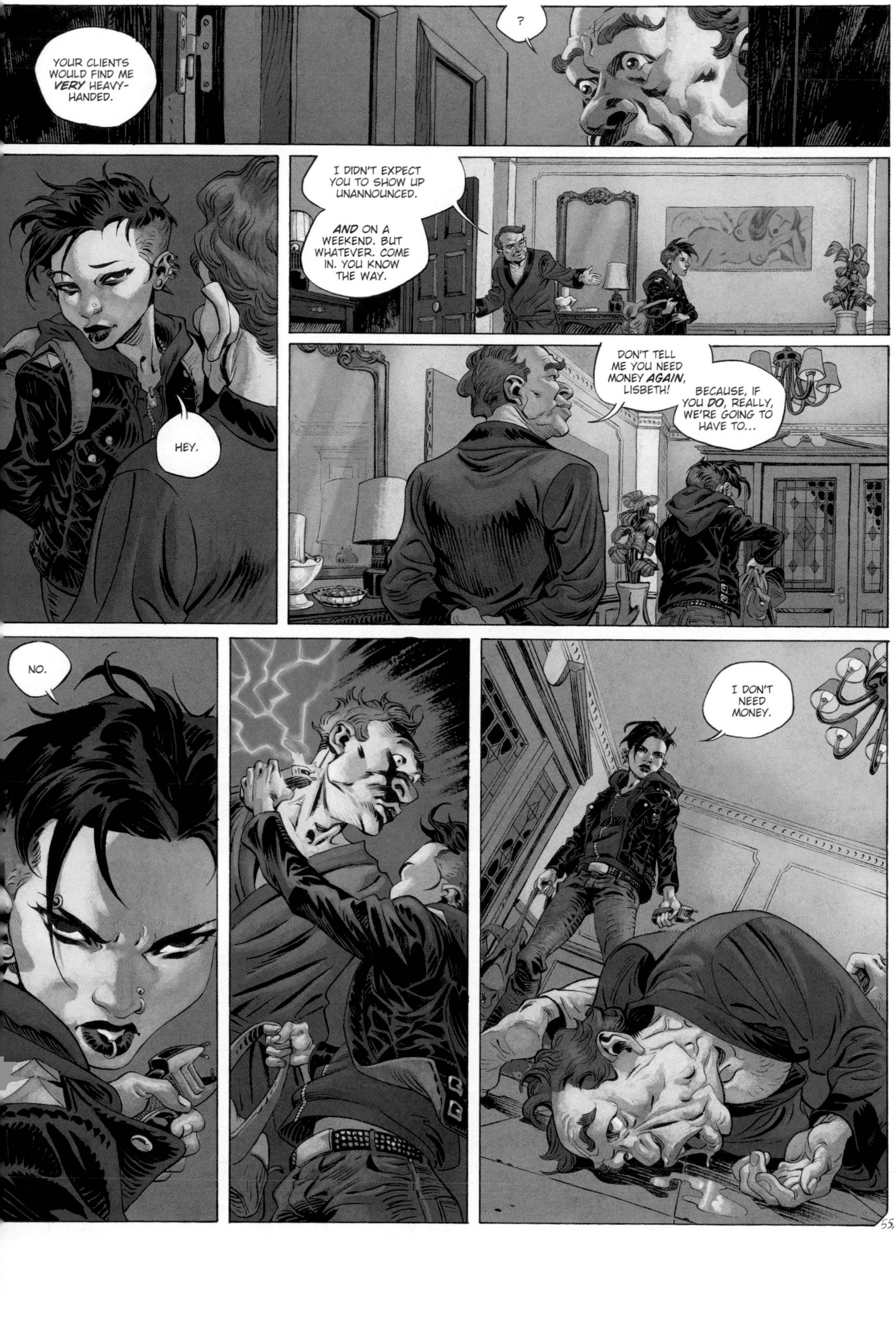
YOUR CLIENTS WOULD FIND ME VERY HEAVY-HANDED.
?
HEY.
I DIDN'T EXPECT YOU TO SHOW UP UNANNOUNCED.
AND ON A WEEKEND. BUT WHATEVER. COME IN. YOU KNOW THE WAY.
DON'T TELL ME YOU NEED MONEY AGAIN, LISBETH!
BECAUSE, IF YOU DO, REALLY, WE'RE GOING TO HAVE TO...
NO.
I DON'T NEED MONEY.

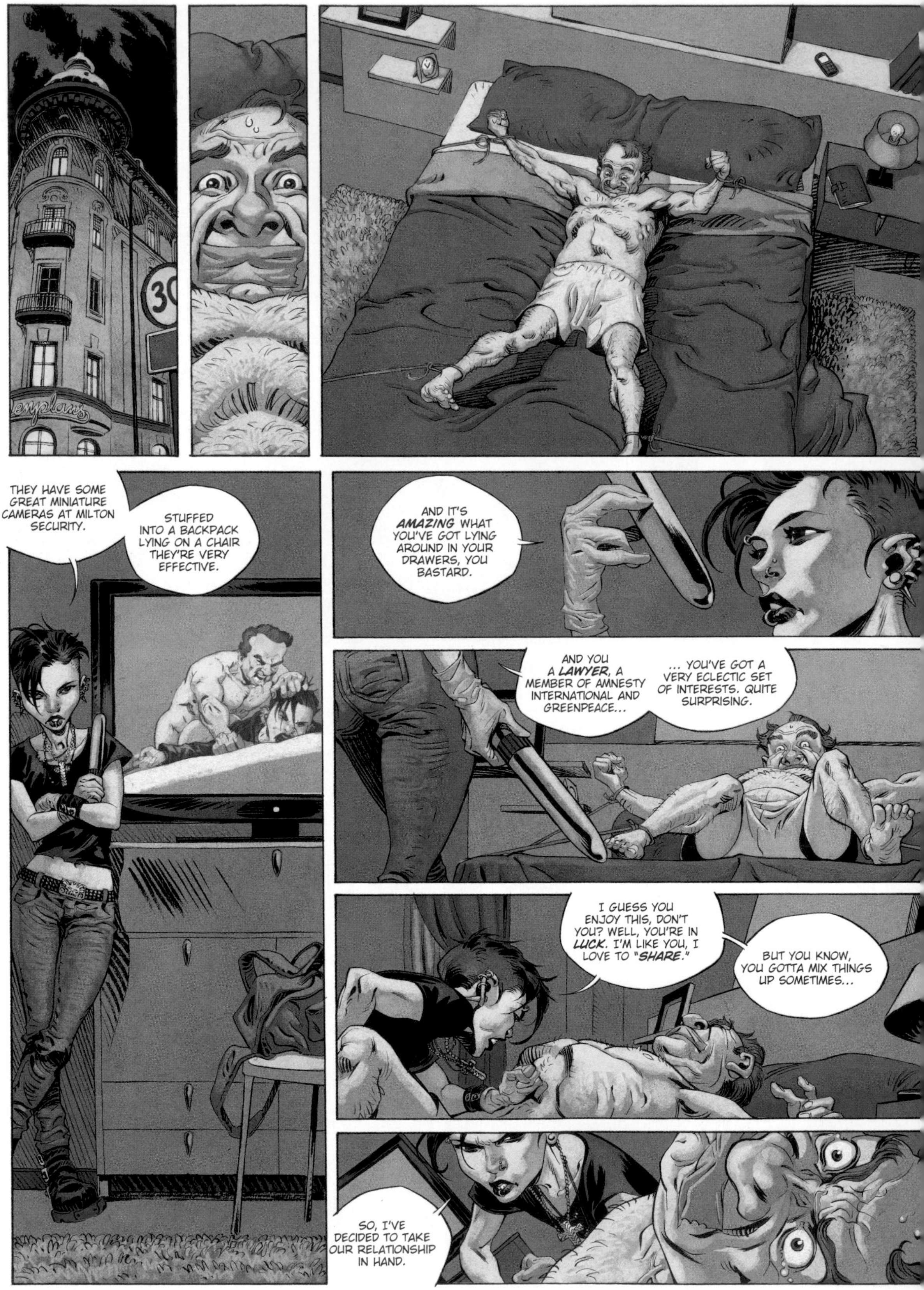
THEY HAVE SOME GREAT MINIATURE CAMERAS AT MILTON SECURITY.
STUFFED INTO A BACKPACK LYING ON A CHAIR THEY'RE VERY EFFECTIVE.
AND IT'S **AMAZING** WHAT YOU'VE GOT LYING AROUND IN YOUR DRAWERS, YOU BASTARD.
AND YOU A **LAWYER**, A MEMBER OF AMNESTY INTERNATIONAL AND GREENPEACE...
... YOU'VE GOT A VERY ECLECTIC SET OF INTERESTS. QUITE SURPRISING.
I GUESS YOU ENJOY THIS, DON'T YOU? WELL, YOU'RE IN **LUCK**. I'M LIKE YOU, I LOVE TO "**SHARE**."
BUT YOU KNOW, YOU GOTTA MIX THINGS UP SOMETIMES...
SO, I'VE DECIDED TO TAKE OUR RELATIONSHIP IN HAND.

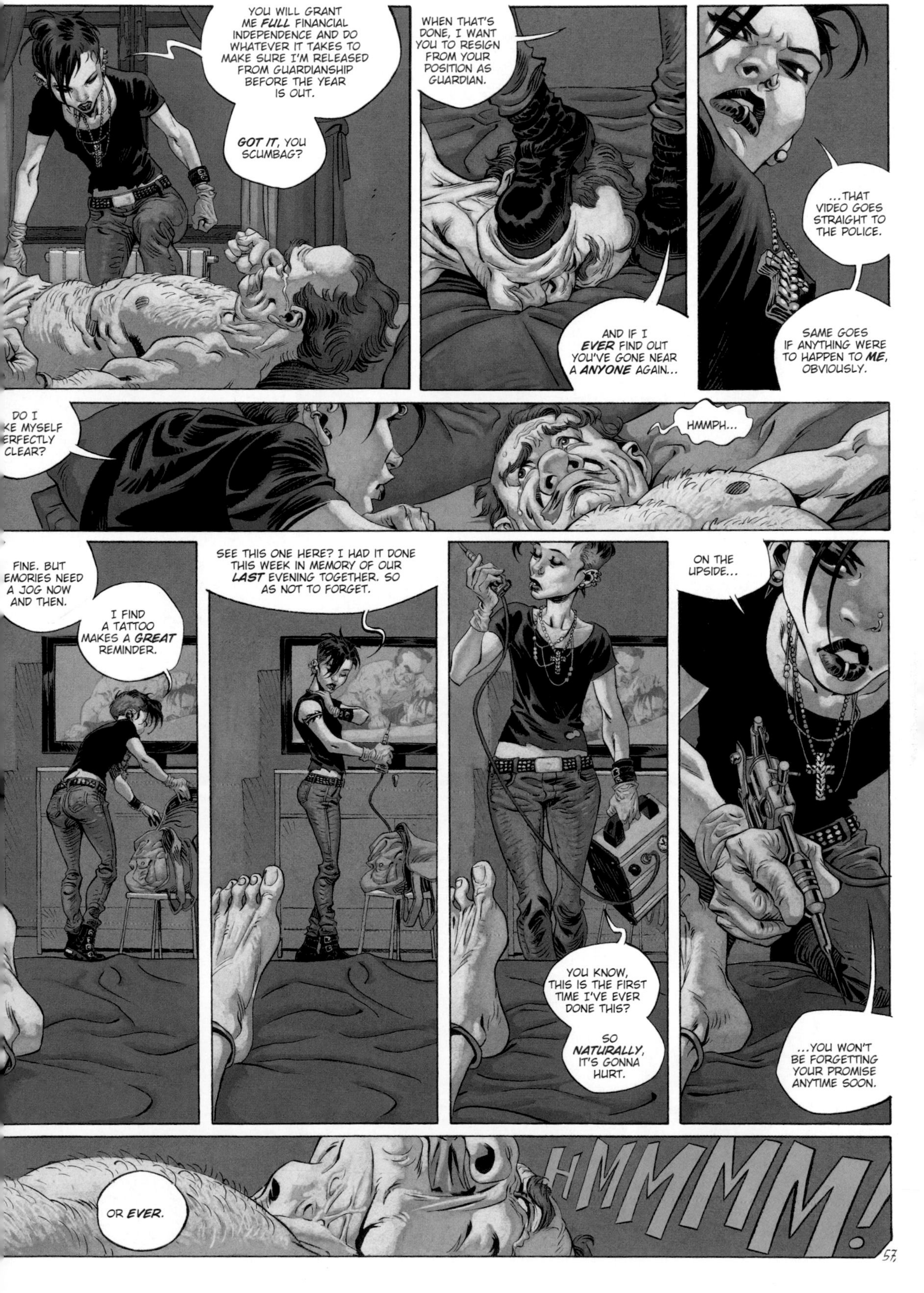
YOU WILL GRANT ME FULL FINANCIAL INDEPENDENCE AND DO WHATEVER IT TAKES TO MAKE SURE I'M RELEASED FROM GUARDIANSHIP BEFORE THE YEAR IS OUT.
GOT IT, YOU SCUMBAG?
WHEN THAT'S DONE, I WANT YOU TO RESIGN FROM YOUR POSITION AS GUARDIAN.
AND IF I EVER FIND OUT YOU'VE GONE NEAR A ANYONE AGAIN...
...THAT VIDEO GOES STRAIGHT TO THE POLICE.
SAME GOES IF ANYTHING WERE TO HAPPEN TO ME, OBVIOUSLY.
DO I KE MYSELF ERFECTLY CLEAR?
HMMPH...
FINE. BUT EMORIES NEED A JOG NOW AND THEN.
I FIND A TATTOO MAKES A GREAT REMINDER.
SEE THIS ONE HERE? I HAD IT DONE THIS WEEK IN MEMORY OF OUR LAST EVENING TOGETHER. SO AS NOT TO FORGET.
YOU KNOW, THIS IS THE FIRST TIME I'VE EVER DONE THIS?
SO NATURALLY, IT'S GONNA HURT.
ON THE UPSIDE...
...YOU WON'T BE FORGETTING YOUR PROMISE ANYTIME SOON.
OR EVER.
HMMMM!

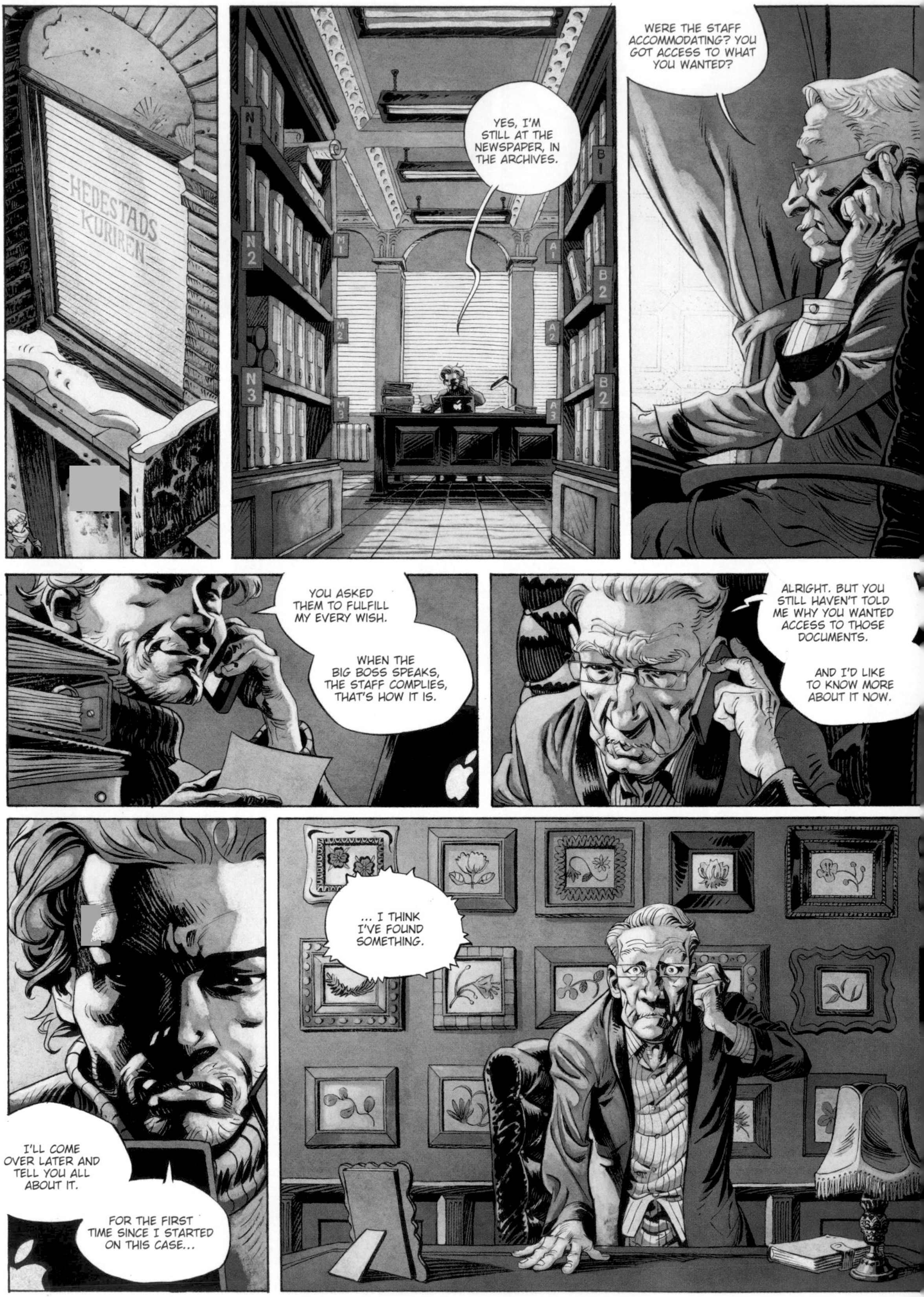
HEDESTADS KURIREN
N1
N2
N3
M1
M2
M3
B1
A1
B2
A2
B2
A3
YES, I'M STILL AT THE NEWSPAPER, IN THE ARCHIVES.
WERE THE STAFF ACCOMMODATING? YOU GOT ACCESS TO WHAT YOU WANTED?
YOU ASKED THEM TO FULFILL MY EVERY WISH.
WHEN THE BIG BOSS SPEAKS, THE STAFF COMPLIES, THAT'S HOW IT IS.
ALRIGHT. BUT YOU STILL HAVEN'T TOLD ME WHY YOU WANTED ACCESS TO THOSE DOCUMENTS.
AND I'D LIKE TO KNOW MORE ABOUT IT NOW.
I'LL COME OVER LATER AND TELL YOU ALL ABOUT IT.
FOR THE FIRST TIME SINCE I STARTED ON THIS CASE...
... I THINK I'VE FOUND SOMETHING.

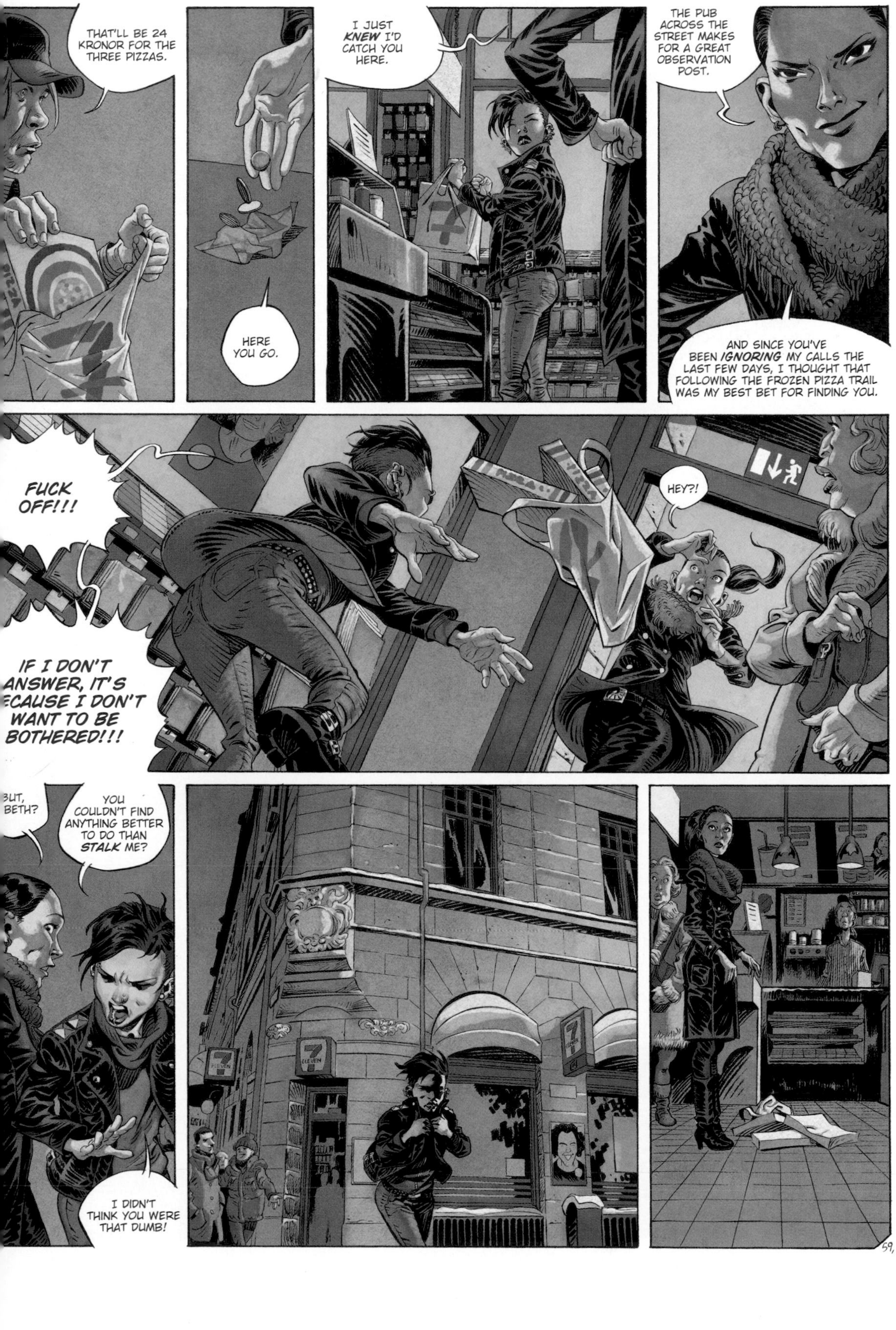
THAT'LL BE 24 KRONOR FOR THE THREE PIZZAS.
HERE YOU GO.
I JUST KNEW I'D CATCH YOU HERE.
THE PUB ACROSS THE STREET MAKES FOR A GREAT OBSERVATION POST.
AND SINCE YOU'VE BEEN IGNORING MY CALLS THE LAST FEW DAYS, I THOUGHT THAT FOLLOWING THE FROZEN PIZZA TRAIL WAS MY BEST BET FOR FINDING YOU.
FUCK OFF!!!
IF I DON'T ANSWER, IT'S BECAUSE I DON'T WANT TO BE BOTHERED!!!
HEY?!
BUT, BETH?
YOU COULDN'T FIND ANYTHING BETTER TO DO THAN STALK ME?
I DIDN'T THINK YOU WERE THAT DUMB!

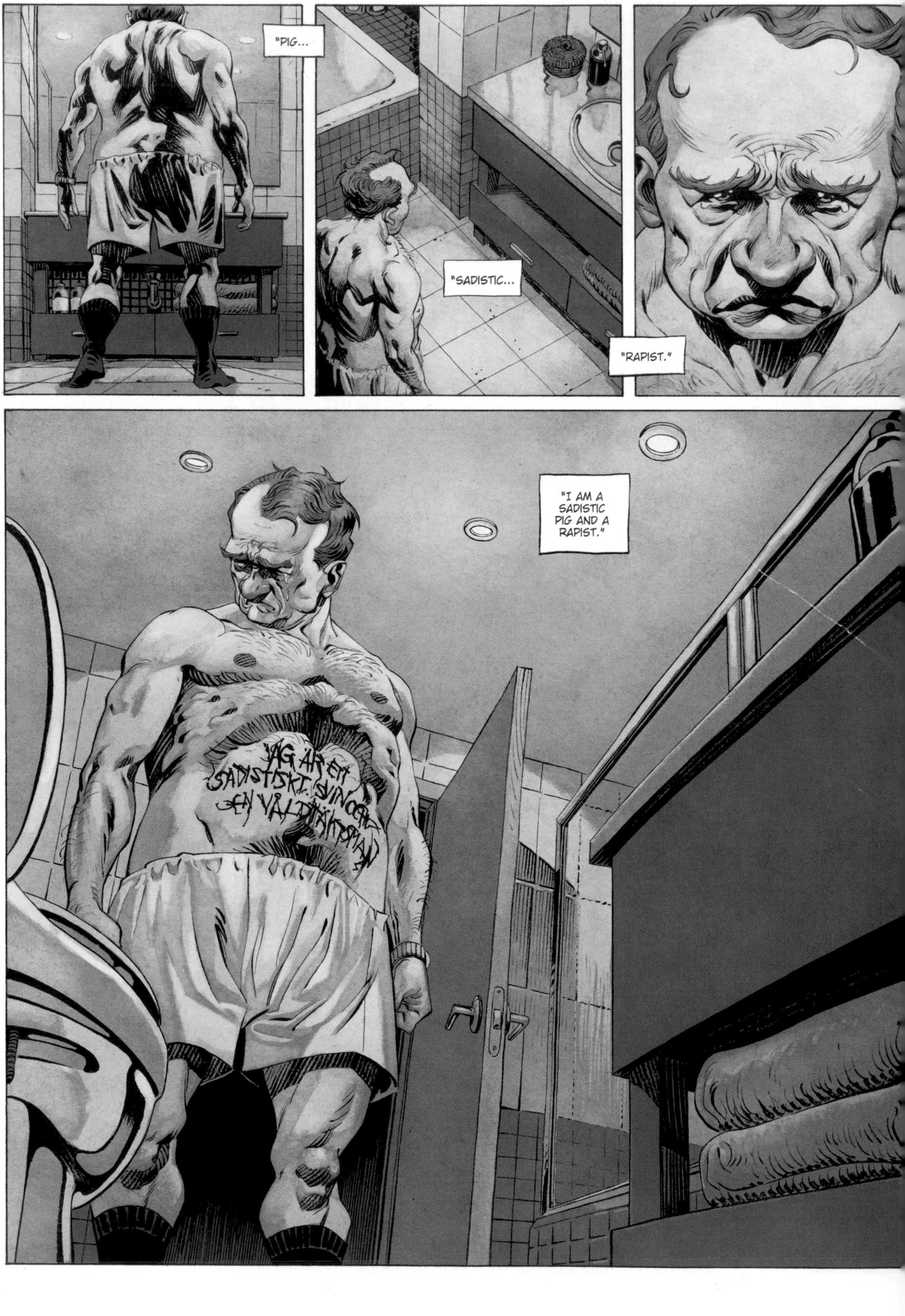
"PIG...
"SADISTIC...
"RAPIST."
"I AM A SADISTIC PIG AND A RAPIST."
JAG ÄR ETT SADISTISKT SVIN OCH EN VÅLDTÄKTSMAN

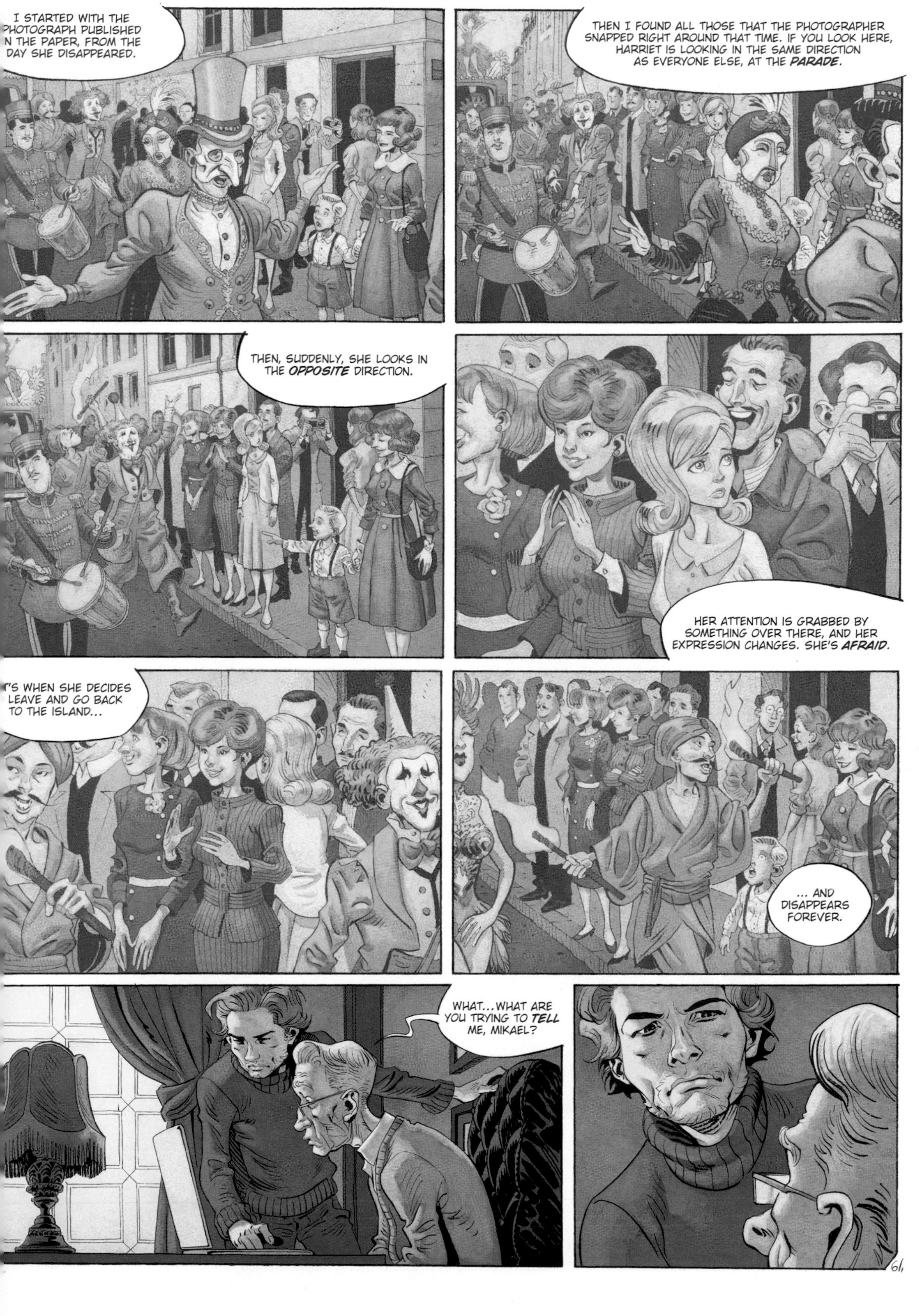
I STARTED WITH THE PHOTOGRAPH PUBLISHED IN THE PAPER, FROM THE DAY SHE DISAPPEARED.
THEN I FOUND ALL THOSE THAT THE PHOTOGRAPHER SNAPPED RIGHT AROUND THAT TIME. IF YOU LOOK HERE, HARRIET IS LOOKING IN THE SAME DIRECTION AS EVERYONE ELSE, AT THE PARADE.
THEN, SUDDENLY, SHE LOOKS IN THE OPPOSITE DIRECTION.
HER ATTENTION IS GRABBED BY SOMETHING OVER THERE, AND HER EXPRESSION CHANGES. SHE'S AFRAID.
'S WHEN SHE DECIDES LEAVE AND GO BACK TO THE ISLAND...
... AND DISAPPEARS FOREVER.
WHAT... WHAT ARE YOU TRYING TO TELL ME, MIKAEL?

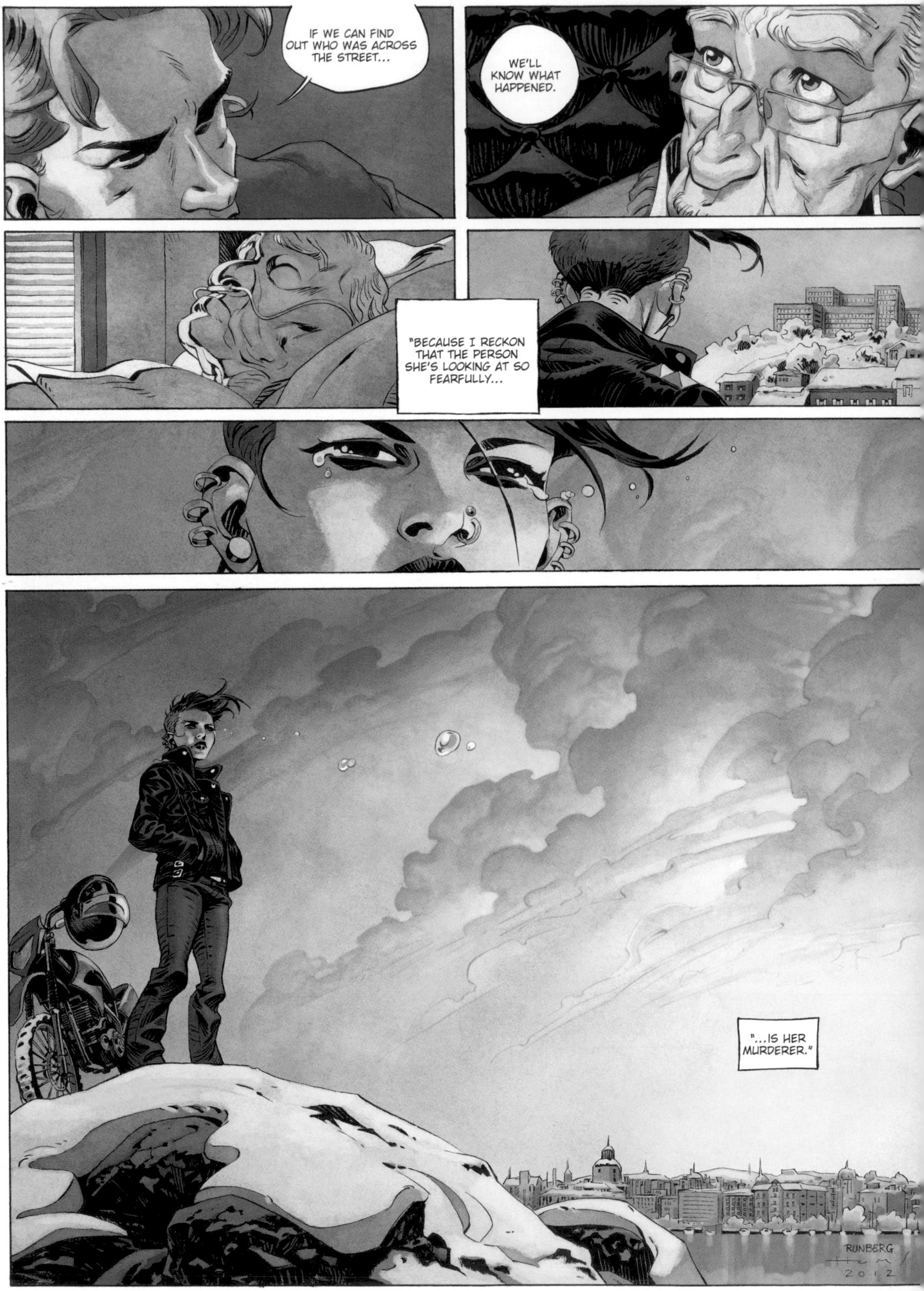
IF WE CAN FIND OUT WHO WAS ACROSS THE STREET...
WE'LL KNOW WHAT HAPPENED.
"BECAUSE I RECKON THAT THE PERSON SHE'S LOOKING AT SO FEARFULLY...
"...IS HER MURDERER."
RUNBERG
2012

MILLENNIUM

THE GIRL WITH THE DRAGON TATTOO

CHAPTER 2

WRITTEN BY
SYLVAIN RUNBERG

ARTWORK BY
HOMS

TRANSLATED BY
RACHEL ZERNER

BASED ON THE NOVEL
TRILOGY BY
STIEG LARSSON

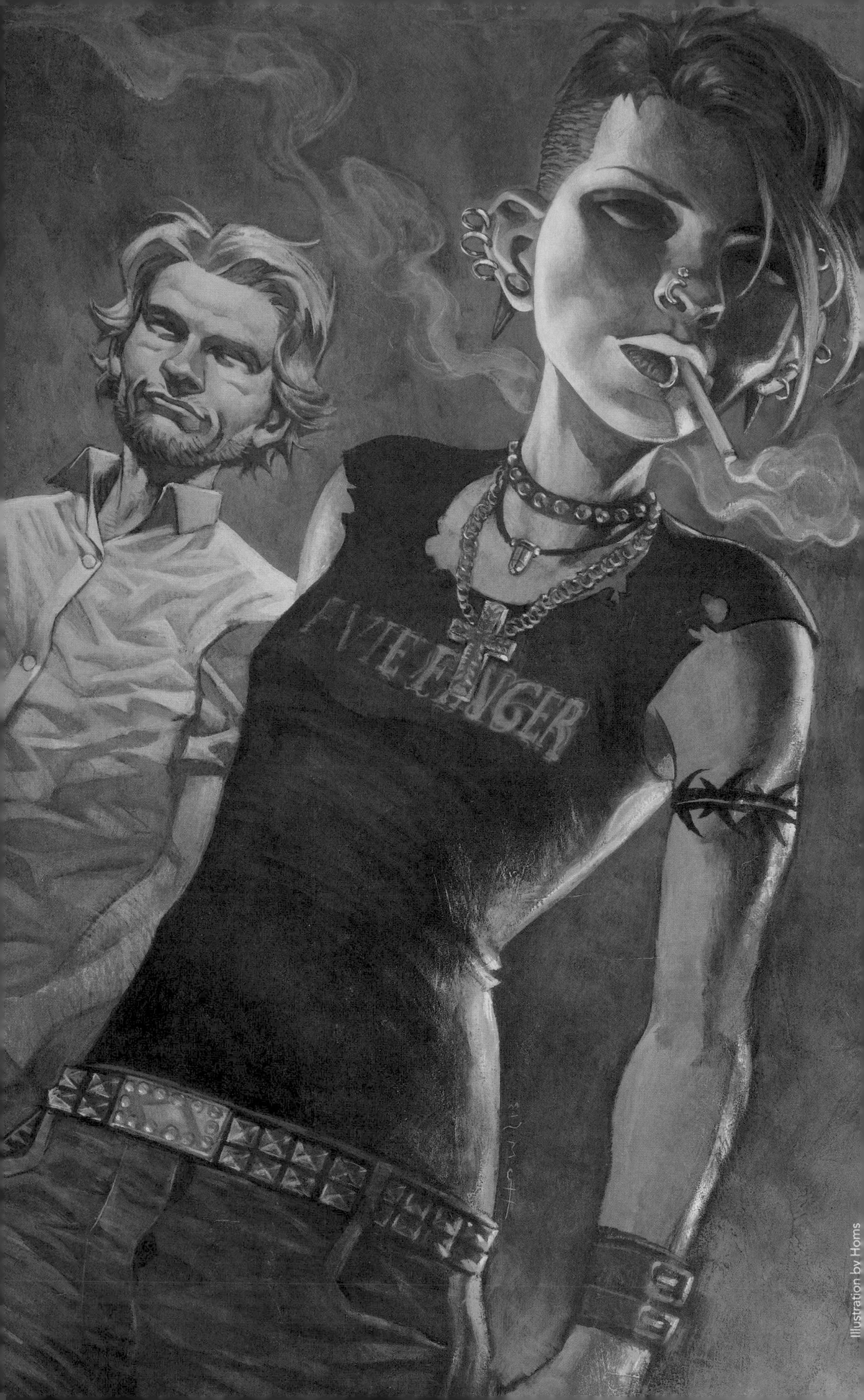

Illustration by Homs

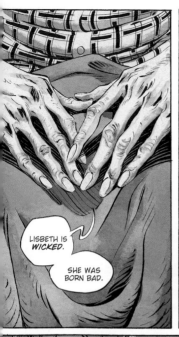
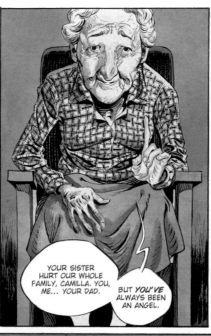

LISBETH IS *WICKED.*

SHE WAS BORN BAD.

YOUR SISTER HURT OUR WHOLE FAMILY, CAMILLA. YOU, ME... YOUR DAD.

BUT *YOU'VE* ALWAYS BEEN AN ANGEL.

MOM.

YOU... YOU'RE CONFUSED AGAIN.

LISBETH...

THAT'S ME.

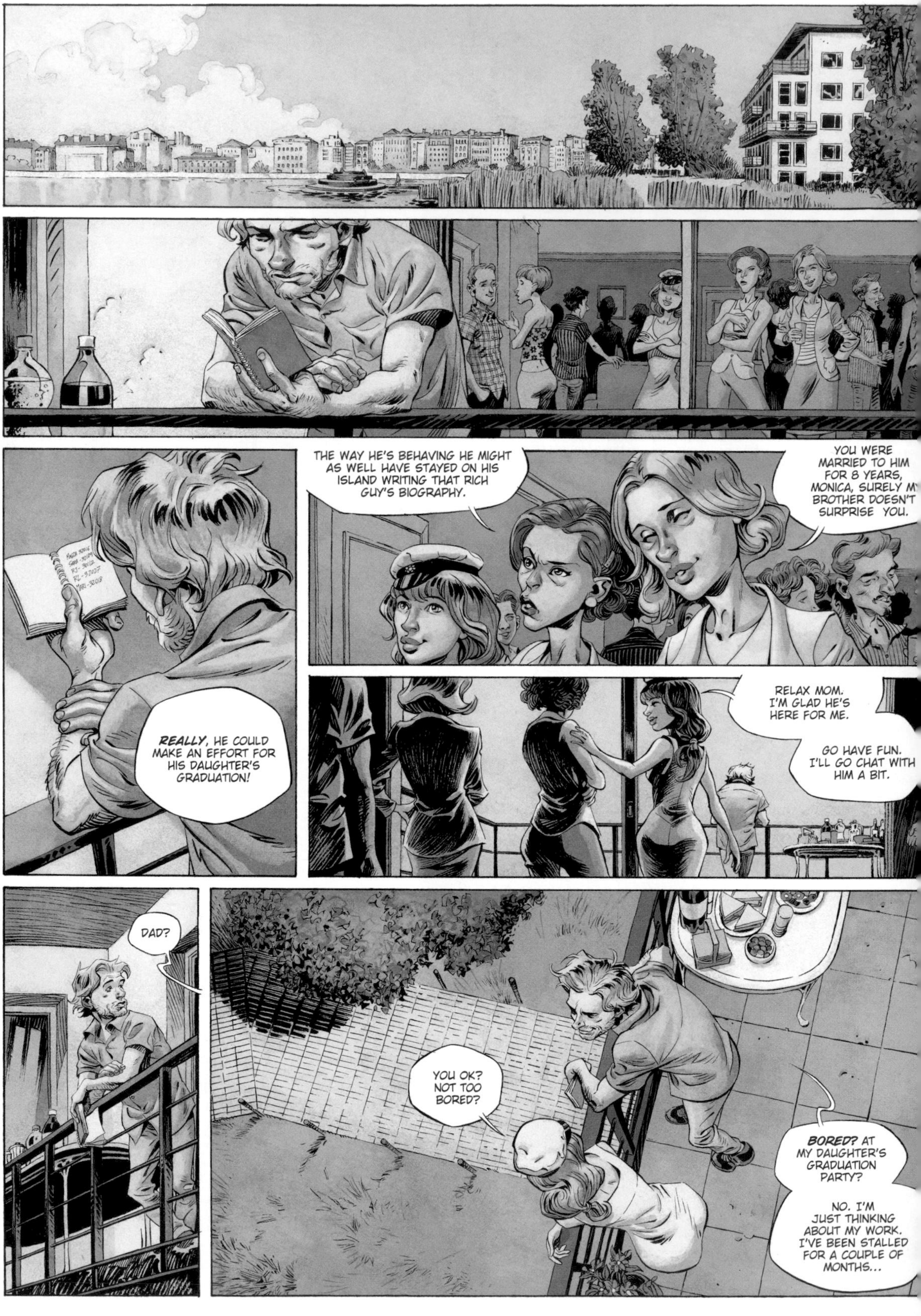
THE WAY HE'S BEHAVING HE MIGHT AS WELL HAVE STAYED ON HIS ISLAND WRITING THAT RICH GUY'S BIOGRAPHY.
YOU WERE MARRIED TO HIM FOR 8 YEARS, MONICA, SURELY MY BROTHER DOESN'T SURPRISE YOU.
REALLY, HE COULD MAKE AN EFFORT FOR HIS DAUGHTER'S GRADUATION!
RELAX MOM. I'M GLAD HE'S HERE FOR ME.
GO HAVE FUN. I'LL GO CHAT WITH HIM A BIT.
DAD?
YOU OK? NOT TOO BORED?
BORED? AT MY DAUGHTER'S GRADUATION PARTY?
NO. I'M JUST THINKING ABOUT MY WORK. I'VE BEEN STALLED FOR A COUPLE OF MONTHS...

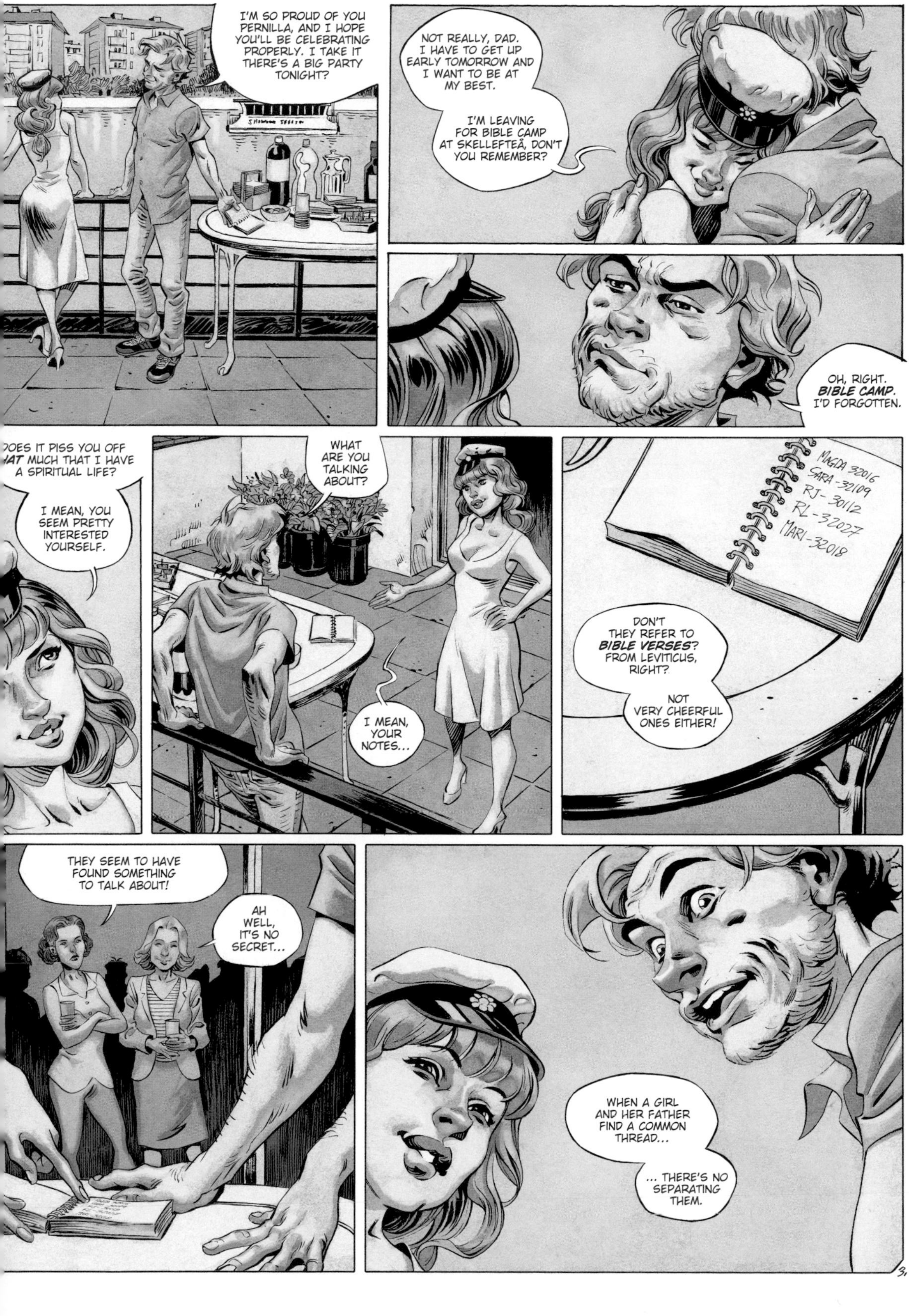
I'M SO PROUD OF YOU PERNILLA, AND I HOPE YOU'LL BE CELEBRATING PROPERLY. I TAKE IT THERE'S A BIG PARTY TONIGHT?
NOT REALLY, DAD. I HAVE TO GET UP EARLY TOMORROW AND I WANT TO BE AT MY BEST.
I'M LEAVING FOR BIBLE CAMP AT SKELLEFTEÅ, DON'T YOU REMEMBER?
OH, RIGHT. BIBLE CAMP. I'D FORGOTTEN.
DOES IT PISS YOU OFF THAT MUCH THAT I HAVE A SPIRITUAL LIFE?
I MEAN, YOU SEEM PRETTY INTERESTED YOURSELF.
WHAT ARE YOU TALKING ABOUT?
I MEAN, YOUR NOTES...
MAGDA-32016
SARA-32109
RJ-30112
RL-32027
MARI-32018
DON'T THEY REFER TO BIBLE VERSES? FROM LEVITICUS, RIGHT?
NOT VERY CHEERFUL ONES EITHER!
THEY SEEM TO HAVE FOUND SOMETHING TO TALK ABOUT!
AH WELL, IT'S NO SECRET...
WHEN A GIRL AND HER FATHER FIND A COMMON THREAD...
... THERE'S NO SEPARATING THEM.

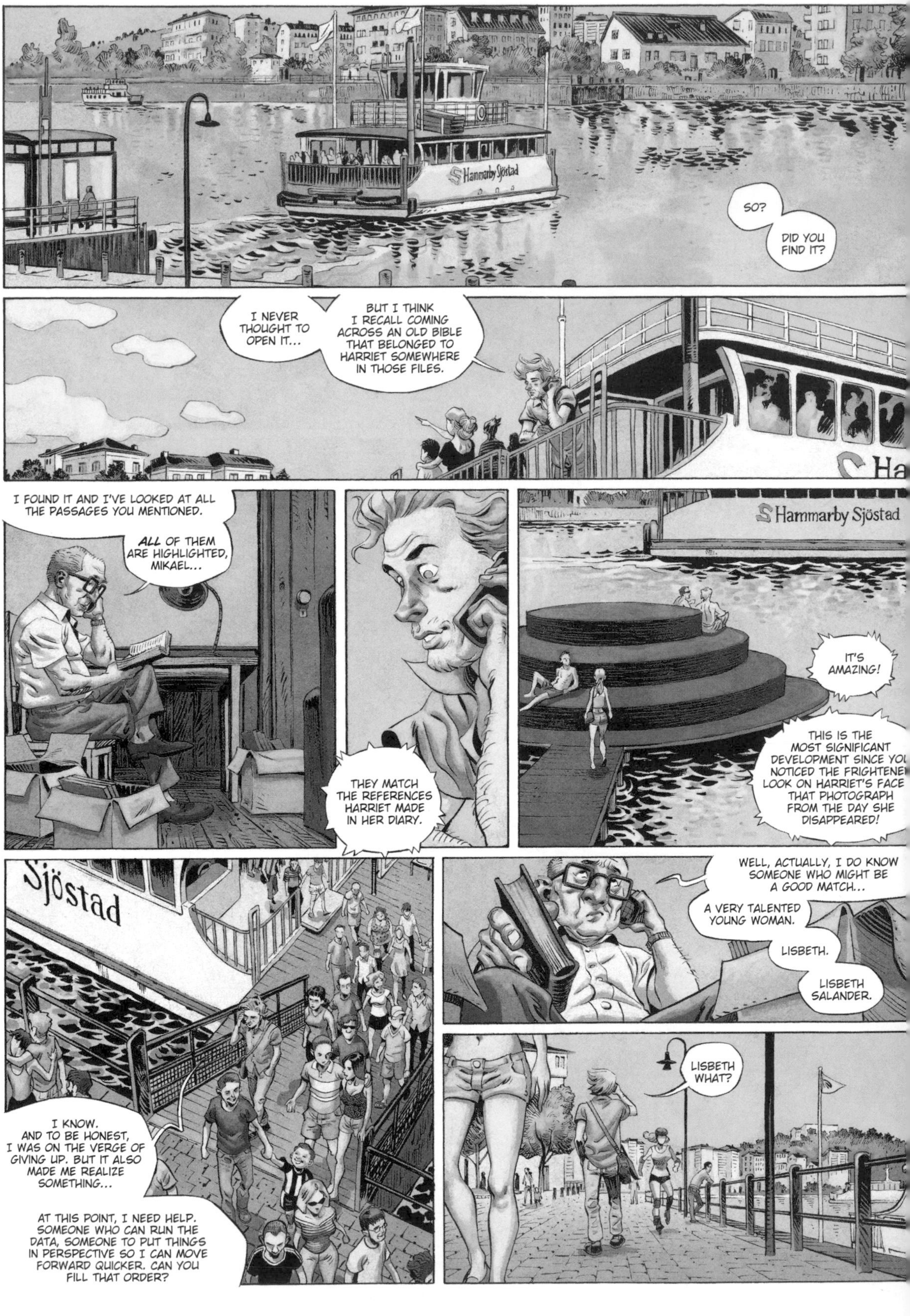
Hammarby Sjöstad
SO?
DID YOU FIND IT?
I NEVER THOUGHT TO OPEN IT...
BUT I THINK I RECALL COMING ACROSS AN OLD BIBLE THAT BELONGED TO HARRIET SOMEWHERE IN THOSE FILES.
I FOUND IT AND I'VE LOOKED AT ALL THE PASSAGES YOU MENTIONED.
ALL OF THEM ARE HIGHLIGHTED, MIKAEL...
THEY MATCH THE REFERENCES HARRIET MADE IN HER DIARY.
Hammarby Sjöstad
IT'S AMAZING!
THIS IS THE MOST SIGNIFICANT DEVELOPMENT SINCE YOU NOTICED THE FRIGHTENE LOOK ON HARRIET'S FACE THAT PHOTOGRAPH FROM THE DAY SHE DISAPPEARED!
Sjöstad
I KNOW. AND TO BE HONEST, I WAS ON THE VERGE OF GIVING UP. BUT IT ALSO MADE ME REALIZE SOMETHING...
AT THIS POINT, I NEED HELP. SOMEONE WHO CAN RUN THE DATA, SOMEONE TO PUT THINGS IN PERSPECTIVE SO I CAN MOVE FORWARD QUICKER. CAN YOU FILL THAT ORDER?
WELL, ACTUALLY, I DO KNOW SOMEONE WHO MIGHT BE A GOOD MATCH...
A VERY TALENTED YOUNG WOMAN.
LISBETH.
LISBETH SALANDER.
LISBETH WHAT?

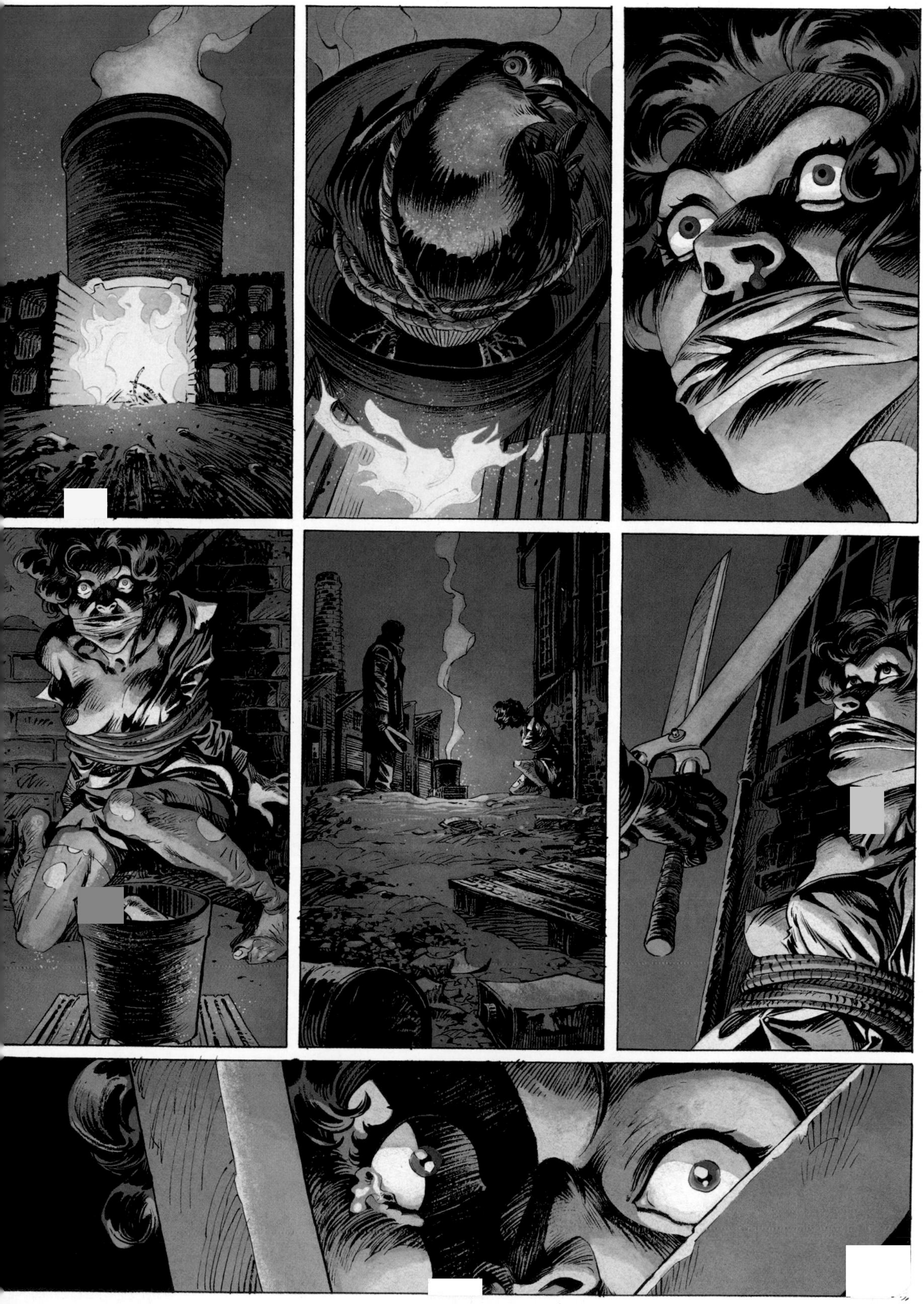

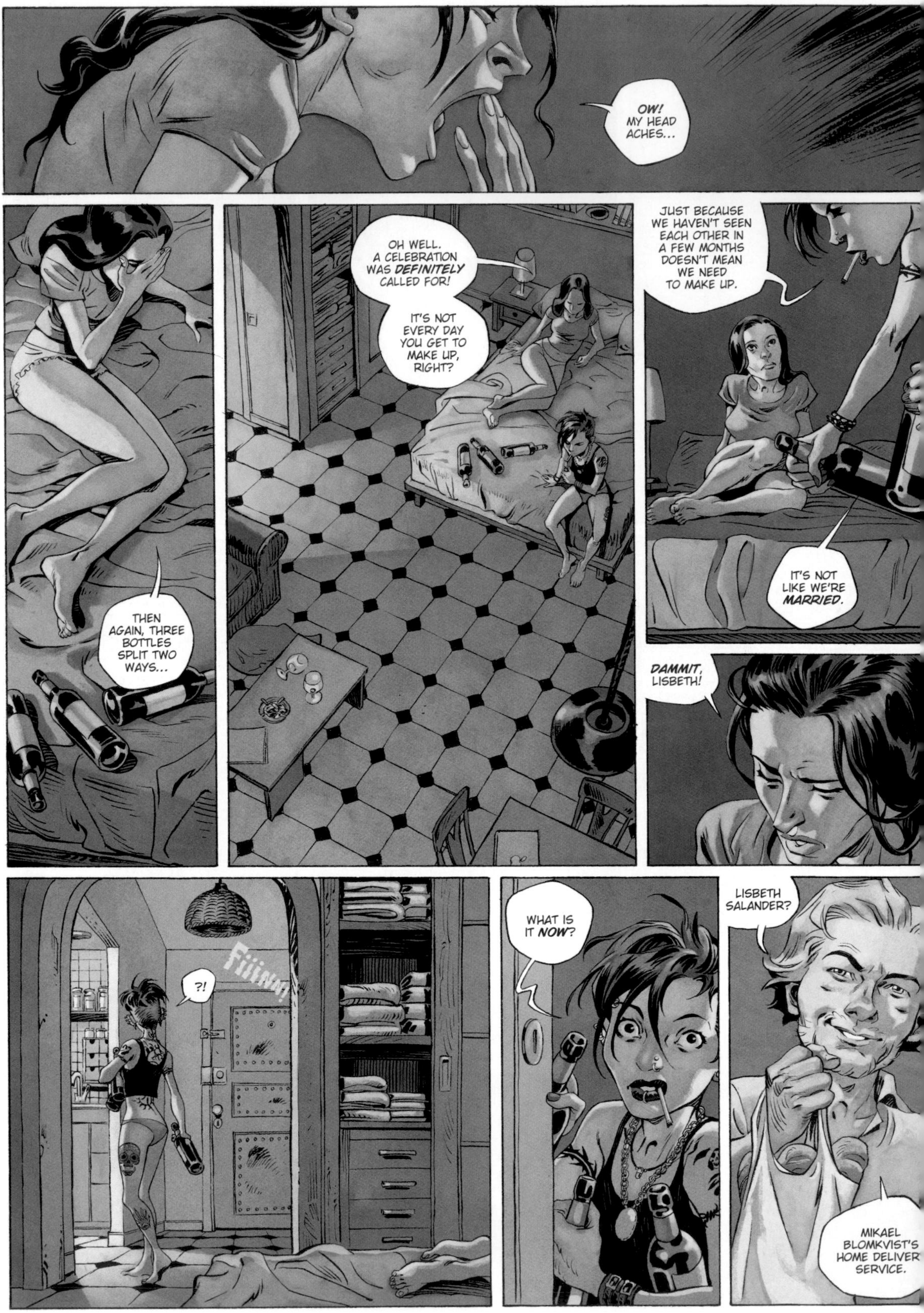
OW! MY HEAD ACHES...
THEN AGAIN, THREE BOTTLES SPLIT TWO WAYS...
OH WELL. A CELEBRATION WAS DEFINITELY CALLED FOR!
IT'S NOT EVERY DAY YOU GET TO MAKE UP, RIGHT?
JUST BECAUSE WE HAVEN'T SEEN EACH OTHER IN A FEW MONTHS DOESN'T MEAN WE NEED TO MAKE UP.
IT'S NOT LIKE WE'RE MARRIED.
DAMMIT, LISBETH!
?!
FIIINN!
WHAT IS IT NOW?
LISBETH SALANDER?
MIKAEL BLOMKVIST'S HOME DELIVER SERVICE.

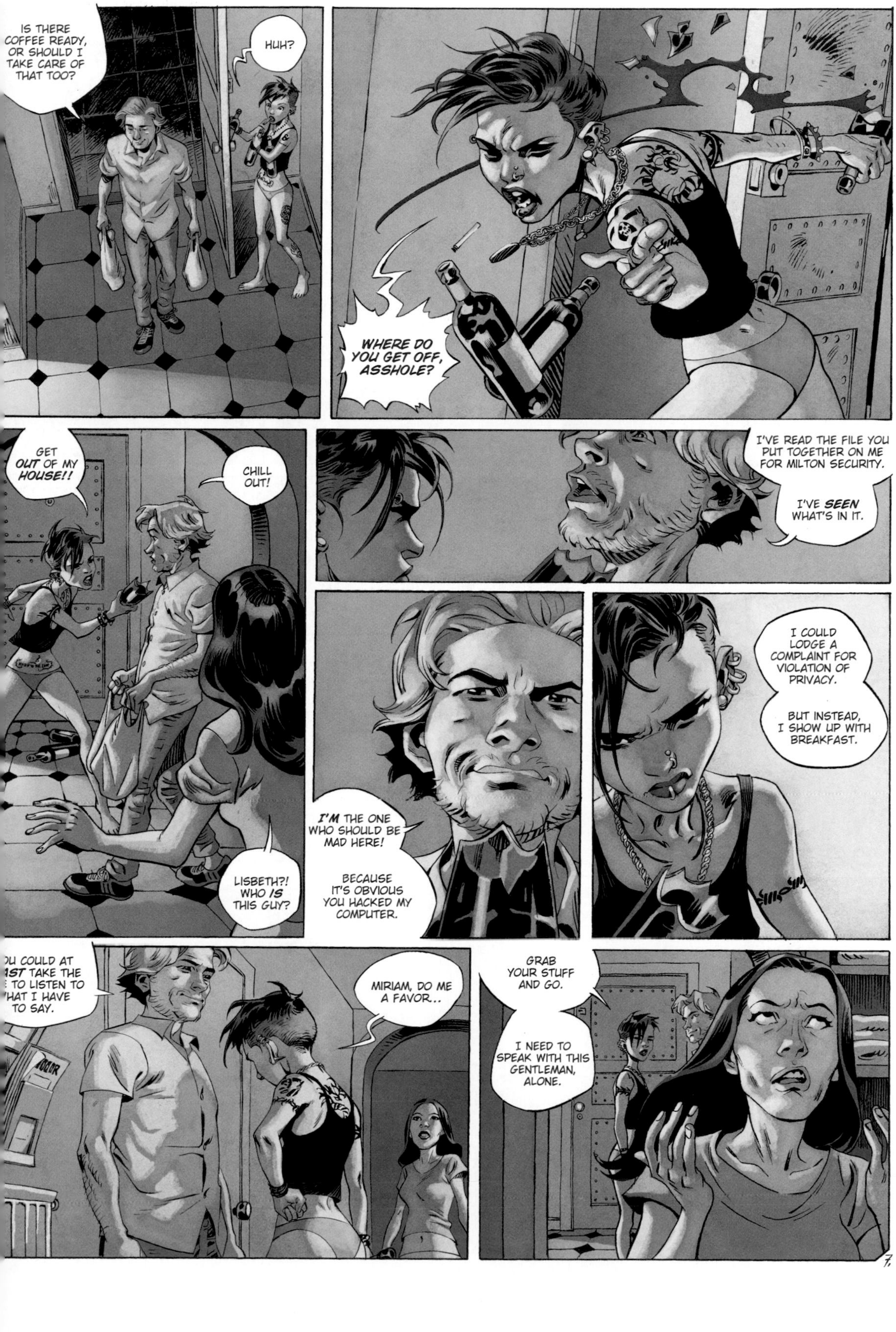

IS THERE COFFEE READY, OR SHOULD I TAKE CARE OF THAT TOO?
HUH?
WHERE DO YOU GET OFF, ASSHOLE?
GET OUT OF MY HOUSE!!
CHILL OUT!
LISBETH?! WHO IS THIS GUY?
I'VE READ THE FILE YOU PUT TOGETHER ON ME FOR MILTON SECURITY.
I'VE SEEN WHAT'S IN IT.
I'M THE ONE WHO SHOULD BE MAD HERE!
BECAUSE IT'S OBVIOUS YOU HACKED MY COMPUTER.
I COULD LODGE A COMPLAINT FOR VIOLATION OF PRIVACY.
BUT INSTEAD, I SHOW UP WITH BREAKFAST.
U COULD AT AST TAKE THE TO LISTEN TO HAT I HAVE TO SAY.
MIRIAM, DO ME A FAVOR...
GRAB YOUR STUFF AND GO.
I NEED TO SPEAK WITH THIS GENTLEMAN, ALONE.

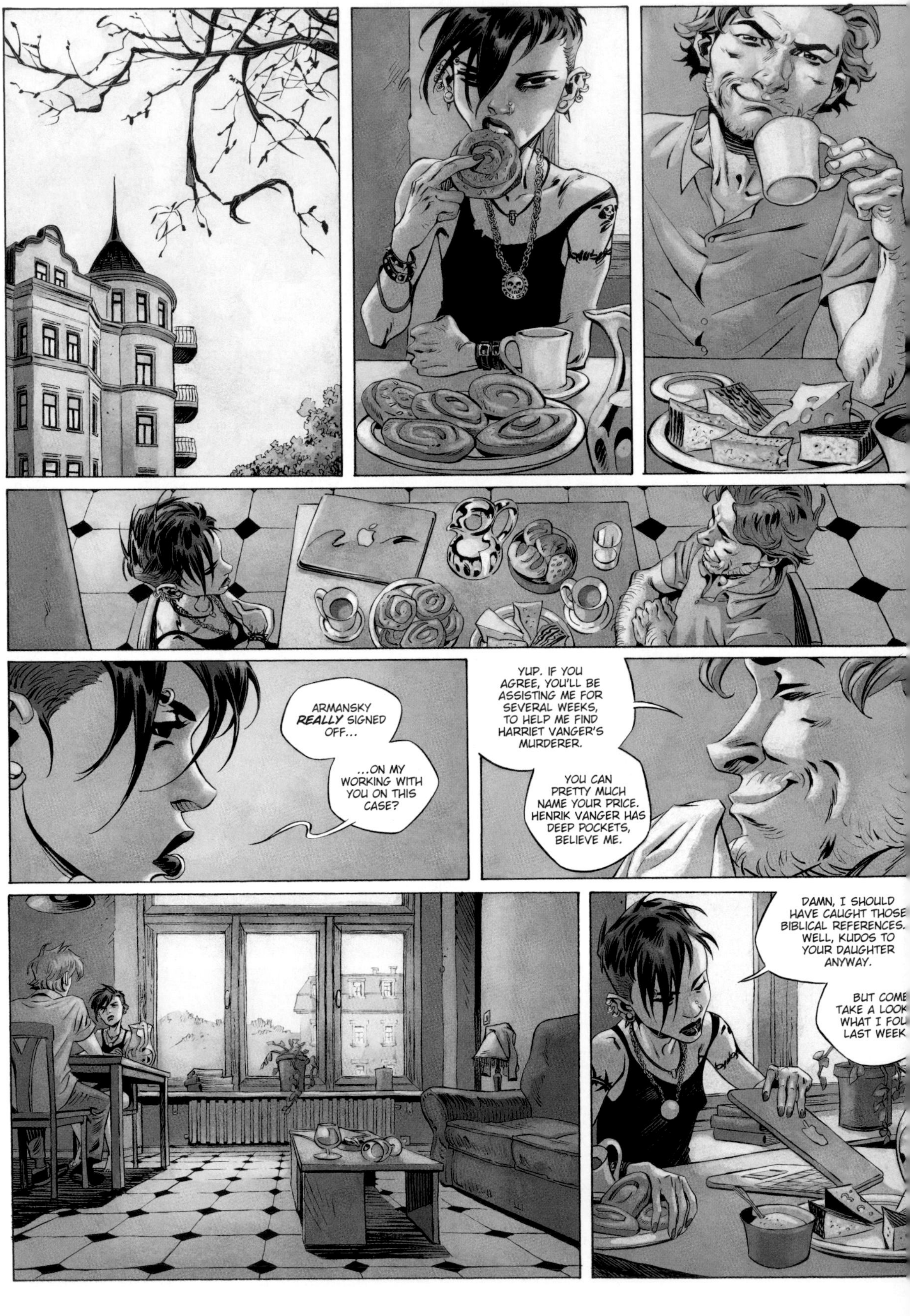
ARMANSKY REALLY SIGNED OFF…
…ON MY WORKING WITH YOU ON THIS CASE?
YUP. IF YOU AGREE, YOU'LL BE ASSISTING ME FOR SEVERAL WEEKS, TO HELP ME FIND HARRIET VANGER'S MURDERER.
YOU CAN PRETTY MUCH NAME YOUR PRICE. HENRIK VANGER HAS DEEP POCKETS, BELIEVE ME.
DAMN, I SHOULD HAVE CAUGHT THOSE BIBLICAL REFERENCES. WELL, KUDOS TO YOUR DAUGHTER ANYWAY.
BUT COME TAKE A LOOK WHAT I FOU LAST WEEK

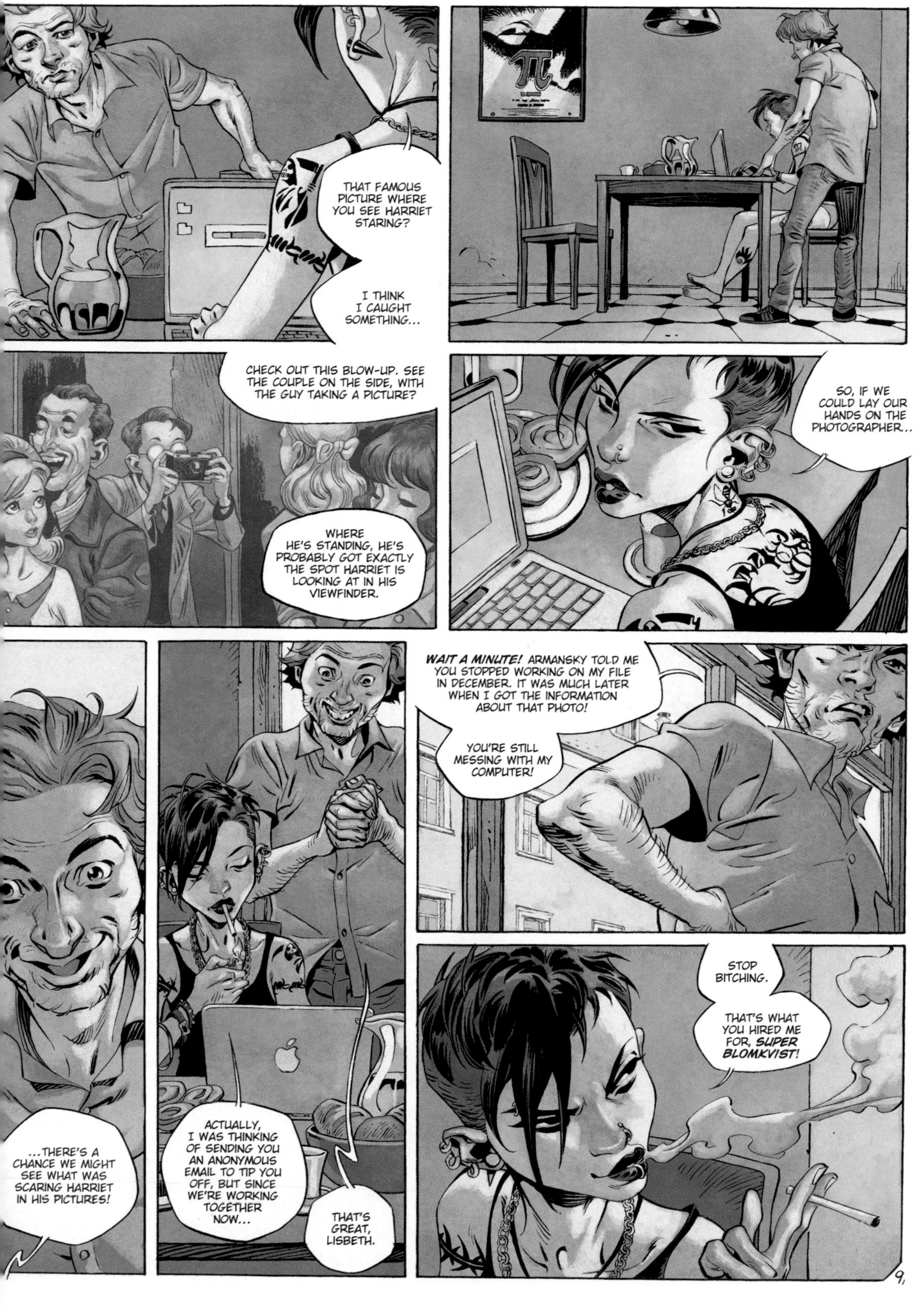
THAT FAMOUS PICTURE WHERE YOU SEE HARRIET STARING?
I THINK I CAUGHT SOMETHING...
CHECK OUT THIS BLOW-UP. SEE THE COUPLE ON THE SIDE, WITH THE GUY TAKING A PICTURE?
WHERE HE'S STANDING, HE'S PROBABLY GOT EXACTLY THE SPOT HARRIET IS LOOKING AT IN HIS VIEWFINDER.
SO, IF WE COULD LAY OUR HANDS ON THE PHOTOGRAPHER...
...THERE'S A CHANCE WE MIGHT SEE WHAT WAS SCARING HARRIET IN HIS PICTURES!
ACTUALLY, I WAS THINKING OF SENDING YOU AN ANONYMOUS EMAIL TO TIP YOU OFF, BUT SINCE WE'RE WORKING TOGETHER NOW...
THAT'S GREAT, LISBETH.
WAIT A MINUTE! ARMANSKY TOLD ME YOU STOPPED WORKING ON MY FILE IN DECEMBER. IT WAS MUCH LATER WHEN I GOT THE INFORMATION ABOUT THAT PHOTO!
YOU'RE STILL MESSING WITH MY COMPUTER!
STOP BITCHING.
THAT'S WHAT YOU HIRED ME FOR, SUPER BLOMKVIST!

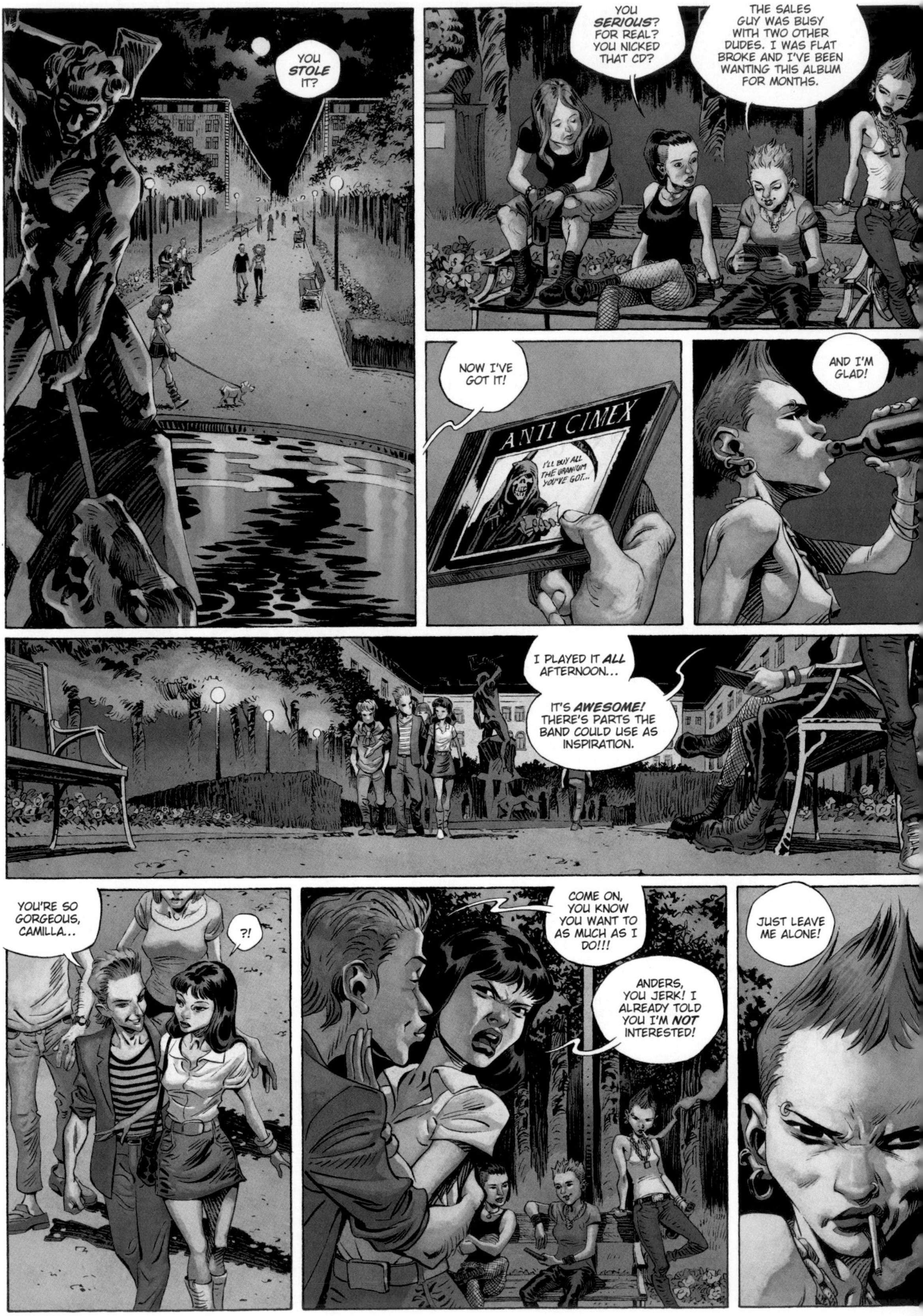
YOU STOLE IT?
YOU SERIOUS? FOR REAL? YOU NICKED THAT CD?
THE SALES GUY WAS BUSY WITH TWO OTHER DUDES. I WAS FLAT BROKE AND I'VE BEEN WANTING THIS ALBUM FOR MONTHS.
NOW I'VE GOT IT!
ANTI CIMEX
I'LL BUY ALL THE URANIUM YOU'VE GOT...
AND I'M GLAD!
I PLAYED IT ALL AFTERNOON...
IT'S AWESOME! THERE'S PARTS THE BAND COULD USE AS INSPIRATION.
YOU'RE SO GORGEOUS, CAMILLA...
?!
COME ON, YOU KNOW YOU WANT TO AS MUCH AS I DO!!!
ANDERS, YOU JERK! I ALREADY TOLD YOU I'M NOT INTERESTED!
JUST LEAVE ME ALONE!

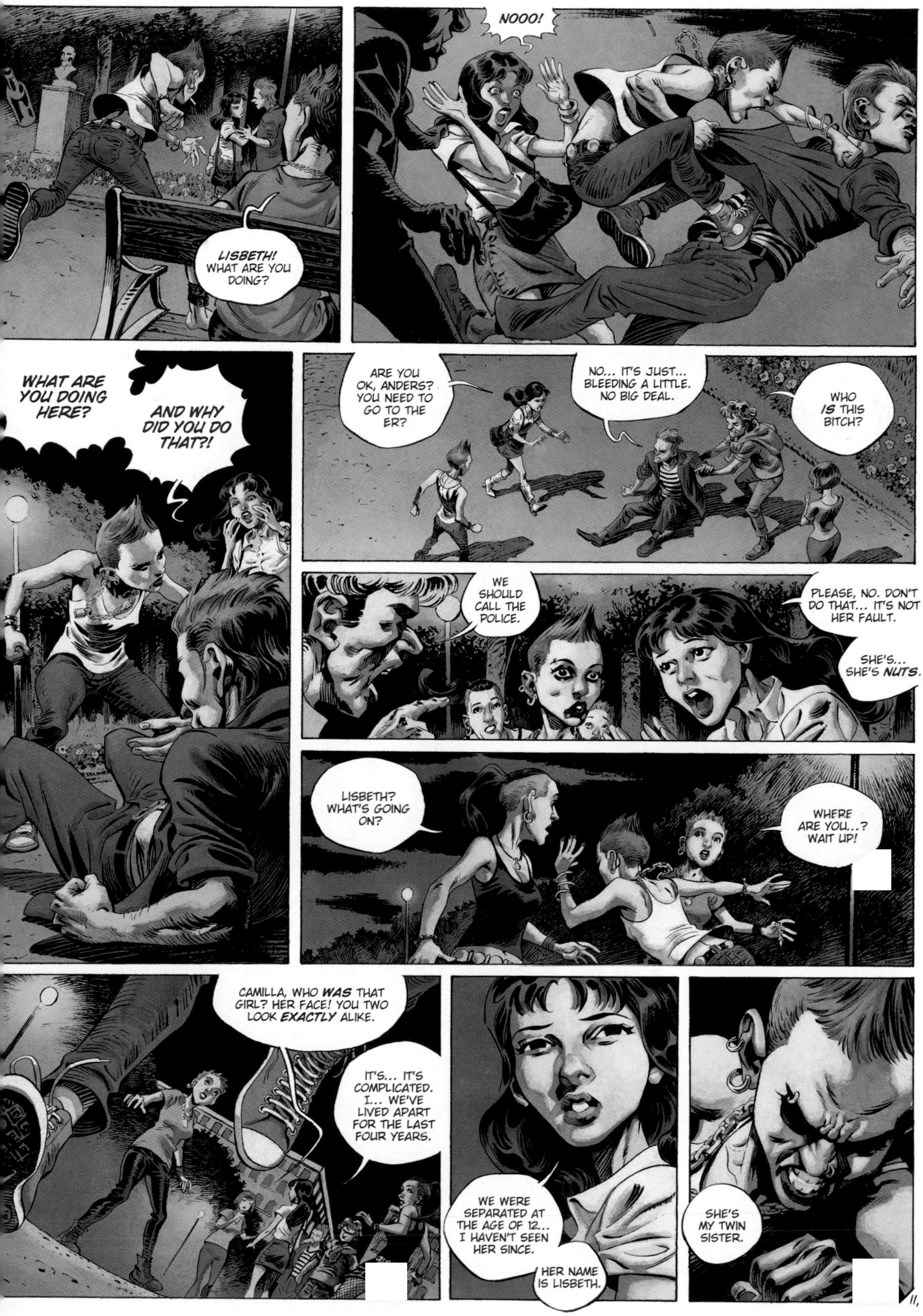
LISBETH! WHAT ARE YOU DOING?
NOOO!
WHAT ARE YOU DOING HERE?
AND WHY DID YOU DO THAT?!
ARE YOU OK, ANDERS? YOU NEED TO GO TO THE ER?
NO... IT'S JUST... BLEEDING A LITTLE. NO BIG DEAL.
WHO *IS* THIS BITCH?
WE SHOULD CALL THE POLICE.
PLEASE, NO. DON'T DO THAT... IT'S NOT HER FAULT.
SHE'S... SHE'S *NUTS*.
LISBETH? WHAT'S GOING ON?
WHERE ARE YOU...? WAIT UP!
CAMILLA, WHO *WAS* THAT GIRL? HER FACE! YOU TWO LOOK *EXACTLY* ALIKE.
IT'S... IT'S COMPLICATED. I... WE'VE LIVED APART FOR THE LAST FOUR YEARS.
WE WERE SEPARATED AT THE AGE OF 12... I HAVEN'T SEEN HER SINCE.
HER NAME IS LISBETH.
SHE'S MY TWIN SISTER.

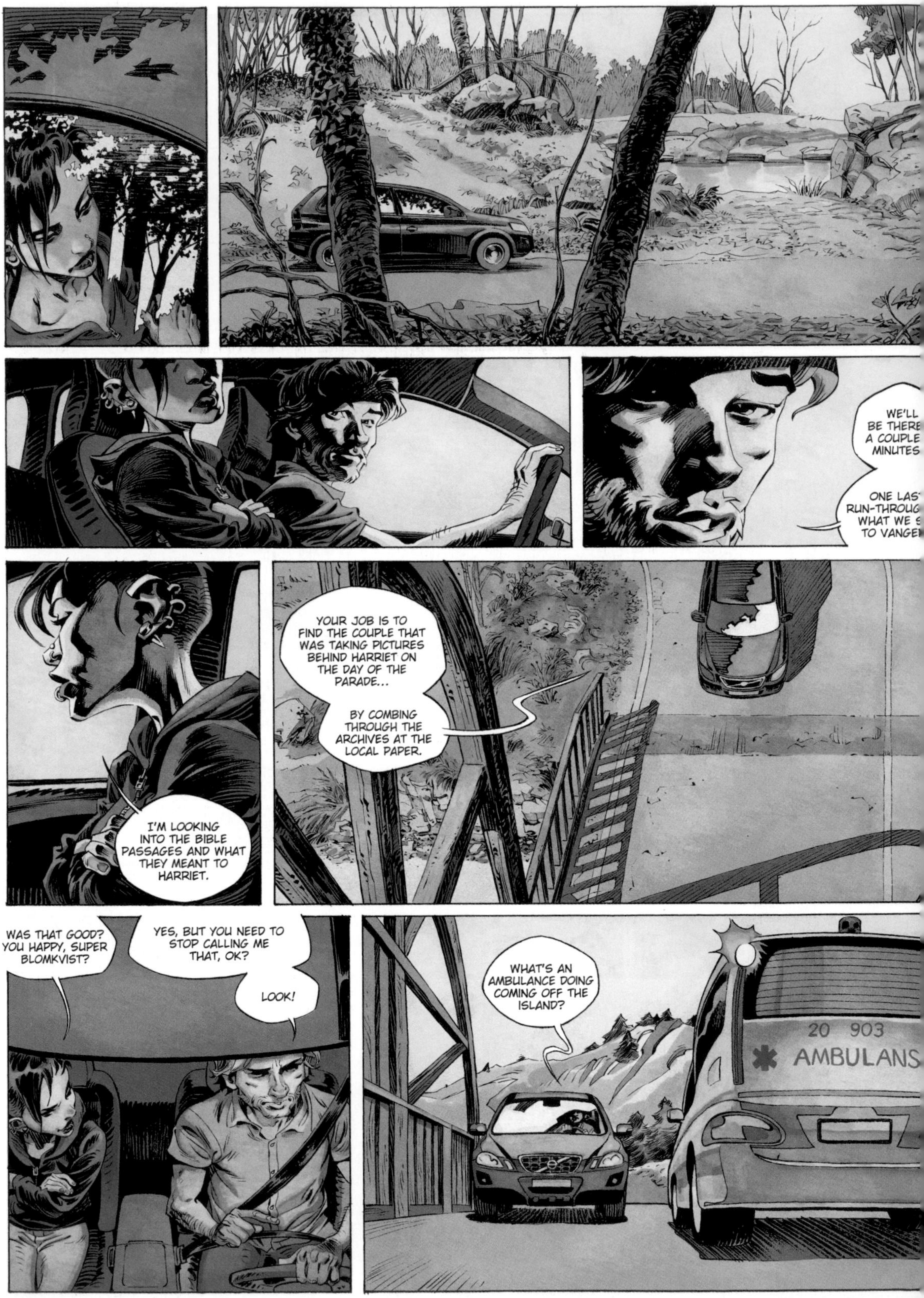
WE'LL BE THERE A COUPLE MINUTES
ONE LAS RUN-THROUG WHAT WE TO VANGE
YOUR JOB IS TO FIND THE COUPLE THAT WAS TAKING PICTURES BEHIND HARRIET ON THE DAY OF THE PARADE...
BY COMBING THROUGH THE ARCHIVES AT THE LOCAL PAPER.
I'M LOOKING INTO THE BIBLE PASSAGES AND WHAT THEY MEANT TO HARRIET.
WAS THAT GOOD? YOU HAPPY, SUPER BLOMKVIST?
YES, BUT YOU NEED TO STOP CALLING ME THAT, OK?
LOOK!
WHAT'S AN AMBULANCE DOING COMING OFF THE ISLAND?
20 903
AMBULANS

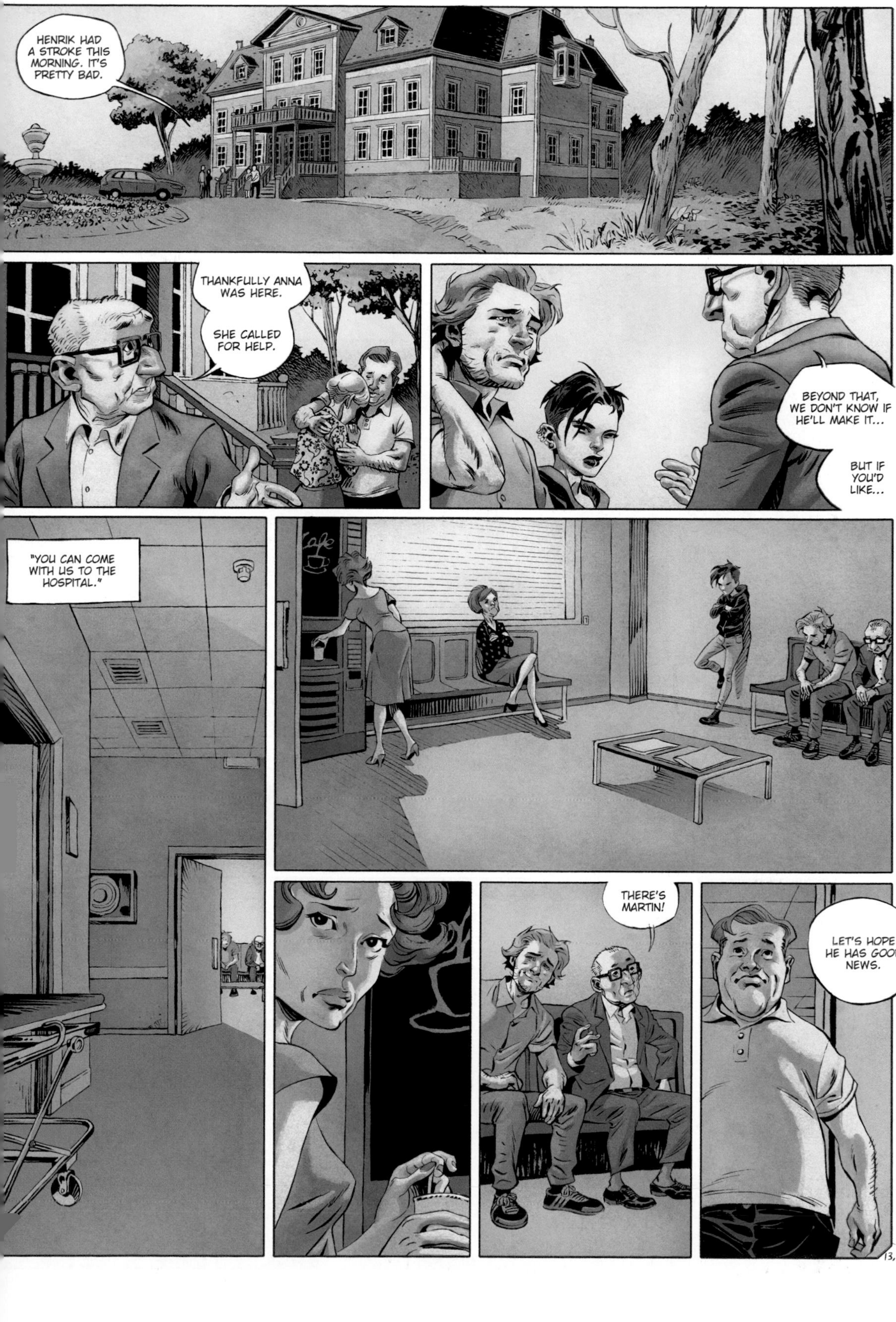
HENRIK HAD A STROKE THIS MORNING. IT'S PRETTY BAD.
THANKFULLY ANNA WAS HERE.
SHE CALLED FOR HELP.
BEYOND THAT, WE DON'T KNOW IF HE'LL MAKE IT...
BUT IF YOU'D LIKE...
"YOU CAN COME WITH US TO THE HOSPITAL."
THERE'S MARTIN!
LET'S HOPE HE HAS GOOD NEWS.

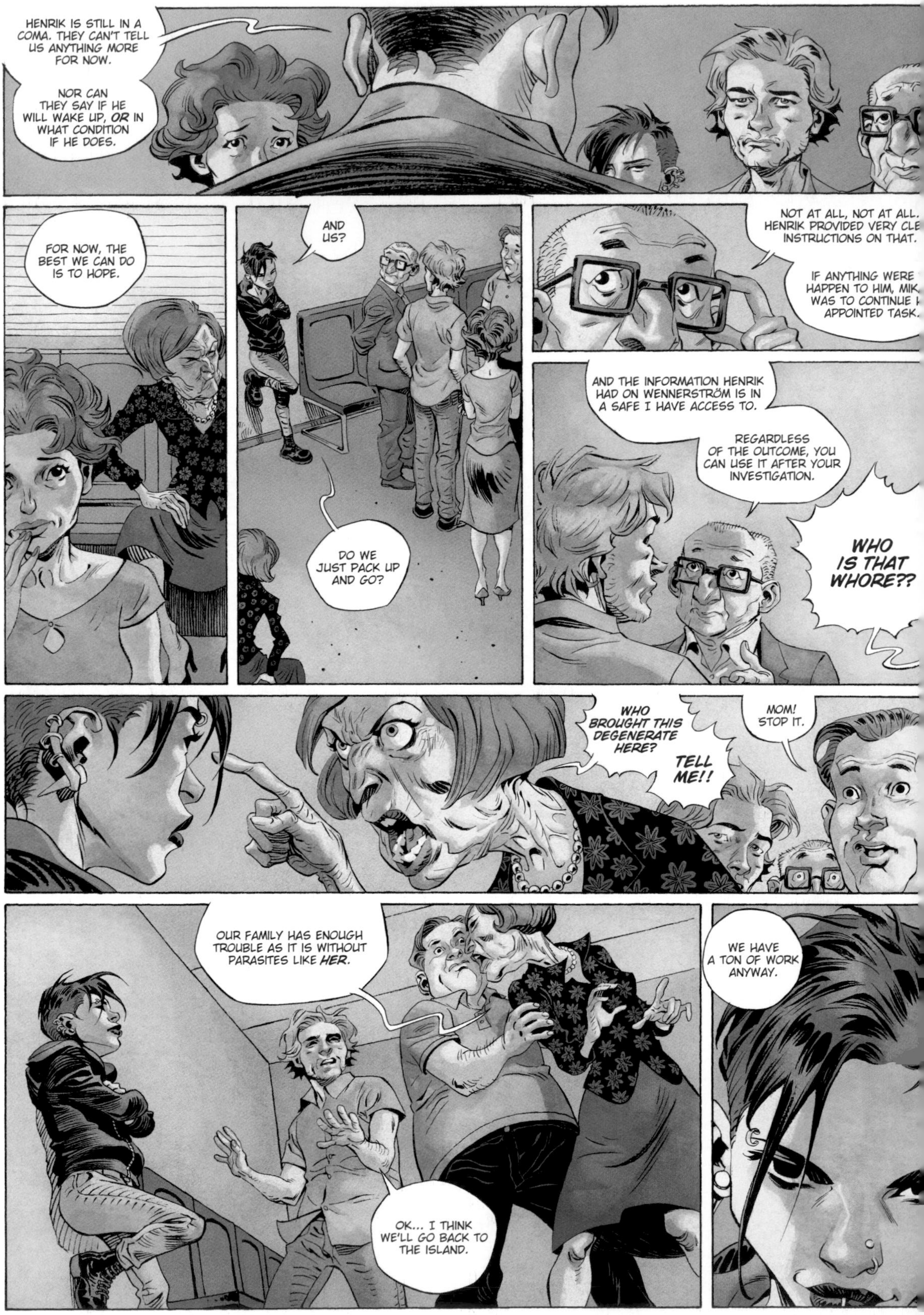

HENRIK IS STILL IN A COMA. THEY CAN'T TELL US ANYTHING MORE FOR NOW.
NOR CAN THEY SAY IF HE WILL WAKE UP, *OR* IN WHAT CONDITION IF HE DOES.
FOR NOW, THE BEST WE CAN DO IS TO HOPE.
AND US?
DO WE JUST PACK UP AND GO?
NOT AT ALL, NOT AT ALL. HENRIK PROVIDED VERY CLE INSTRUCTIONS ON THAT.
IF ANYTHING WERE HAPPEN TO HIM, MIK WAS TO CONTINUE APPOINTED TASK.
AND THE INFORMATION HENRIK HAD ON WENNERSTRÖM IS IN A SAFE I HAVE ACCESS TO.
REGARDLESS OF THE OUTCOME, YOU CAN USE IT AFTER YOUR INVESTIGATION.
WHO IS THAT WHORE??
WHO BROUGHT THIS DEGENERATE HERE?
TELL ME!!
MOM! STOP IT.
OUR FAMILY HAS ENOUGH TROUBLE AS IT IS WITHOUT PARASITES LIKE *HER*.
OK... I THINK WE'LL GO BACK TO THE ISLAND.
WE HAVE A TON OF WORK ANYWAY.

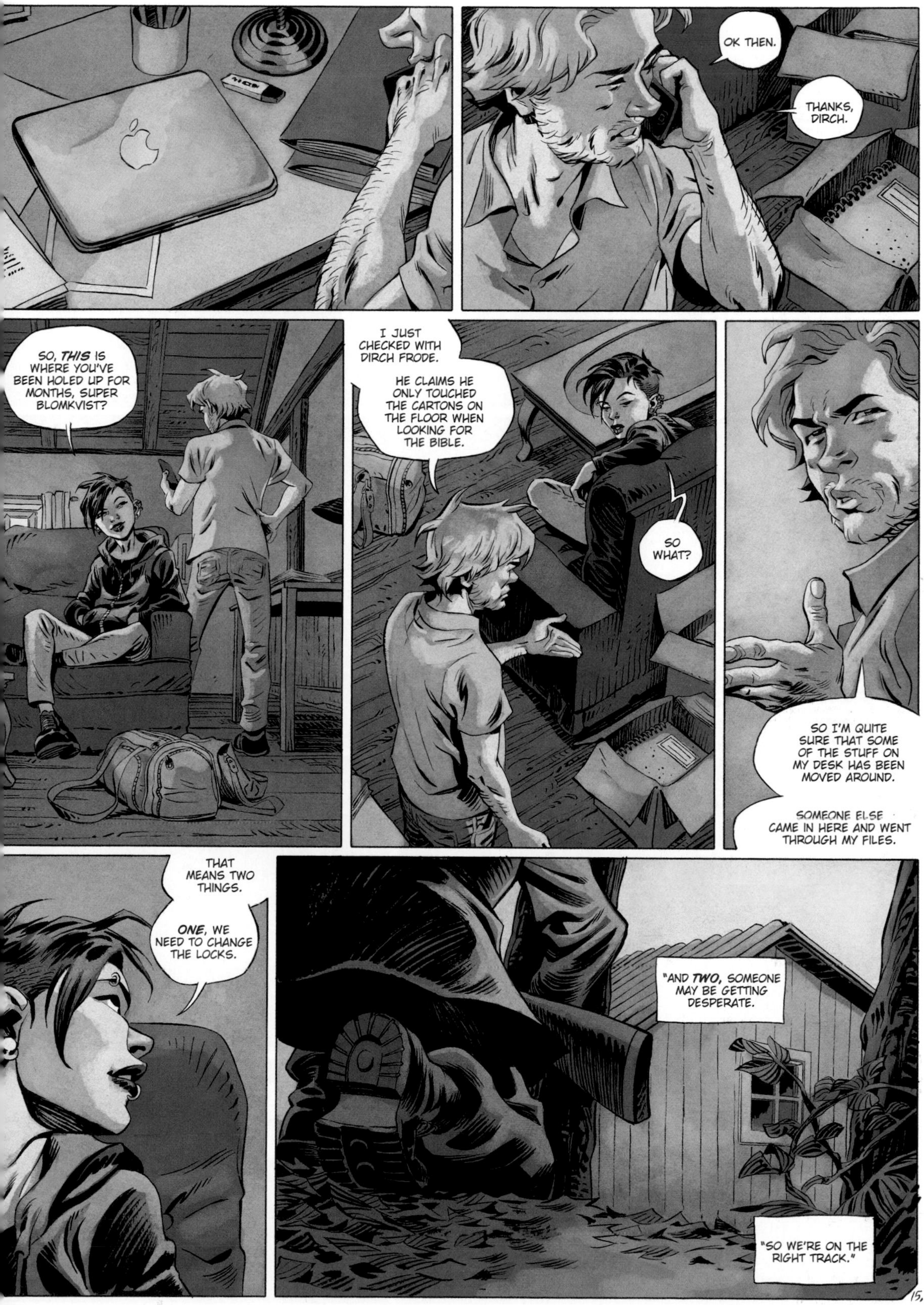
OK THEN.
THANKS, DIRCH.
SO, THIS IS WHERE YOU'VE BEEN HOLED UP FOR MONTHS, SUPER BLOMKVIST?
I JUST CHECKED WITH DIRCH FRODE.
HE CLAIMS HE ONLY TOUCHED THE CARTONS ON THE FLOOR WHEN LOOKING FOR THE BIBLE.
SO WHAT?
SO I'M QUITE SURE THAT SOME OF THE STUFF ON MY DESK HAS BEEN MOVED AROUND.
SOMEONE ELSE CAME IN HERE AND WENT THROUGH MY FILES.
THAT MEANS TWO THINGS.
ONE, WE NEED TO CHANGE THE LOCKS.
"AND TWO, SOMEONE MAY BE GETTING DESPERATE.
"SO WE'RE ON THE RIGHT TRACK."

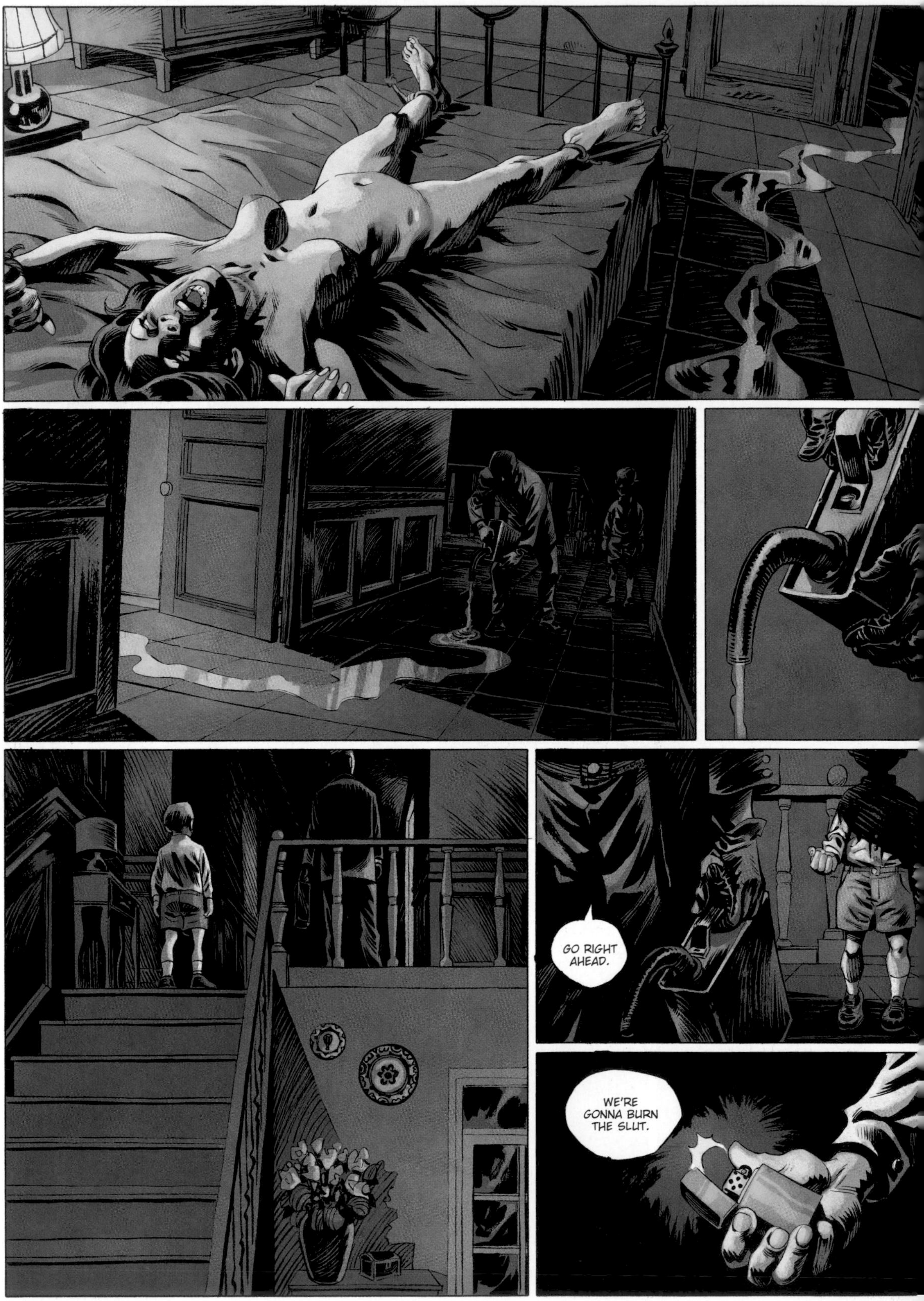
GO RIGHT AHEAD.
WE'RE GONNA BURN THE SLUT.

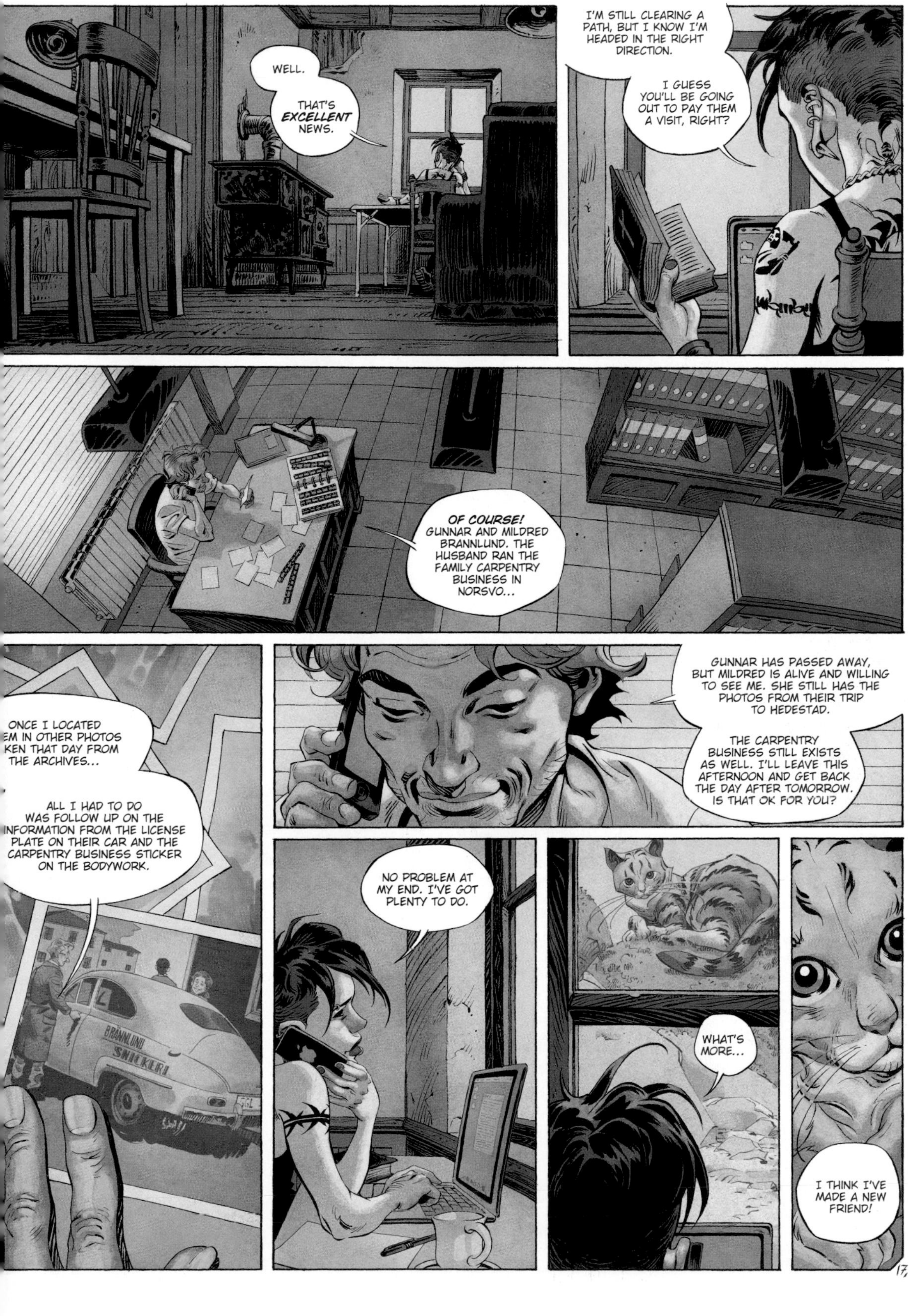
WELL.
THAT'S *EXCELLENT* NEWS.
I'M STILL CLEARING A PATH, BUT I KNOW I'M HEADED IN THE RIGHT DIRECTION.
I GUESS YOU'LL BE GOING OUT TO PAY THEM A VISIT, RIGHT?
OF COURSE! GUNNAR AND MILDRED BRANNLUND. THE HUSBAND RAN THE FAMILY CARPENTRY BUSINESS IN NORSVO...
ONCE I LOCATED EM IN OTHER PHOTOS KEN THAT DAY FROM THE ARCHIVES...
ALL I HAD TO DO WAS FOLLOW UP ON THE INFORMATION FROM THE LICENSE PLATE ON THEIR CAR AND THE CARPENTRY BUSINESS STICKER ON THE BODYWORK.
BRÄNNLUND SNICKERI
GUNNAR HAS PASSED AWAY, BUT MILDRED IS ALIVE AND WILLING TO SEE ME. SHE STILL HAS THE PHOTOS FROM THEIR TRIP TO HEDESTAD.
THE CARPENTRY BUSINESS STILL EXISTS AS WELL. I'LL LEAVE THIS AFTERNOON AND GET BACK THE DAY AFTER TOMORROW. IS THAT OK FOR YOU?
NO PROBLEM AT MY END. I'VE GOT PLENTY TO DO.
WHAT'S MORE...
I THINK I'VE MADE A NEW FRIEND!

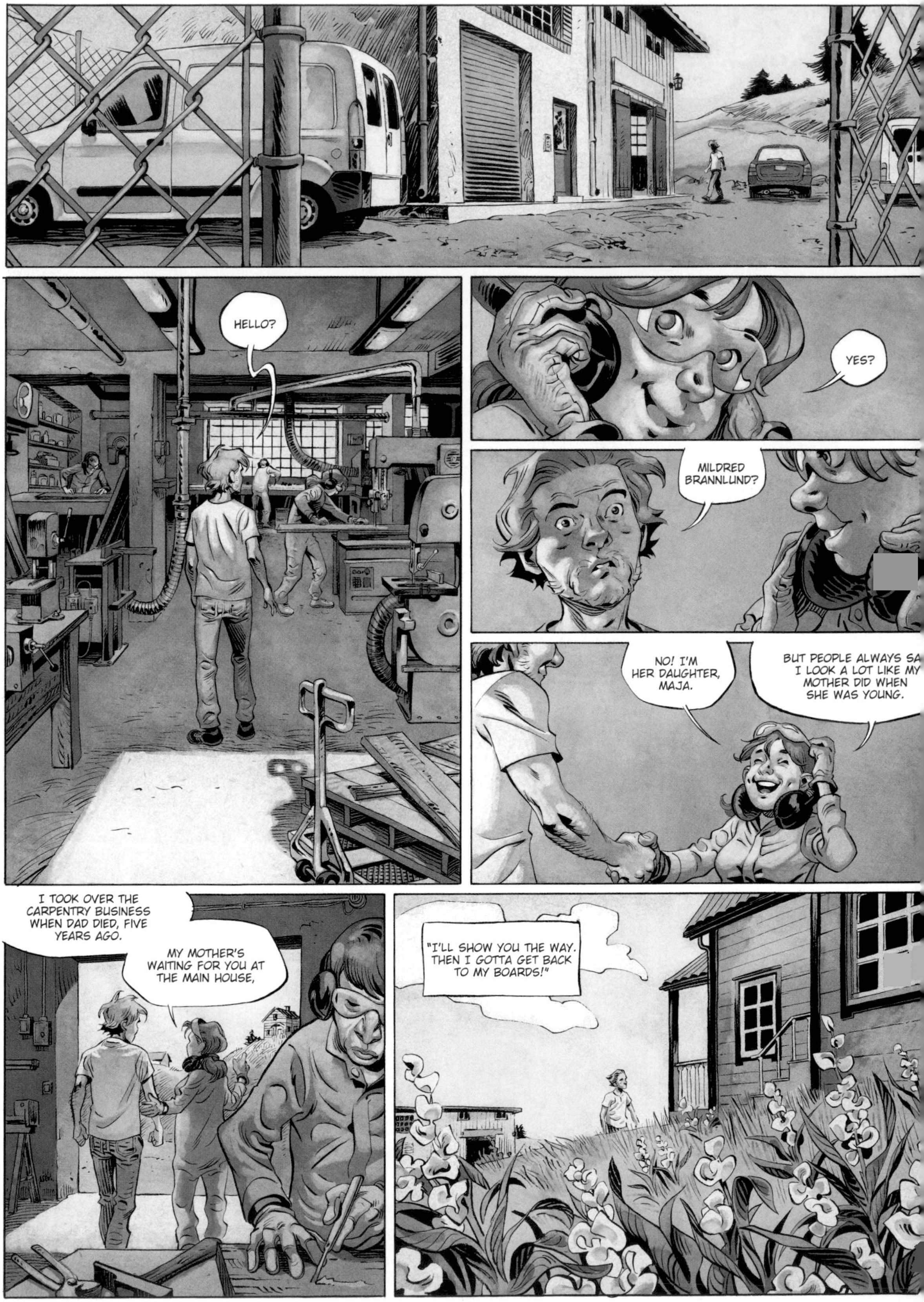
HELLO?
YES?
MILDRED BRANNLUND?
NO! I'M HER DAUGHTER, MAJA.
BUT PEOPLE ALWAYS SA I LOOK A LOT LIKE MY MOTHER DID WHEN SHE WAS YOUNG.
I TOOK OVER THE CARPENTRY BUSINESS WHEN DAD DIED, FIVE YEARS AGO.
MY MOTHER'S WAITING FOR YOU AT THE MAIN HOUSE,
"I'LL SHOW YOU THE WAY. THEN I GOTTA GET BACK TO MY BOARDS!"

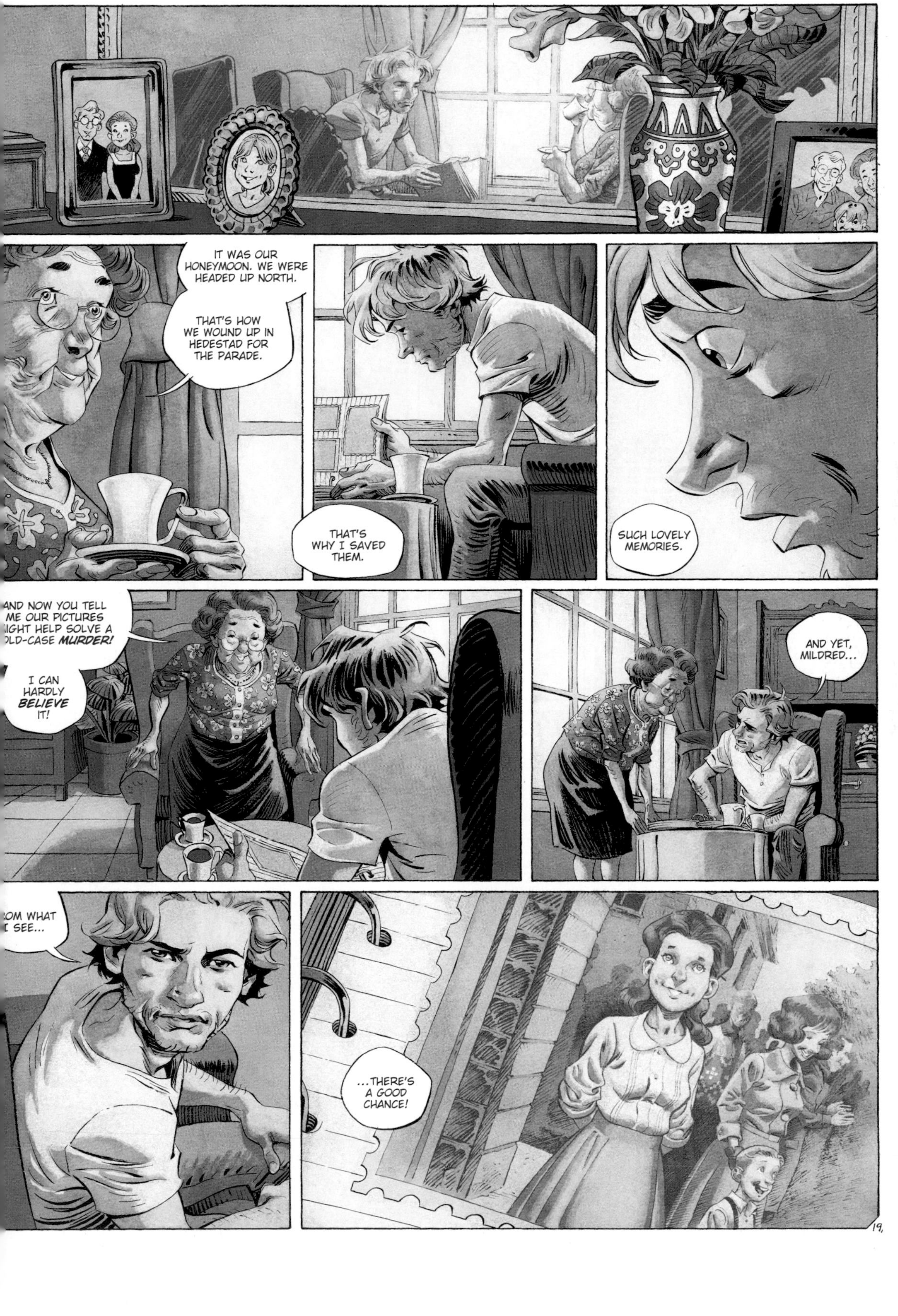

IT WAS OUR HONEYMOON. WE WERE HEADED UP NORTH.
THAT'S HOW WE WOUND UP IN HEDESTAD FOR THE PARADE.
THAT'S WHY I SAVED THEM.
SUCH LOVELY MEMORIES.
AND NOW YOU TELL ME OUR PICTURES IGHT HELP SOLVE A OLD-CASE MURDER!
I CAN HARDLY BELIEVE IT!
AND YET, MILDRED...
ROM WHAT I SEE...
...THERE'S A GOOD CHANCE!

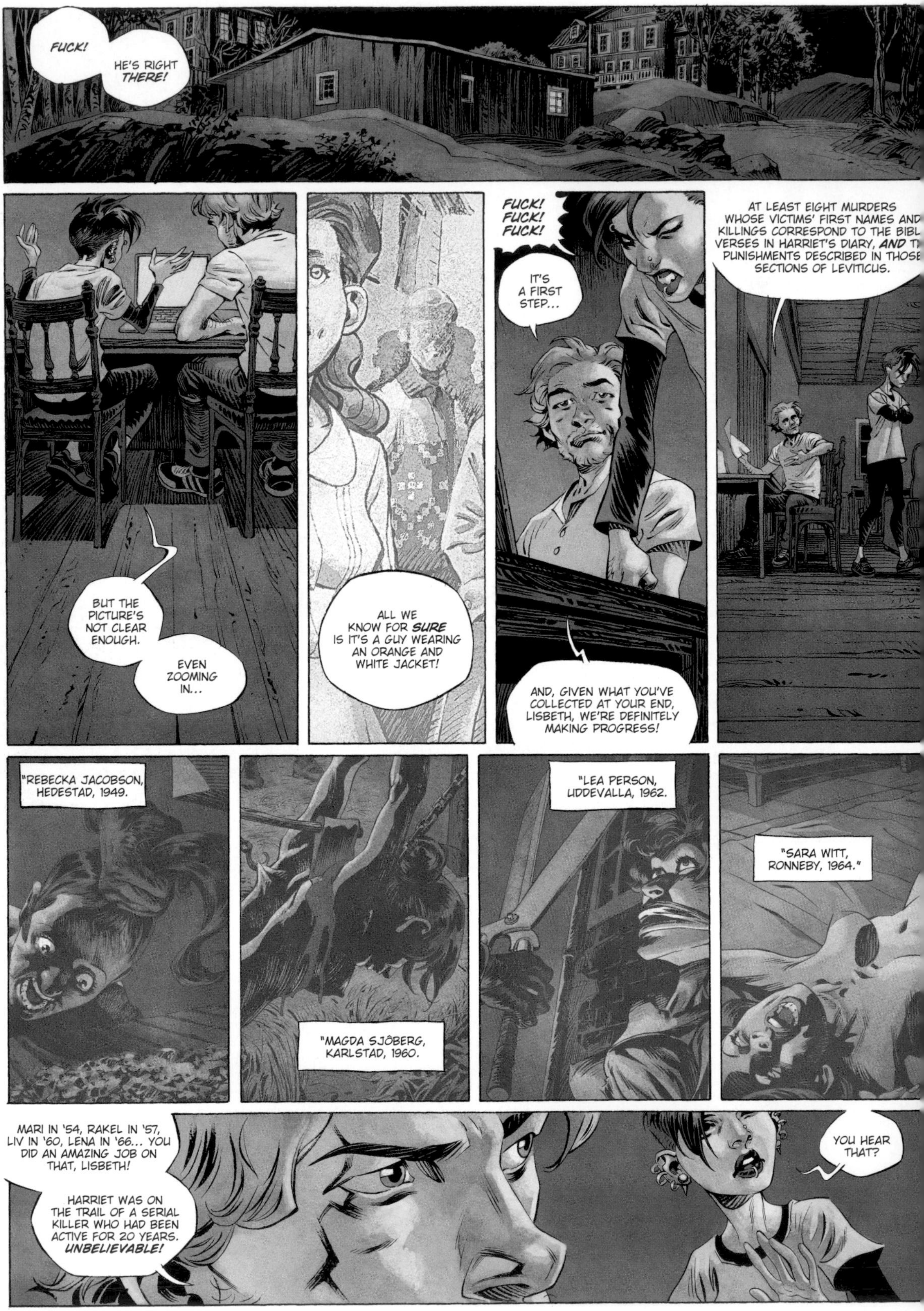
FUCK!
HE'S RIGHT *THERE!*
BUT THE PICTURE'S NOT CLEAR ENOUGH.
EVEN ZOOMING IN...
ALL WE KNOW FOR *SURE* IS IT'S A GUY WEARING AN ORANGE AND WHITE JACKET!
FUCK! FUCK! FUCK!
IT'S A FIRST STEP...
AND, GIVEN WHAT YOU'VE COLLECTED AT YOUR END, LISBETH, WE'RE DEFINITELY MAKING PROGRESS!
AT LEAST EIGHT MURDERS WHOSE VICTIMS' FIRST NAMES AND KILLINGS CORRESPOND TO THE BIBL VERSES IN HARRIET'S DIARY, *AND* TH PUNISHMENTS DESCRIBED IN THOSE SECTIONS OF LEVITICUS.
"REBECKA JACOBSON, HEDESTAD, 1949.
"MAGDA SJÖBERG, KARLSTAD, 1960.
"LEA PERSON, UDDEVALLA, 1962.
"SARA WITT, RONNEBY, 1964."
MARI IN '54, RAKEL IN '57, LIV IN '60, LENA IN '66... YOU DID AN AMAZING JOB ON THAT, LISBETH!
HARRIET WAS ON THE TRAIL OF A SERIAL KILLER WHO HAD BEEN ACTIVE FOR 20 YEARS. *UNBELIEVABLE!*
YOU HEAR THAT?

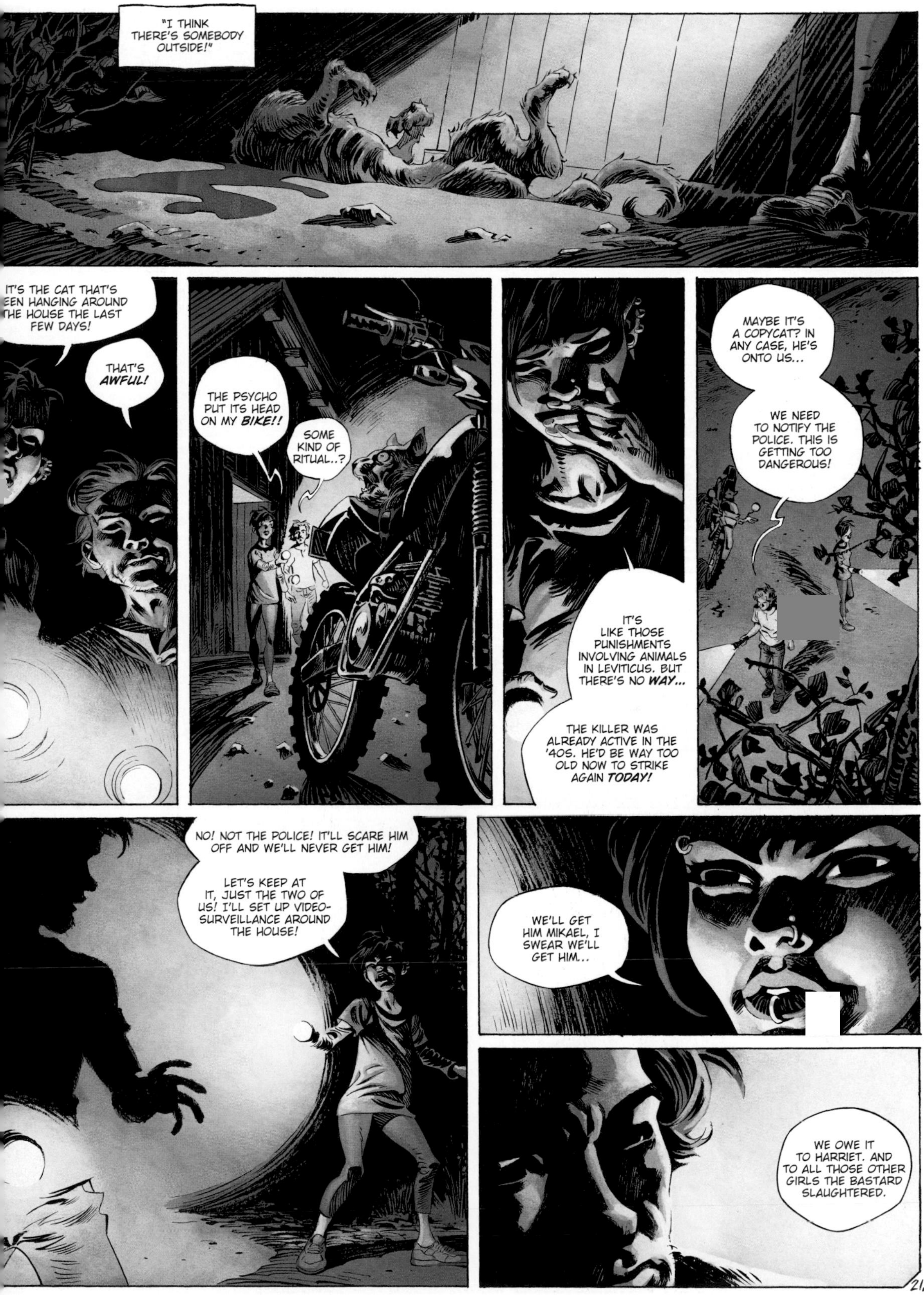
"I THINK THERE'S SOMEBODY OUTSIDE!"
IT'S THE CAT THAT'S EEN HANGING AROUND THE HOUSE THE LAST FEW DAYS!
THAT'S AWFUL!
THE PSYCHO PUT ITS HEAD ON MY BIKE!!
SOME KIND OF RITUAL..?
IT'S LIKE THOSE PUNISHMENTS INVOLVING ANIMALS IN LEVITICUS. BUT THERE'S NO WAY...
THE KILLER WAS ALREADY ACTIVE IN THE '40S. HE'D BE WAY TOO OLD NOW TO STRIKE AGAIN TODAY!
MAYBE IT'S A COPYCAT? IN ANY CASE, HE'S ONTO US...
WE NEED TO NOTIFY THE POLICE. THIS IS GETTING TOO DANGEROUS!
NO! NOT THE POLICE! IT'LL SCARE HIM OFF AND WE'LL NEVER GET HIM!
LET'S KEEP AT IT, JUST THE TWO OF US! I'LL SET UP VIDEO-SURVEILLANCE AROUND THE HOUSE!
WE'LL GET HIM MIKAEL, I SWEAR WE'LL GET HIM..
WE OWE IT TO HARRIET. AND TO ALL THOSE OTHER GIRLS THE BASTARD SLAUGHTERED.

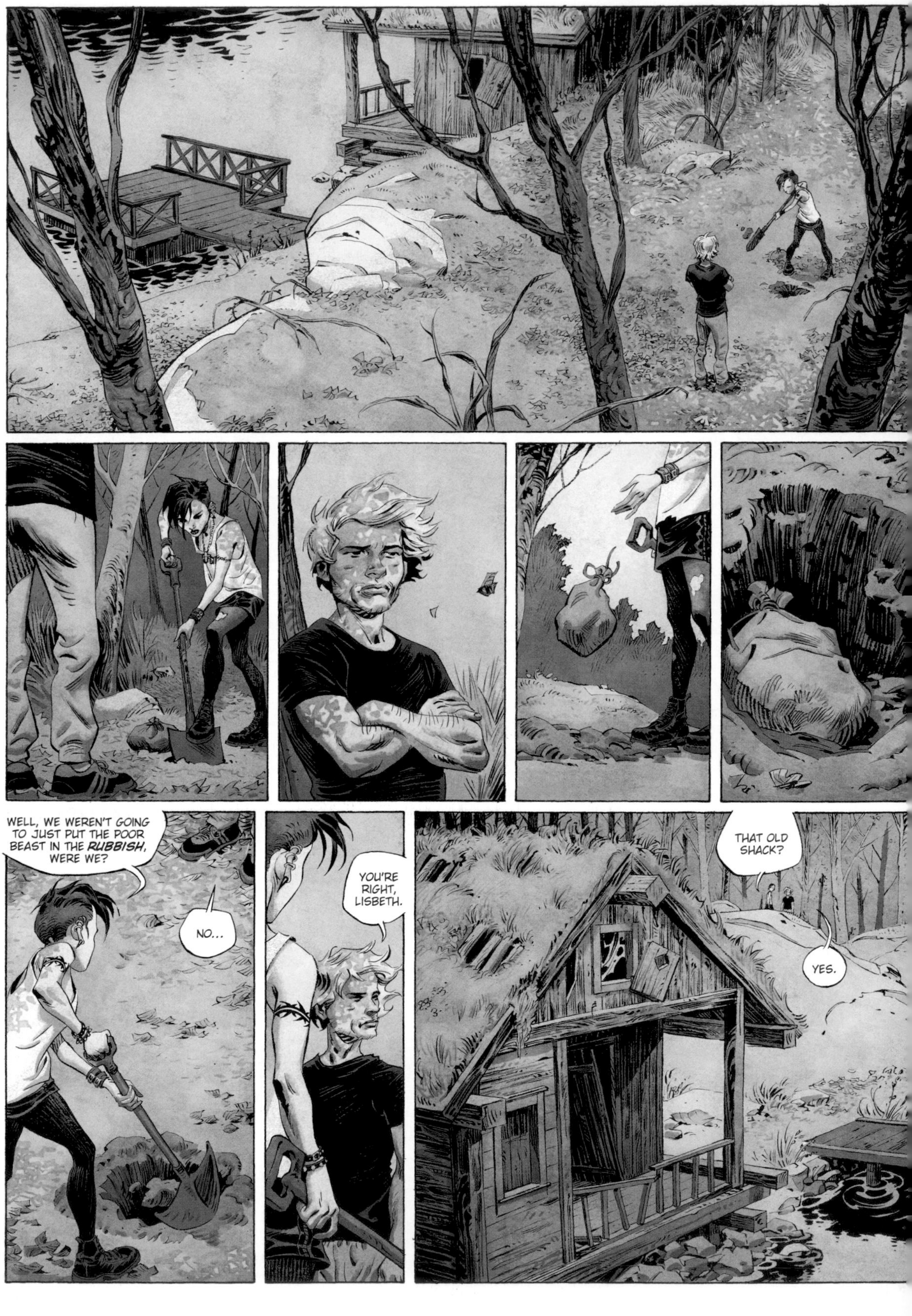
WELL, WE WEREN'T GOING TO JUST PUT THE POOR BEAST IN THE RUBBISH, WERE WE?
NO...
YOU'RE RIGHT, LISBETH.
THAT OLD SHACK?
YES.

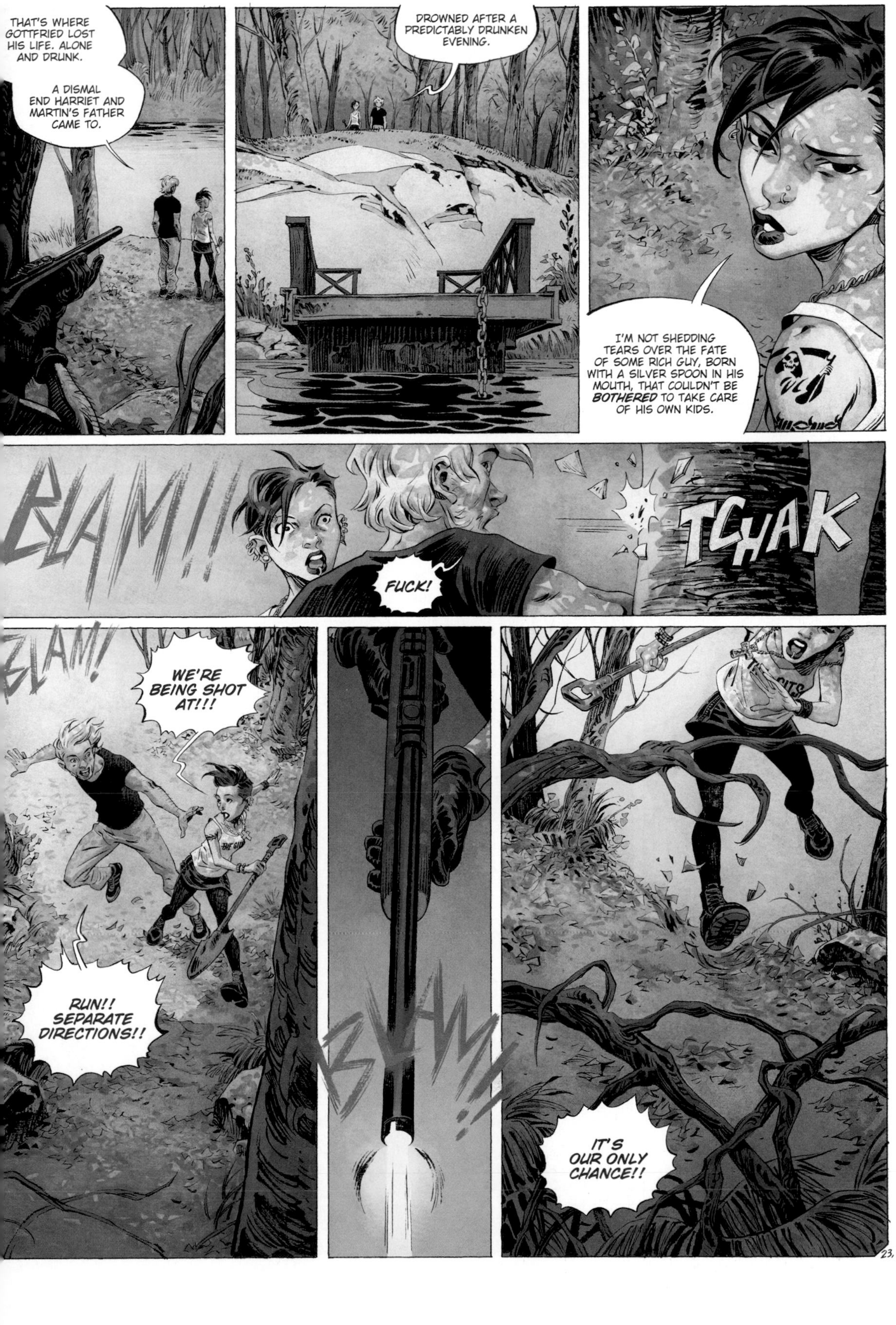
THAT'S WHERE GOTTFRIED LOST HIS LIFE. ALONE AND DRUNK.
A DISMAL END HARRIET AND MARTIN'S FATHER CAME TO.
DROWNED AFTER A PREDICTABLY DRUNKEN EVENING.
I'M NOT SHEDDING TEARS OVER THE FATE OF SOME RICH GUY, BORN WITH A SILVER SPOON IN HIS MOUTH, THAT COULDN'T BE BOTHERED TO TAKE CARE OF HIS OWN KIDS.
BLAM!!
TCHAK
FUCK!
BLAM!
WE'RE BEING SHOT AT!!!
RUN!! SEPARATE DIRECTIONS!!
BLAM!!
IT'S OUR ONLY CHANCE!!

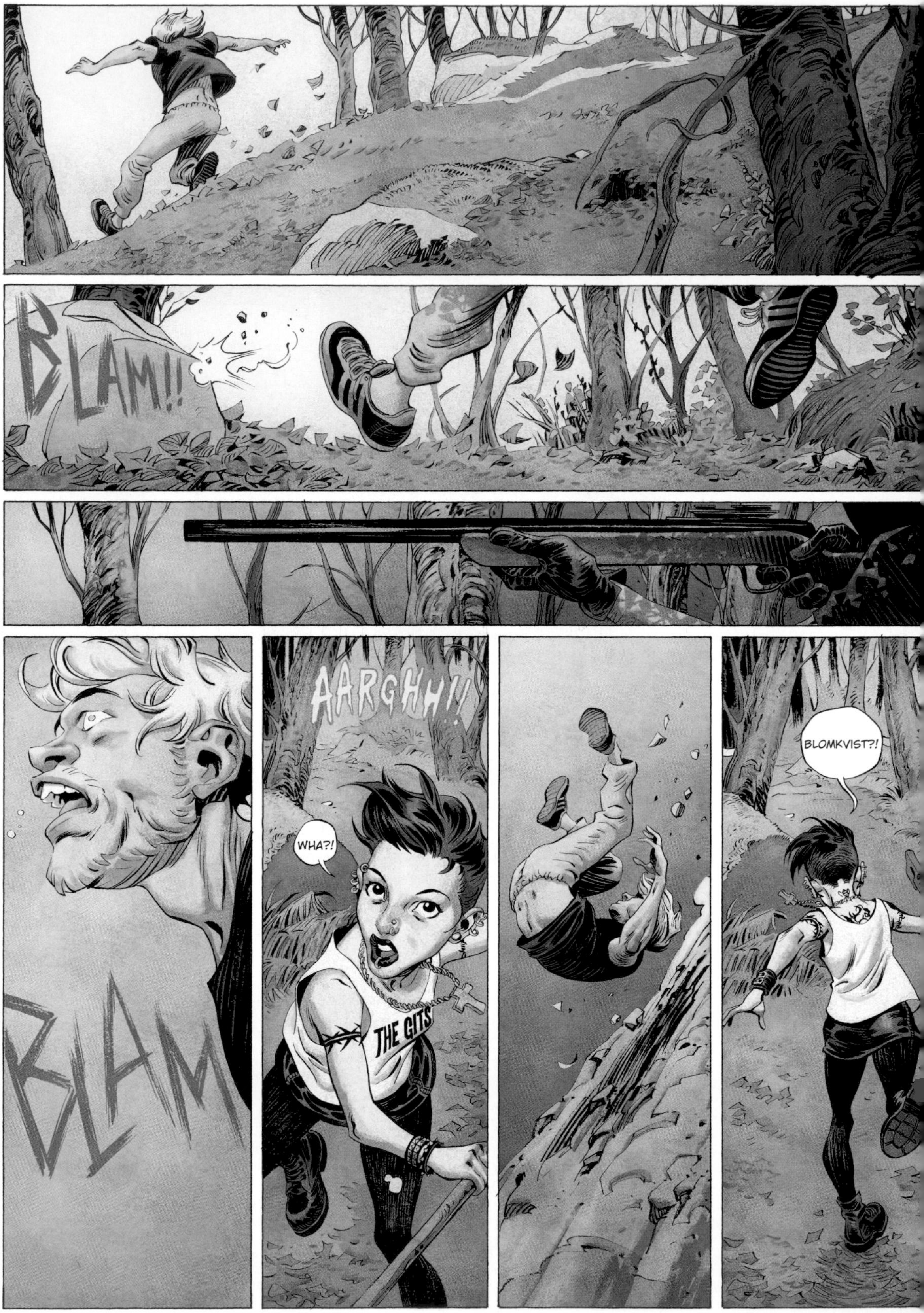
BLAM!!
BLAM
AARGHH!!
WHA?!
THE GITS
BLOMKVIST?!

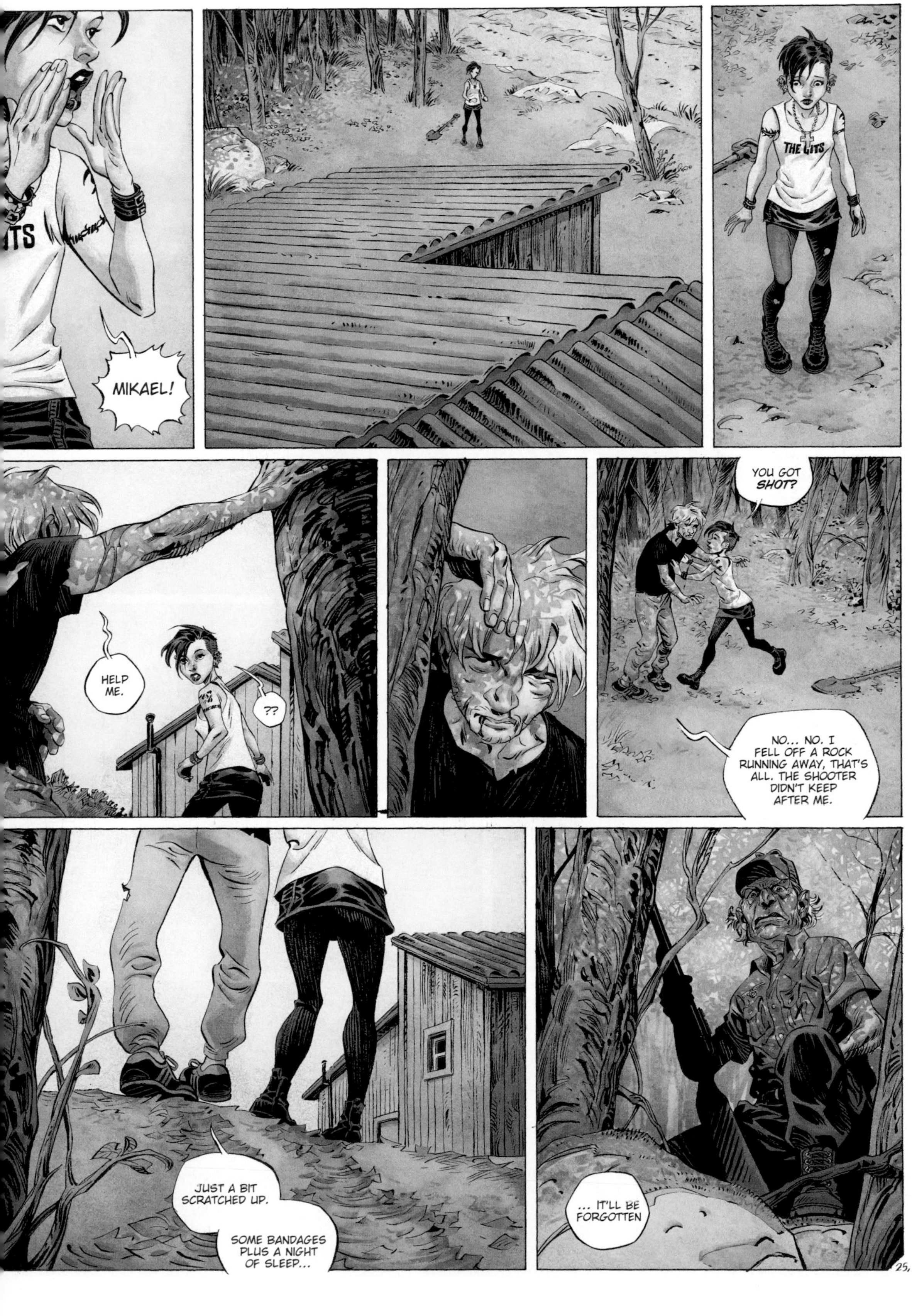
MIKAEL!
HELP ME.
??
YOU GOT SHOT?
NO... NO. I FELL OFF A ROCK RUNNING AWAY, THAT'S ALL. THE SHOOTER DIDN'T KEEP AFTER ME.
JUST A BIT SCRATCHED UP.
SOME BANDAGES PLUS A NIGHT OF SLEEP...
... IT'LL BE FORGOTTEN

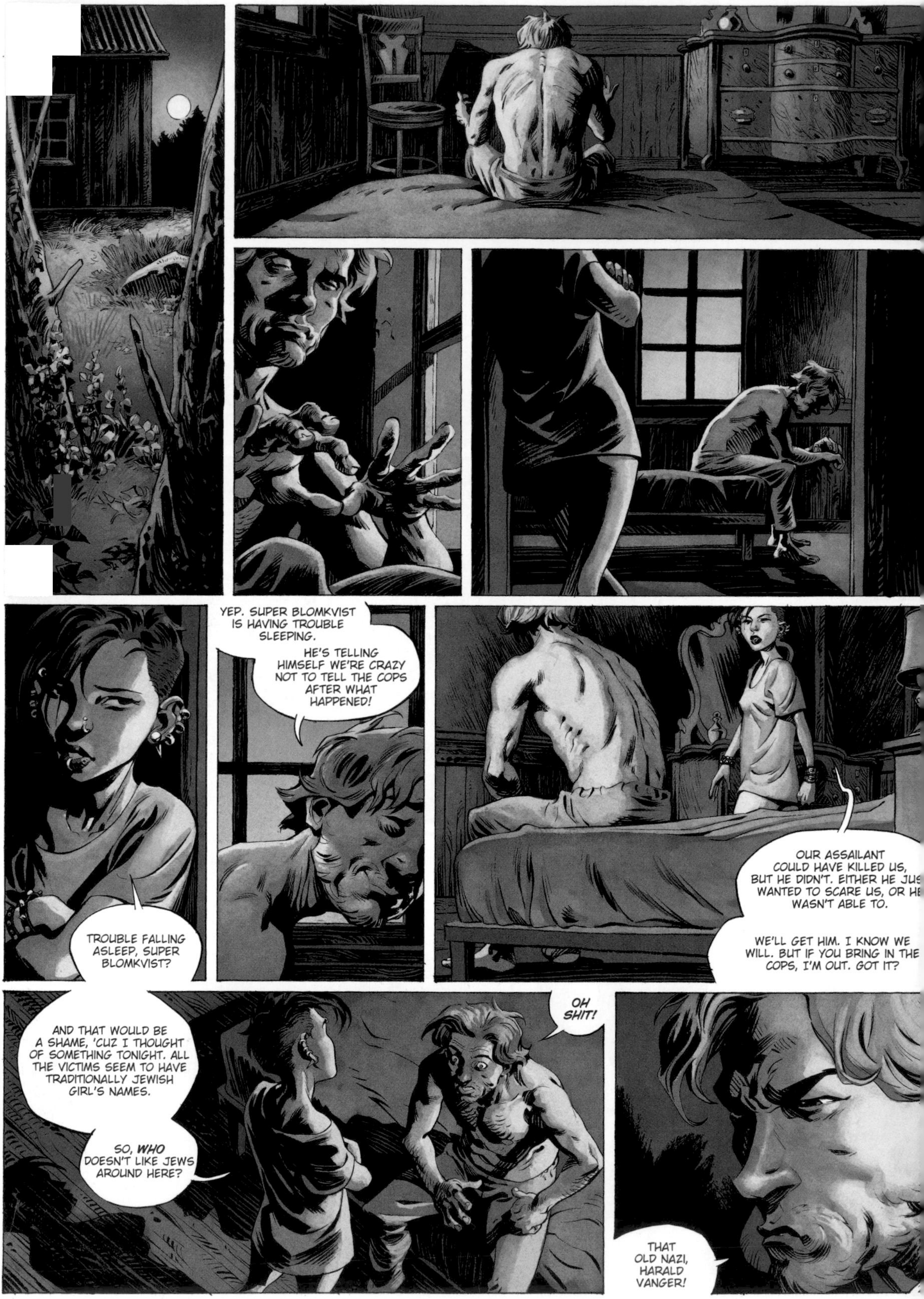
YEP. SUPER BLOMKVIST IS HAVING TROUBLE SLEEPING.
HE'S TELLING HIMSELF WE'RE CRAZY NOT TO TELL THE COPS AFTER WHAT HAPPENED!
TROUBLE FALLING ASLEEP, SUPER BLOMKVIST?
OUR ASSAILANT COULD HAVE KILLED US, BUT HE DIDN'T. EITHER HE JUS WANTED TO SCARE US, OR HE WASN'T ABLE TO.
WE'LL GET HIM. I KNOW WE WILL. BUT IF YOU BRING IN THE COPS, I'M OUT. GOT IT?
AND THAT WOULD BE A SHAME, 'CUZ I THOUGHT OF SOMETHING TONIGHT. ALL THE VICTIMS SEEM TO HAVE TRADITIONALLY JEWISH GIRL'S NAMES.
SO, WHO DOESN'T LIKE JEWS AROUND HERE?
OH SHIT!
THAT OLD NAZI, HARALD VANGER!

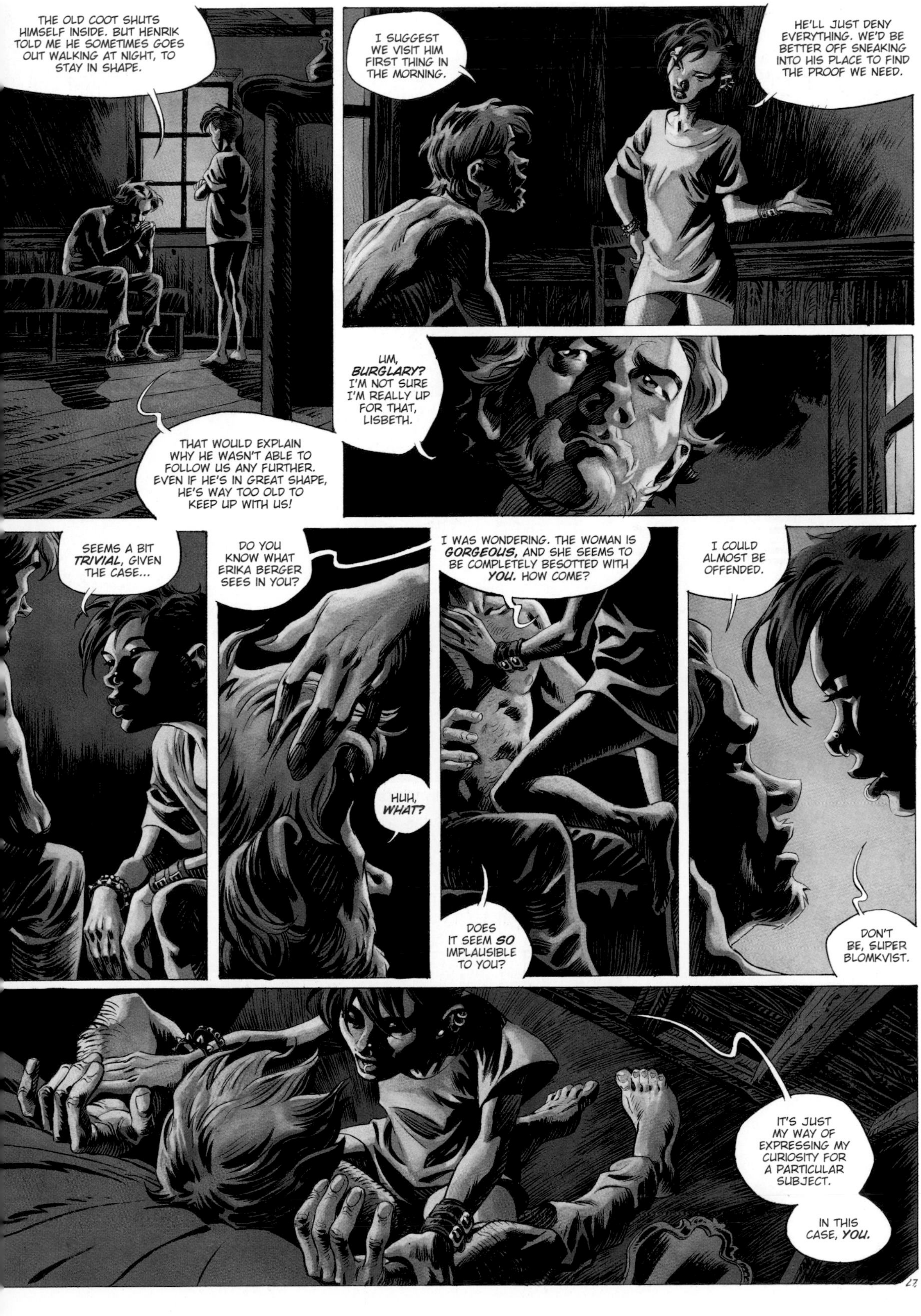
THE OLD COOT SHUTS HIMSELF INSIDE. BUT HENRIK TOLD ME HE SOMETIMES GOES OUT WALKING AT NIGHT, TO STAY IN SHAPE.
THAT WOULD EXPLAIN WHY HE WASN'T ABLE TO FOLLOW US ANY FURTHER. EVEN IF HE'S IN GREAT SHAPE, HE'S WAY TOO OLD TO KEEP UP WITH US!
I SUGGEST WE VISIT HIM FIRST THING IN THE MORNING.
HE'LL JUST DENY EVERYTHING. WE'D BE BETTER OFF SNEAKING INTO HIS PLACE TO FIND THE PROOF WE NEED.
UM, BURGLARY? I'M NOT SURE I'M REALLY UP FOR THAT, LISBETH.
SEEMS A BIT TRIVIAL, GIVEN THE CASE...
DO YOU KNOW WHAT ERIKA BERGER SEES IN YOU?
HUH, WHAT?
I WAS WONDERING. THE WOMAN IS GORGEOUS, AND SHE SEEMS TO BE COMPLETELY BESOTTED WITH YOU. HOW COME?
DOES IT SEEM SO IMPLAUSIBLE TO YOU?
I COULD ALMOST BE OFFENDED.
DON'T BE, SUPER BLOMKVIST.
IT'S JUST MY WAY OF EXPRESSING MY CURIOSITY FOR A PARTICULAR SUBJECT.
IN THIS CASE, YOU.

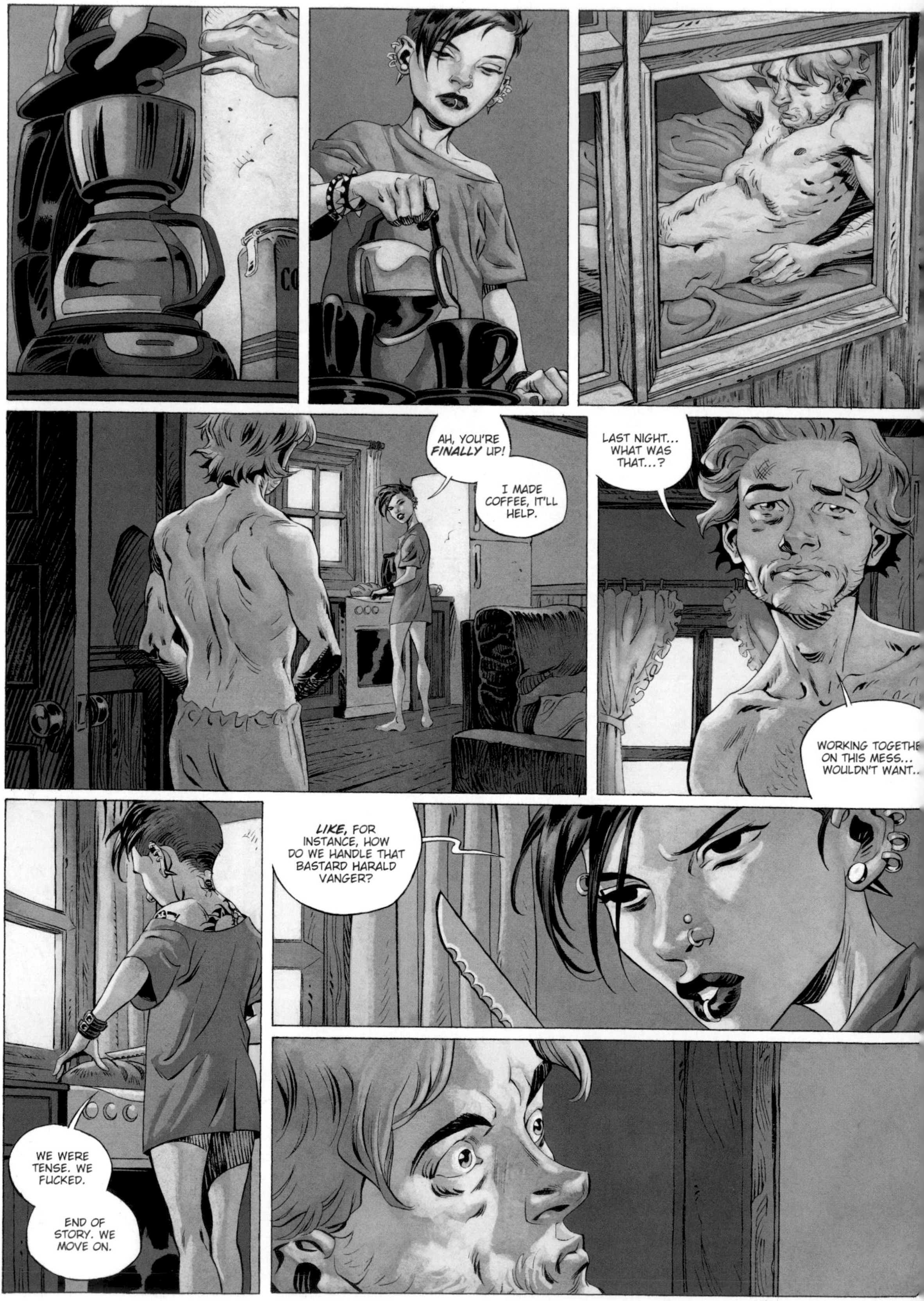
AH, YOU'RE *FINALLY* UP!
I MADE COFFEE, IT'LL HELP.
LAST NIGHT... WHAT WAS THAT...?
WORKING TOGETHE ON THIS MESS... WOULDN'T WANT...
WE WERE TENSE. WE FUCKED.
END OF STORY. WE MOVE ON.
LIKE, FOR INSTANCE, HOW DO WE HANDLE THAT BASTARD HARALD VANGER?

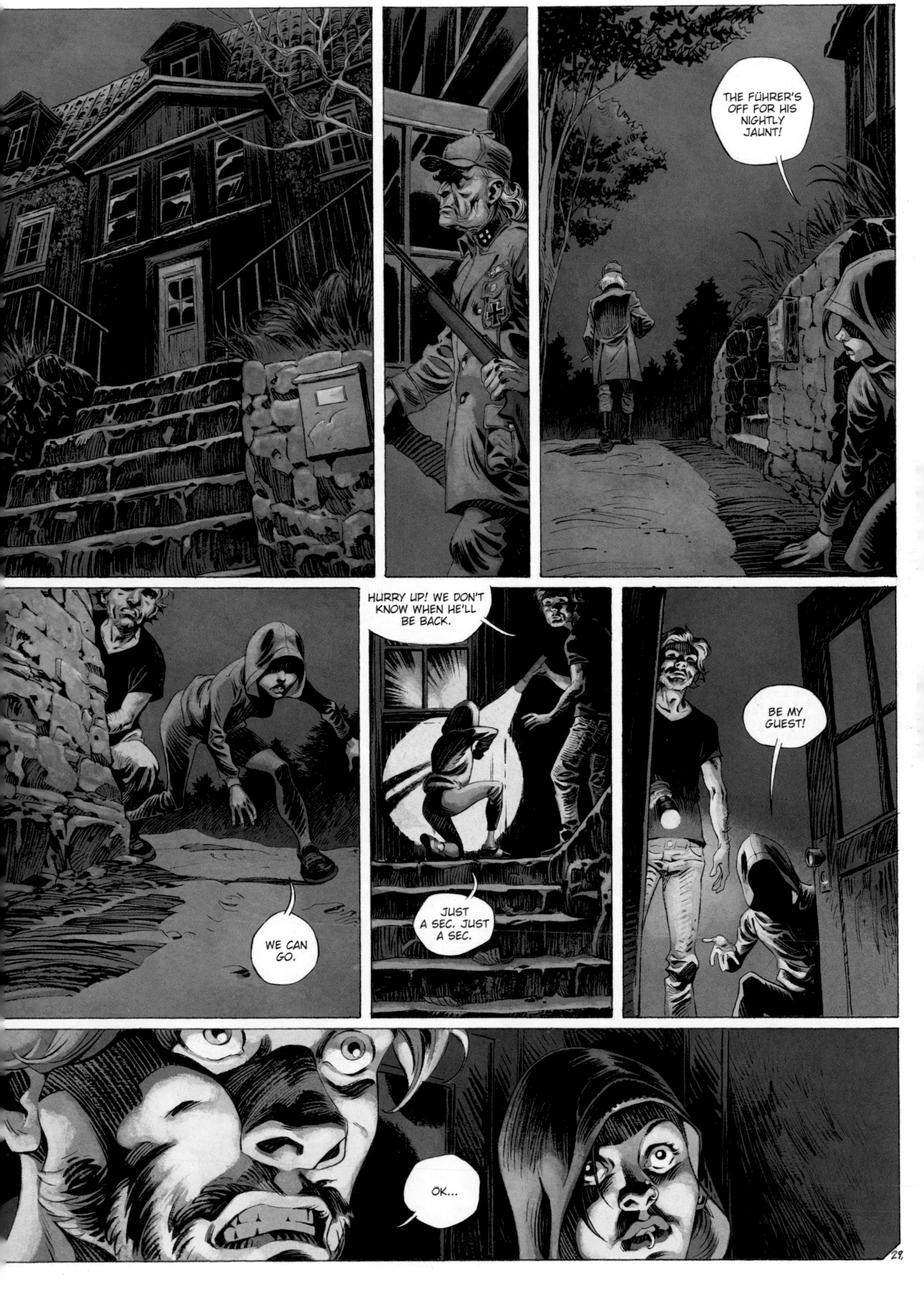
THE FÜHRER'S OFF FOR HIS NIGHTLY JAUNT!
WE CAN GO.
HURRY UP! WE DON'T KNOW WHEN HE'LL BE BACK.
JUST A SEC. JUST A SEC.
BE MY GUEST!
OK...

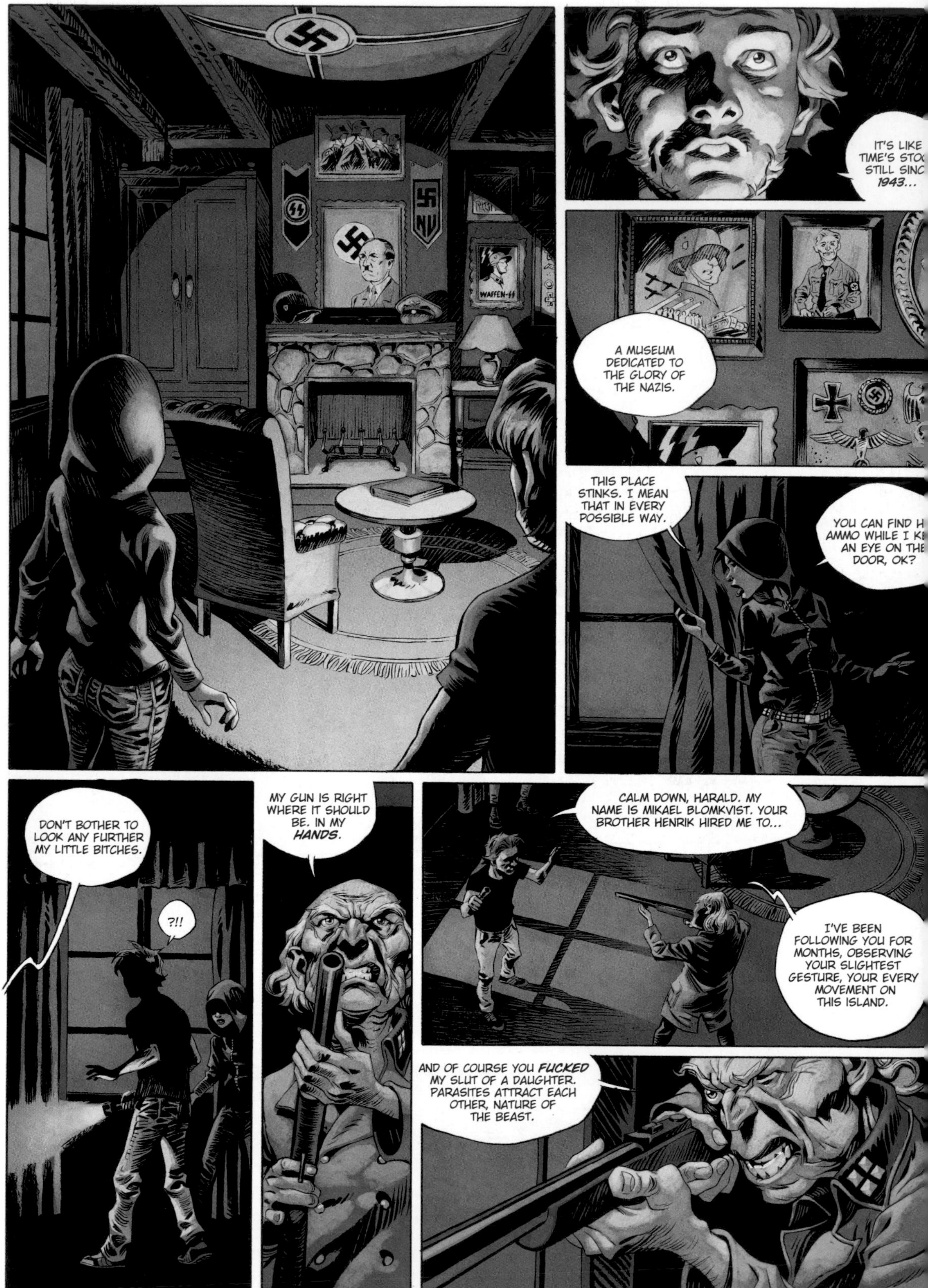
WAFFEN-SS
IT'S LIKE TIME'S STO STILL SINC *1943...*
A MUSEUM DEDICATED TO THE GLORY OF THE NAZIS.
THIS PLACE STINKS. I MEAN THAT IN EVERY POSSIBLE WAY.
YOU CAN FIND H AMMO WHILE I KE AN EYE ON THE DOOR, OK?
DON'T BOTHER TO LOOK ANY FURTHER MY LITTLE BITCHES.
?!!
MY GUN IS RIGHT WHERE IT SHOULD BE. IN MY ***HANDS***.
CALM DOWN, HARALD. MY NAME IS MIKAEL BLOMKVIST. YOUR BROTHER HENRIK HIRED ME TO...
I'VE BEEN FOLLOWING YOU FOR MONTHS, OBSERVING YOUR SLIGHTEST GESTURE, YOUR EVERY MOVEMENT ON THIS ISLAND.
AND OF COURSE YOU ***FUCKED*** MY SLUT OF A DAUGHTER. PARASITES ATTRACT EACH OTHER, NATURE OF THE BEAST.

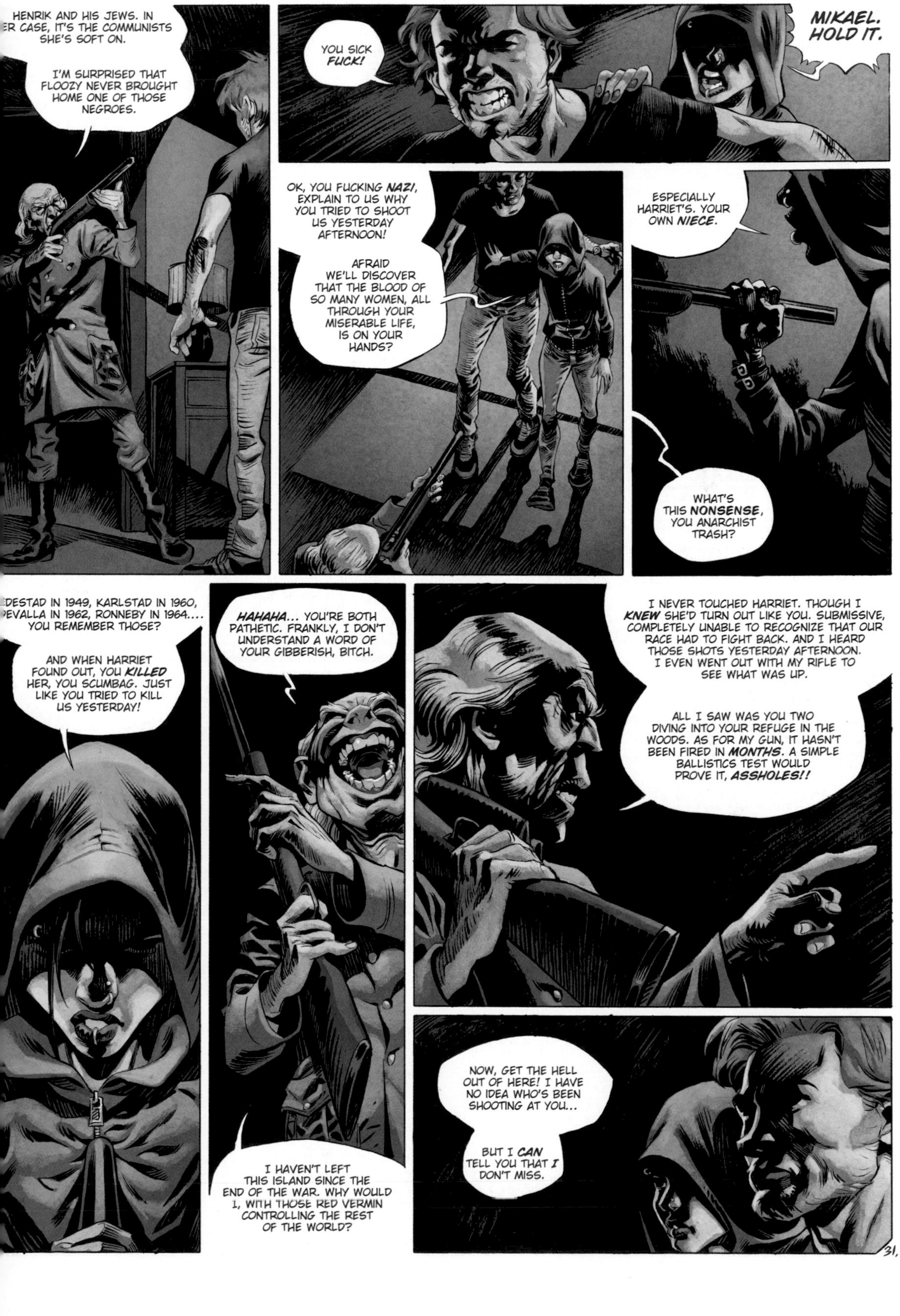
HENRIK AND HIS JEWS. IN ER CASE, IT'S THE COMMUNISTS SHE'S SOFT ON.
I'M SURPRISED THAT FLOOZY NEVER BROUGHT HOME ONE OF THOSE NEGROES.
YOU SICK FUCK!
MIKAEL. HOLD IT.
OK, YOU FUCKING NAZI, EXPLAIN TO US WHY YOU TRIED TO SHOOT US YESTERDAY AFTERNOON!
AFRAID WE'LL DISCOVER THAT THE BLOOD OF SO MANY WOMEN, ALL THROUGH YOUR MISERABLE LIFE, IS ON YOUR HANDS?
ESPECIALLY HARRIET'S. YOUR OWN NIECE.
WHAT'S THIS NONSENSE, YOU ANARCHIST TRASH?
EDESTAD IN 1949, KARLSTAD IN 1960, DEVALLA IN 1962, RONNEBY IN 1964.... YOU REMEMBER THOSE?
AND WHEN HARRIET FOUND OUT, YOU KILLED HER, YOU SCUMBAG. JUST LIKE YOU TRIED TO KILL US YESTERDAY!
HAHAHA... YOU'RE BOTH PATHETIC. FRANKLY, I DON'T UNDERSTAND A WORD OF YOUR GIBBERISH, BITCH.
I HAVEN'T LEFT THIS ISLAND SINCE THE END OF THE WAR. WHY WOULD I, WITH THOSE RED VERMIN CONTROLLING THE REST OF THE WORLD?
I NEVER TOUCHED HARRIET. THOUGH I KNEW SHE'D TURN OUT LIKE YOU. SUBMISSIVE, COMPLETELY UNABLE TO RECOGNIZE THAT OUR RACE HAD TO FIGHT BACK. AND I HEARD THOSE SHOTS YESTERDAY AFTERNOON. I EVEN WENT OUT WITH MY RIFLE TO SEE WHAT WAS UP.
ALL I SAW WAS YOU TWO DIVING INTO YOUR REFUGE IN THE WOODS. AS FOR MY GUN, IT HASN'T BEEN FIRED IN MONTHS. A SIMPLE BALLISTICS TEST WOULD PROVE IT, ASSHOLES!!
NOW, GET THE HELL OUT OF HERE! I HAVE NO IDEA WHO'S BEEN SHOOTING AT YOU...
BUT I CAN TELL YOU THAT I DON'T MISS.

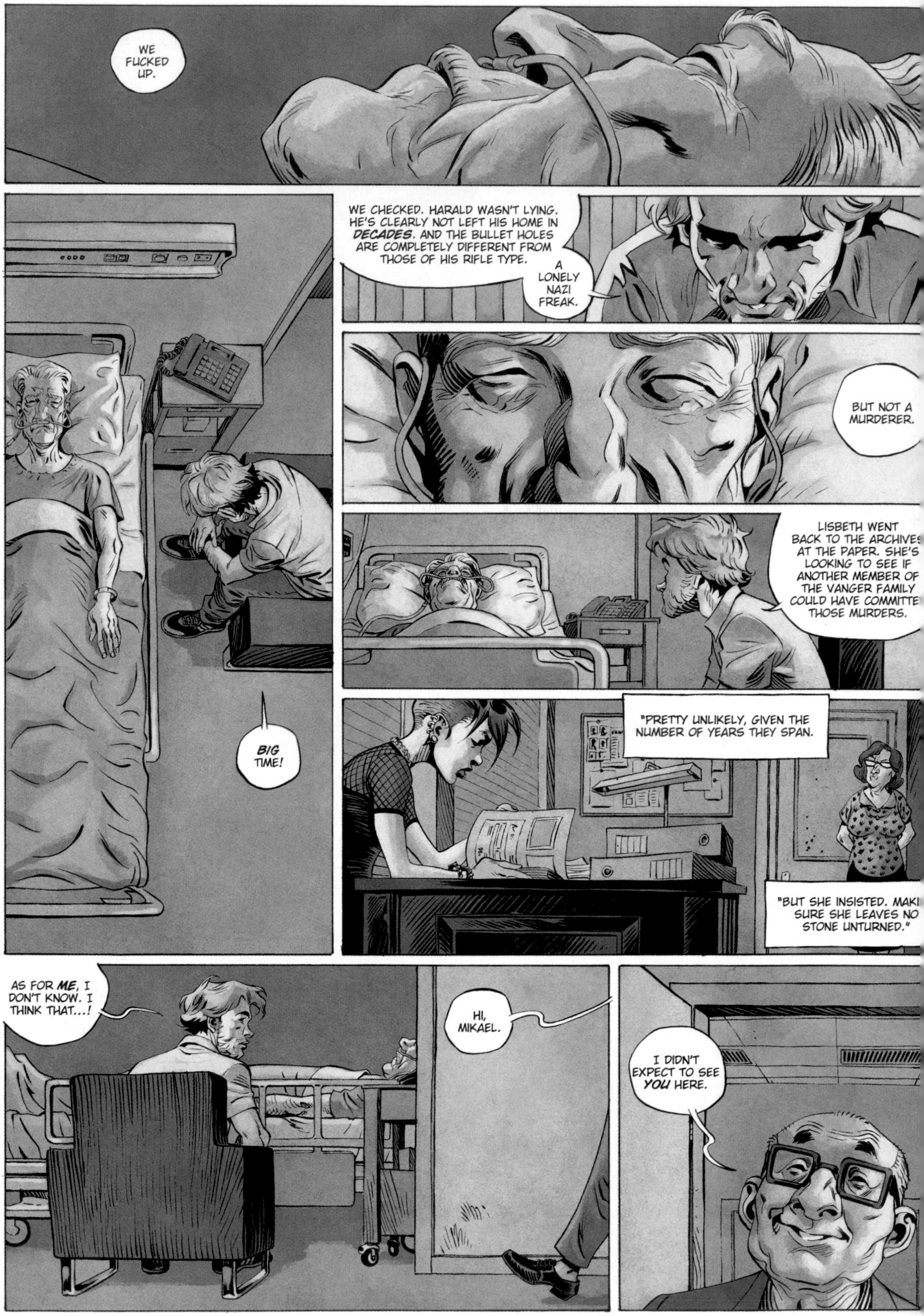
WE FUCKED UP.
BIG TIME!
WE CHECKED. HARALD WASN'T LYING. HE'S CLEARLY NOT LEFT HIS HOME IN DECADES. AND THE BULLET HOLES ARE COMPLETELY DIFFERENT FROM THOSE OF HIS RIFLE TYPE.
A LONELY NAZI FREAK.
BUT NOT A MURDERER.
LISBETH WENT BACK TO THE ARCHIVES AT THE PAPER. SHE'S LOOKING TO SEE IF ANOTHER MEMBER OF THE VANGER FAMILY COULD HAVE COMMITTE THOSE MURDERS.
"PRETTY UNLIKELY, GIVEN THE NUMBER OF YEARS THEY SPAN.
"BUT SHE INSISTED. MAKI SURE SHE LEAVES NO STONE UNTURNED."
AS FOR ME, I DON'T KNOW. I THINK THAT...!
HI, MIKAEL.
I DIDN'T EXPECT TO SEE YOU HERE.

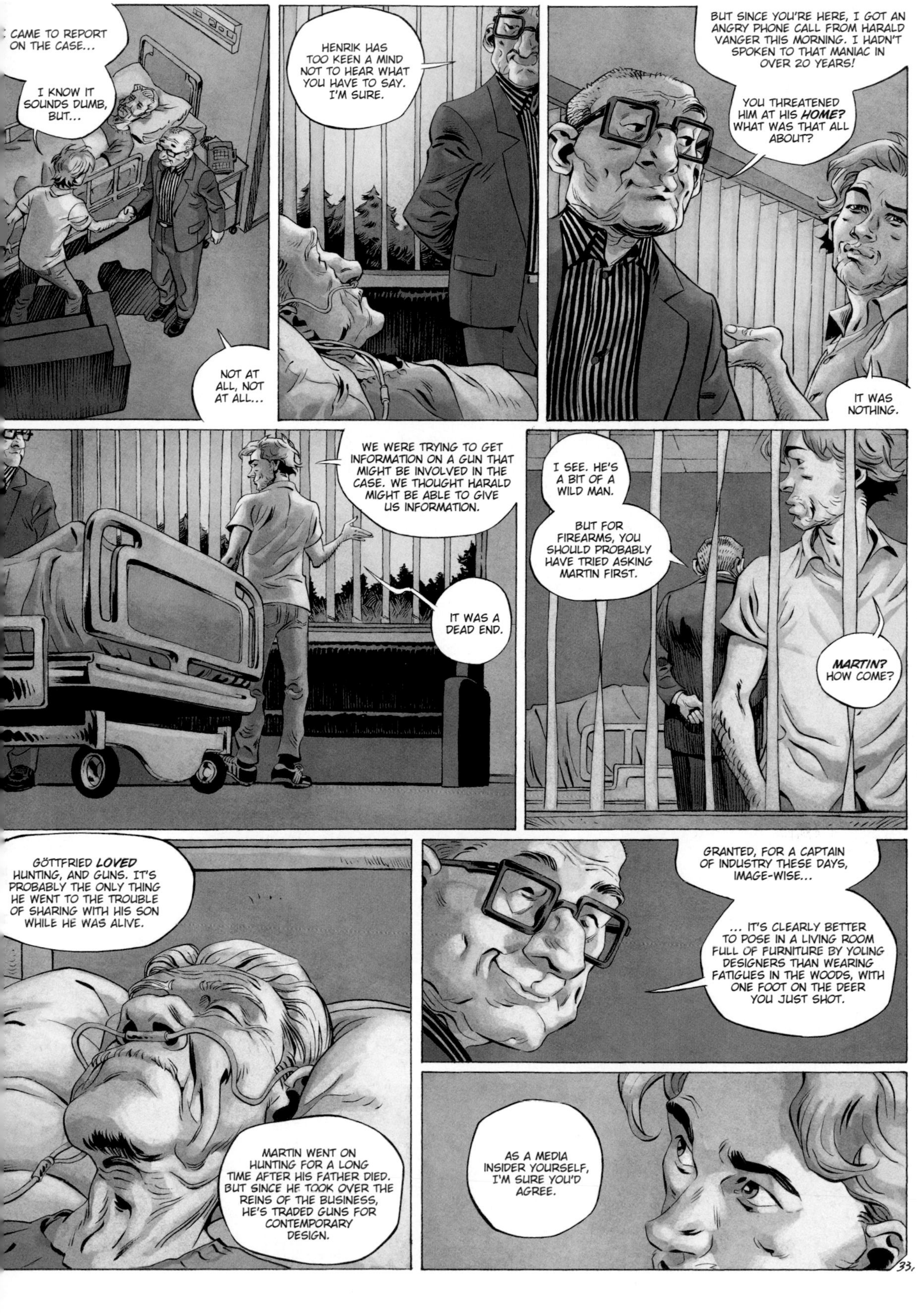
CAME TO REPORT ON THE CASE...
I KNOW IT SOUNDS DUMB, BUT...
NOT AT ALL, NOT AT ALL...
HENRIK HAS TOO KEEN A MIND NOT TO HEAR WHAT YOU HAVE TO SAY. I'M SURE.
BUT SINCE YOU'RE HERE, I GOT AN ANGRY PHONE CALL FROM HARALD VANGER THIS MORNING. I HADN'T SPOKEN TO THAT MANIAC IN OVER 20 YEARS!
YOU THREATENED HIM AT HIS HOME? WHAT WAS THAT ALL ABOUT?
IT WAS NOTHING.
WE WERE TRYING TO GET INFORMATION ON A GUN THAT MIGHT BE INVOLVED IN THE CASE. WE THOUGHT HARALD MIGHT BE ABLE TO GIVE US INFORMATION.
IT WAS A DEAD END.
I SEE. HE'S A BIT OF A WILD MAN.
BUT FOR FIREARMS, YOU SHOULD PROBABLY HAVE TRIED ASKING MARTIN FIRST.
MARTIN? HOW COME?
GÖTTFRIED LOVED HUNTING, AND GUNS. IT'S PROBABLY THE ONLY THING HE WENT TO THE TROUBLE OF SHARING WITH HIS SON WHILE HE WAS ALIVE.
MARTIN WENT ON HUNTING FOR A LONG TIME AFTER HIS FATHER DIED. BUT SINCE HE TOOK OVER THE REINS OF THE BUSINESS, HE'S TRADED GUNS FOR CONTEMPORARY DESIGN.
GRANTED, FOR A CAPTAIN OF INDUSTRY THESE DAYS, IMAGE-WISE...
... IT'S CLEARLY BETTER TO POSE IN A LIVING ROOM FULL OF FURNITURE BY YOUNG DESIGNERS THAN WEARING FATIGUES IN THE WOODS, WITH ONE FOOT ON THE DEER YOU JUST SHOT.
AS A MEDIA INSIDER YOURSELF, I'M SURE YOU'D AGREE.

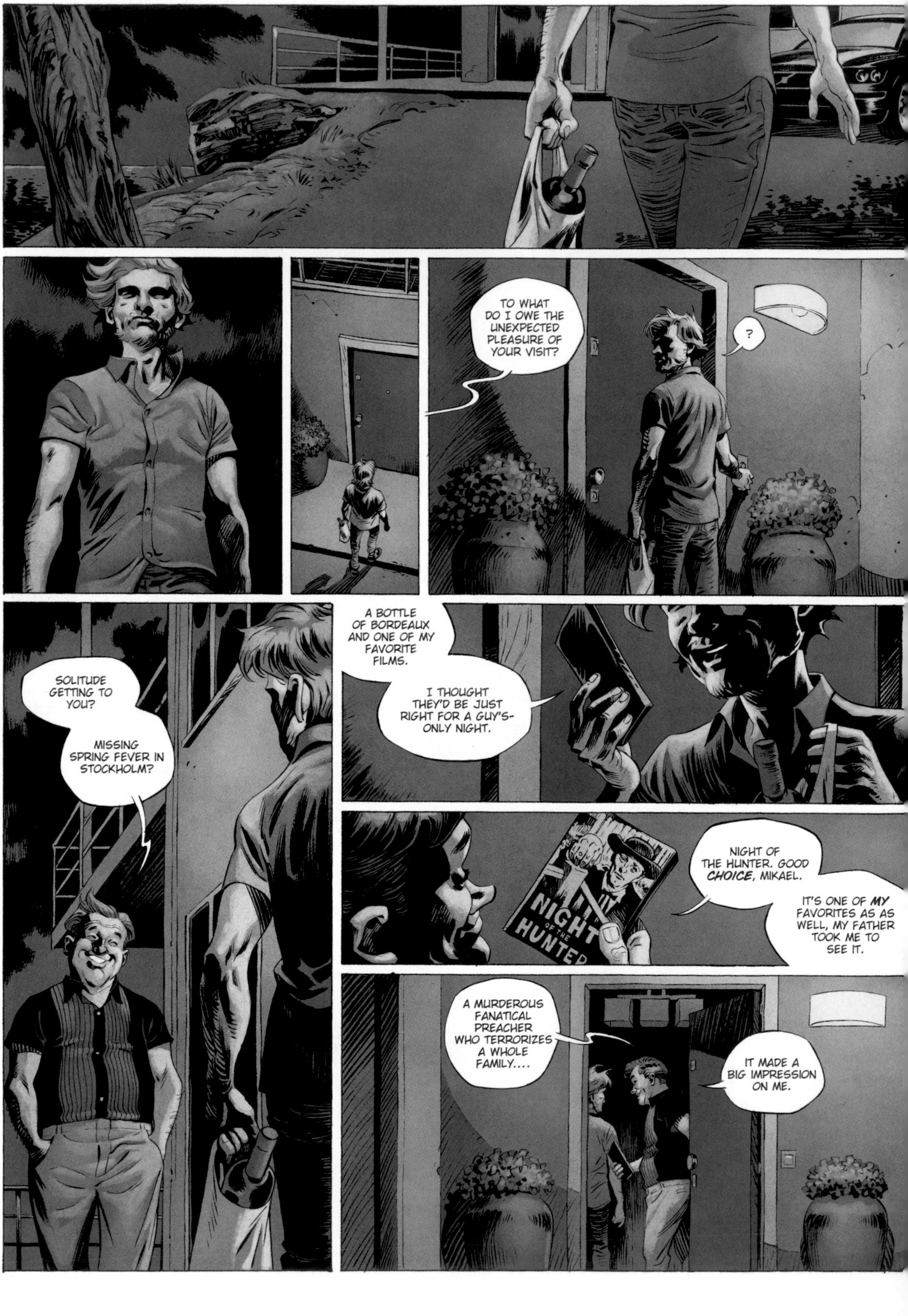
TO WHAT DO I OWE THE UNEXPECTED PLEASURE OF YOUR VISIT?
?
SOLITUDE GETTING TO YOU?
MISSING SPRING FEVER IN STOCKHOLM?
A BOTTLE OF BORDEAUX AND ONE OF MY FAVORITE FILMS.
I THOUGHT THEY'D BE JUST RIGHT FOR A GUY'S-ONLY NIGHT.
NIGHT OF THE HUNTER
NIGHT OF THE HUNTER. GOOD CHOICE, MIKAEL.
IT'S ONE OF MY FAVORITES AS AS WELL, MY FATHER TOOK ME TO SEE IT.
A MURDEROUS FANATICAL PREACHER WHO TERRORIZES A WHOLE FAMILY....
IT MADE A BIG IMPRESSION ON ME.

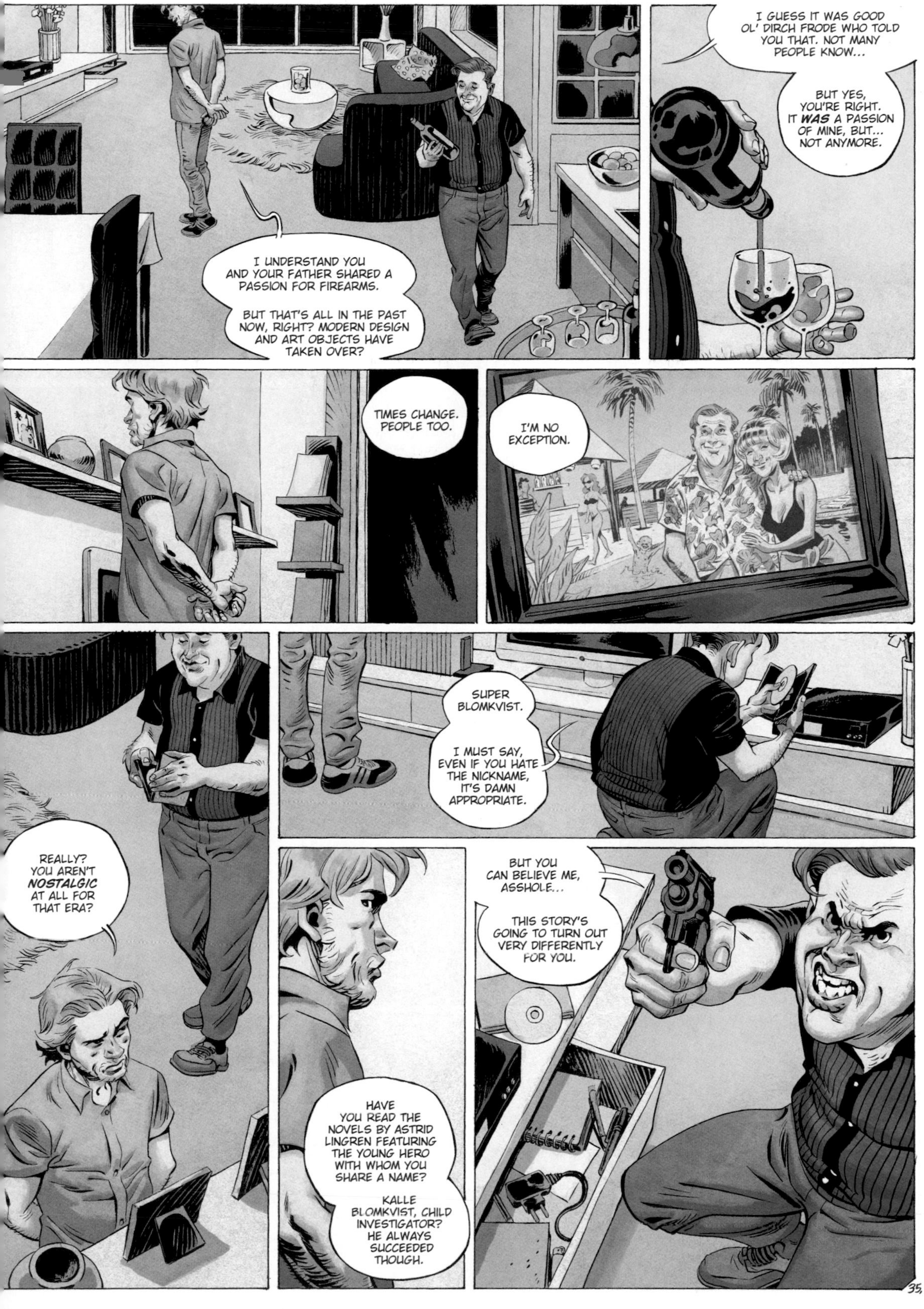
I UNDERSTAND YOU AND YOUR FATHER SHARED A PASSION FOR FIREARMS.
BUT THAT'S ALL IN THE PAST NOW, RIGHT? MODERN DESIGN AND ART OBJECTS HAVE TAKEN OVER?
I GUESS IT WAS GOOD OL' DIRCH FRODE WHO TOLD YOU THAT. NOT MANY PEOPLE KNOW...
BUT YES, YOU'RE RIGHT. IT WAS A PASSION OF MINE, BUT... NOT ANYMORE.
TIMES CHANGE. PEOPLE TOO.
I'M NO EXCEPTION.
REALLY? YOU AREN'T NOSTALGIC AT ALL FOR THAT ERA?
SUPER BLOMKVIST.
I MUST SAY, EVEN IF YOU HATE THE NICKNAME, IT'S DAMN APPROPRIATE.
HAVE YOU READ THE NOVELS BY ASTRID LINGREN FEATURING THE YOUNG HERO WITH WHOM YOU SHARE A NAME?
KALLE BLOMKVIST, CHILD INVESTIGATOR? HE ALWAYS SUCCEEDED THOUGH.
BUT YOU CAN BELIEVE ME, ASSHOLE...
THIS STORY'S GOING TO TURN OUT VERY DIFFERENTLY FOR YOU.

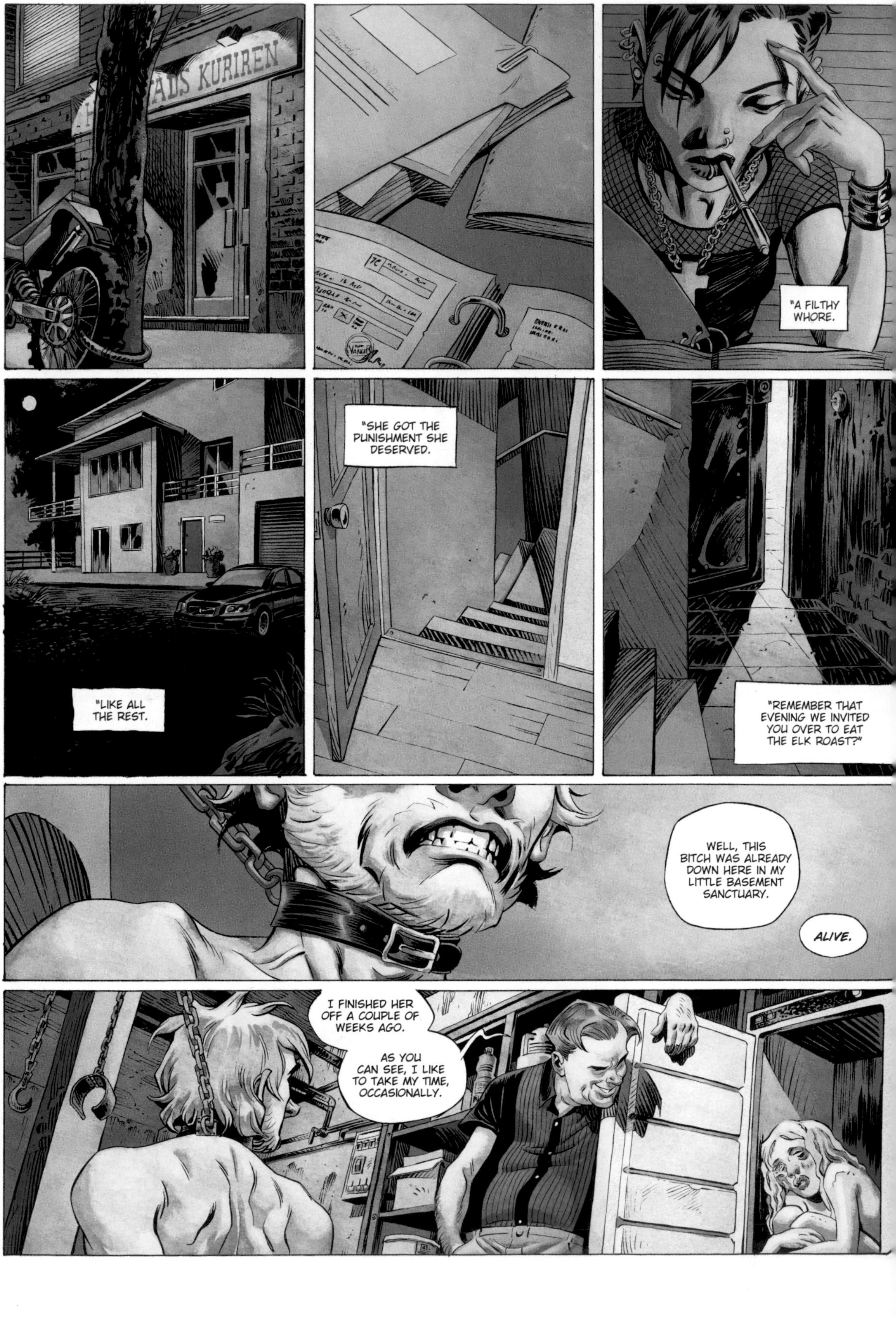

KURIREN
"A FILTHY WHORE.
"LIKE ALL THE REST.
"SHE GOT THE PUNISHMENT SHE DESERVED.
"REMEMBER THAT EVENING WE INVITED YOU OVER TO EAT THE ELK ROAST?"
WELL, THIS BITCH WAS ALREADY DOWN HERE IN MY LITTLE BASEMENT SANCTUARY.
ALIVE.
I FINISHED HER OFF A COUPLE OF WEEKS AGO.
AS YOU CAN SEE, I LIKE TO TAKE MY TIME, OCCASIONALLY.

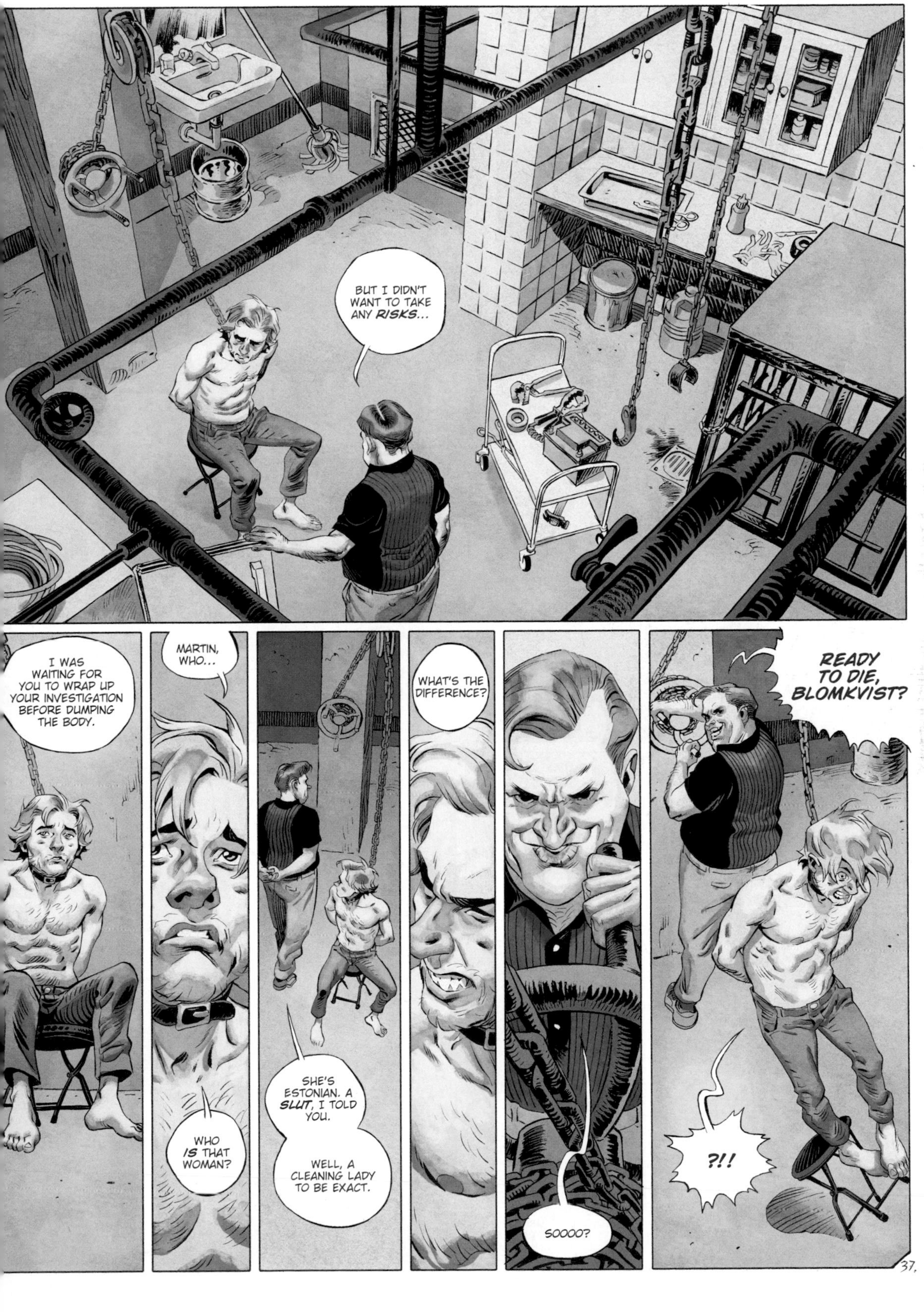
BUT I DIDN'T WANT TO TAKE ANY *RISKS*...
I WAS WAITING FOR YOU TO WRAP UP YOUR INVESTIGATION BEFORE DUMPING THE BODY.
MARTIN, WHO...
WHO *IS* THAT WOMAN?
WHAT'S THE DIFFERENCE?
SHE'S ESTONIAN. A *SLUT*, I TOLD YOU.
WELL, A CLEANING LADY TO BE EXACT.
SOOOO?
READY TO DIE, BLOMKVIST?
?!!

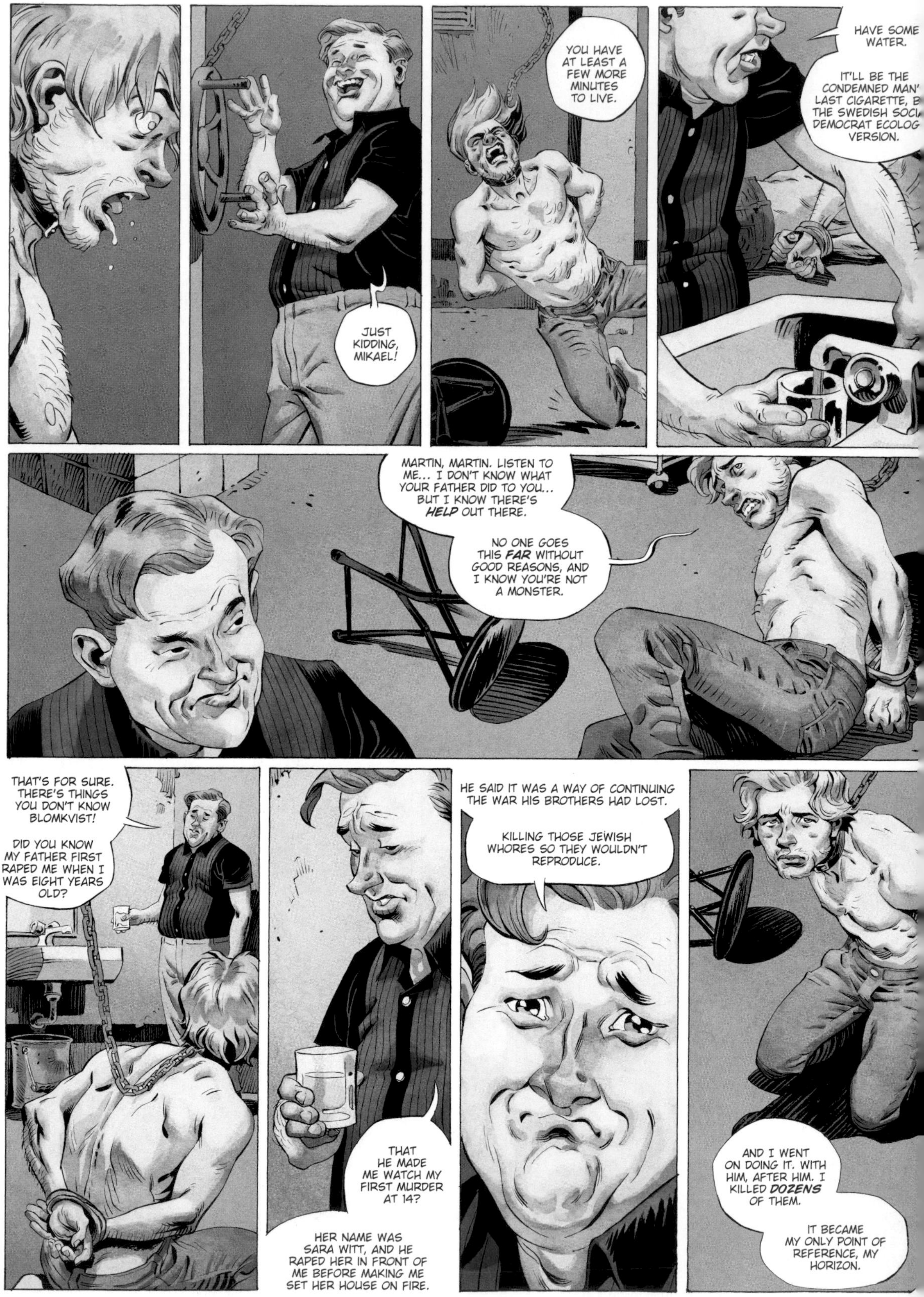
JUST KIDDING, MIKAEL!
YOU HAVE AT LEAST A FEW MORE MINUTES TO LIVE.
HAVE SOME WATER.
IT'LL BE THE CONDEMNED MAN' LAST CIGARETTE, B THE SWEDISH SOCI DEMOCRAT ECOLOG VERSION.
MARTIN, MARTIN. LISTEN TO ME... I DON'T KNOW WHAT YOUR FATHER DID TO YOU... BUT I KNOW THERE'S HELP OUT THERE.
NO ONE GOES THIS FAR WITHOUT GOOD REASONS, AND I KNOW YOU'RE NOT A MONSTER.
THAT'S FOR SURE. THERE'S THINGS YOU DON'T KNOW BLOMKVIST!
DID YOU KNOW MY FATHER FIRST RAPED ME WHEN I WAS EIGHT YEARS OLD?
THAT HE MADE ME WATCH MY FIRST MURDER AT 14?
HER NAME WAS SARA WITT, AND HE RAPED HER IN FRONT OF ME BEFORE MAKING ME SET HER HOUSE ON FIRE.
HE SAID IT WAS A WAY OF CONTINUING THE WAR HIS BROTHERS HAD LOST.
KILLING THOSE JEWISH WHORES SO THEY WOULDN'T REPRODUCE.
AND I WENT ON DOING IT. WITH HIM, AFTER HIM. I KILLED DOZENS OF THEM.
IT BECAME MY ONLY POINT OF REFERENCE, MY HORIZON.

GÖTTFRIED WAS A SLIMEBALL, MARTIN. HE *USED* YOU!

THERE'S *STILL* TIME TO CHANGE ALL THAT.

THINK OF EVA. THAT SHE CAN LOVE YOU SHOWS THAT THE HUMAN BEING INSIDE, THE *REAL* MARTIN, STILL EXISTS.

THERE'S STILL *HOPE!*

EVA. MY SWEET EVA.

EVA IS A CUNT. SHE'S UNBEARABLE AND PRETENTIOUS.

BUT HAVING HER BY MY SIDE IS THE BEST COVER EVER!!

AND YES, MY FATHER WAS WRONG!!

WHY BE LIMITED TO JEWISH BITCHES, WHEN THERE ARE SO MANY USELESS FEMALES TO PLAY WITH?

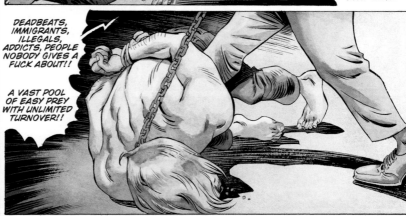

DEADBEATS, IMMIGRANTS, ILLEGALS, ADDICTS, PEOPLE NOBODY GIVES A FUCK ABOUT!!

A VAST POOL OF EASY PREY WITH UNLIMITED TURNOVER!!

"AND I'M NOT GOING TO LET YOU SPOIL MY FUN."

OH SHIT! THE ORANGE AND WHITE JACKET!

MARTIN VANGER.

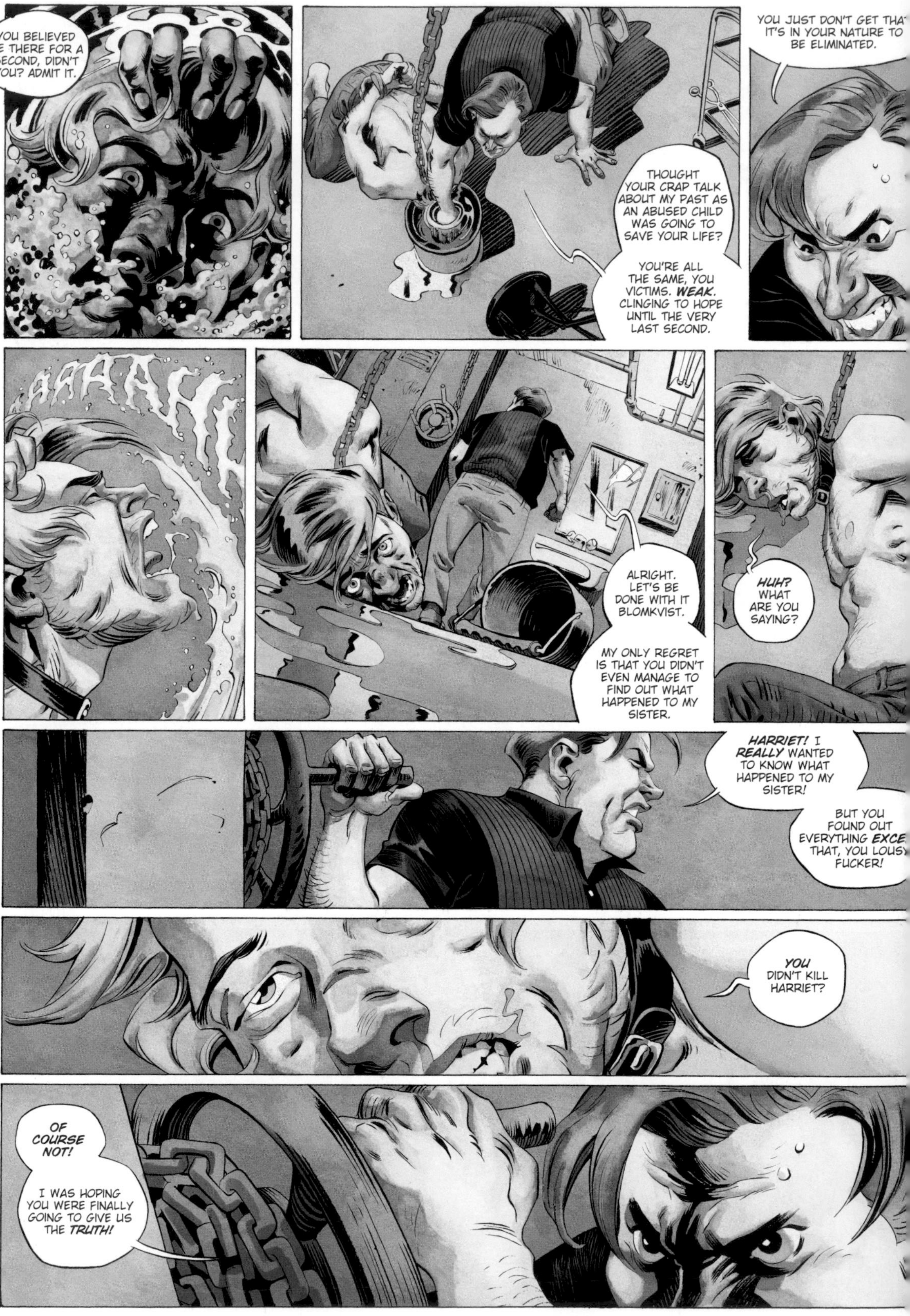
YOU BELIEVED ME THERE FOR A SECOND, DIDN'T YOU? ADMIT IT.
THOUGHT YOUR CRAP TALK ABOUT MY PAST AS AN ABUSED CHILD WAS GOING TO SAVE YOUR LIFE?
YOU'RE ALL THE SAME, YOU VICTIMS. WEAK. CLINGING TO HOPE UNTIL THE VERY LAST SECOND.
YOU JUST DON'T GET THA IT'S IN YOUR NATURE TO BE ELIMINATED.
ALRIGHT. LET'S BE DONE WITH IT BLOMKVIST.
MY ONLY REGRET IS THAT YOU DIDN'T EVEN MANAGE TO FIND OUT WHAT HAPPENED TO MY SISTER.
HUH? WHAT ARE YOU SAYING?
HARRIET! I REALLY WANTED TO KNOW WHAT HAPPENED TO MY SISTER!
BUT YOU FOUND OUT EVERYTHING EXCE THAT, YOU LOUS FUCKER!
YOU DIDN'T KILL HARRIET?
OF COURSE NOT!
I WAS HOPING YOU WERE FINALLY GOING TO GIVE US THE TRUTH!

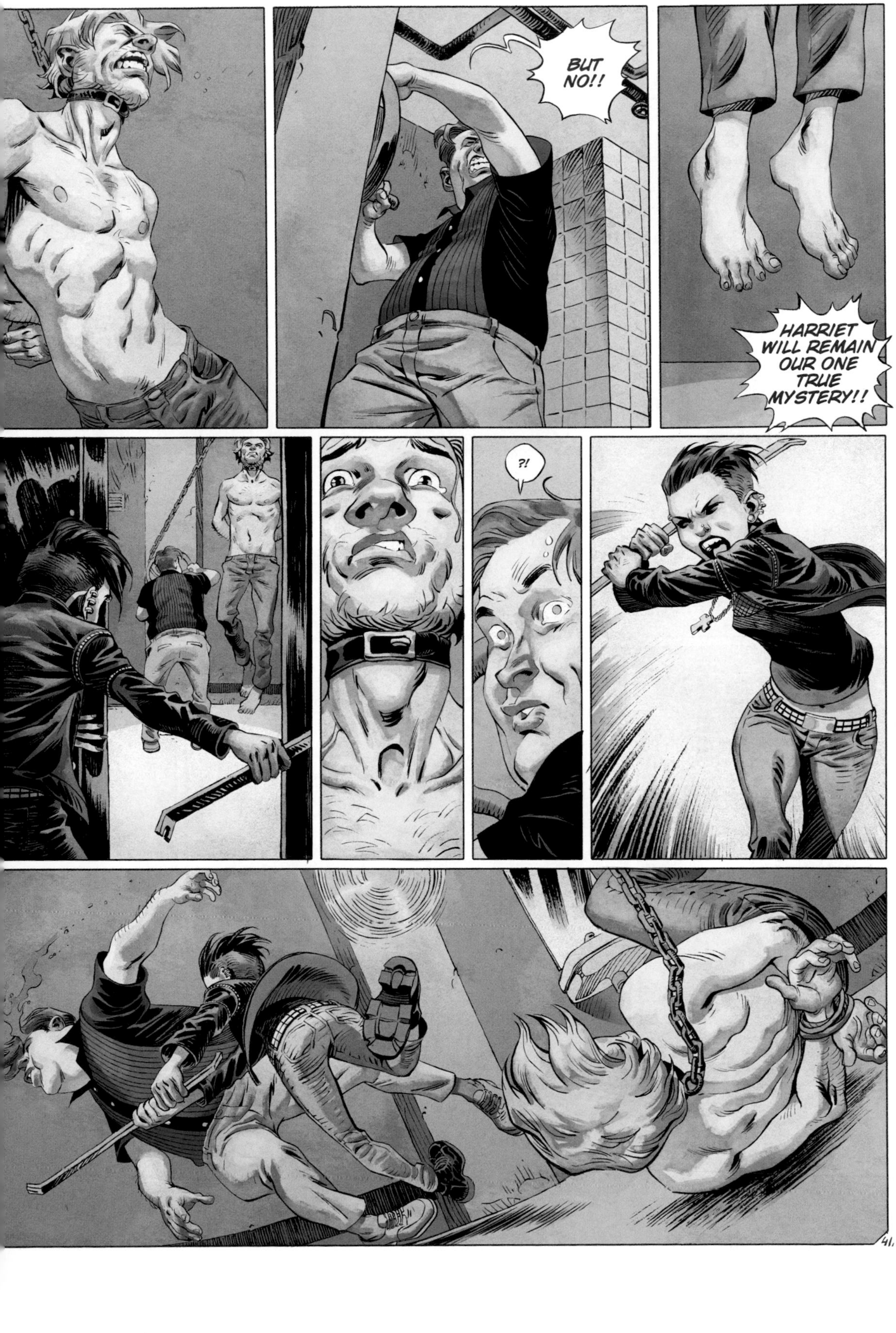
BUT NO!!
HARRIET WILL REMAIN OUR ONE TRUE MYSTERY!!
?!

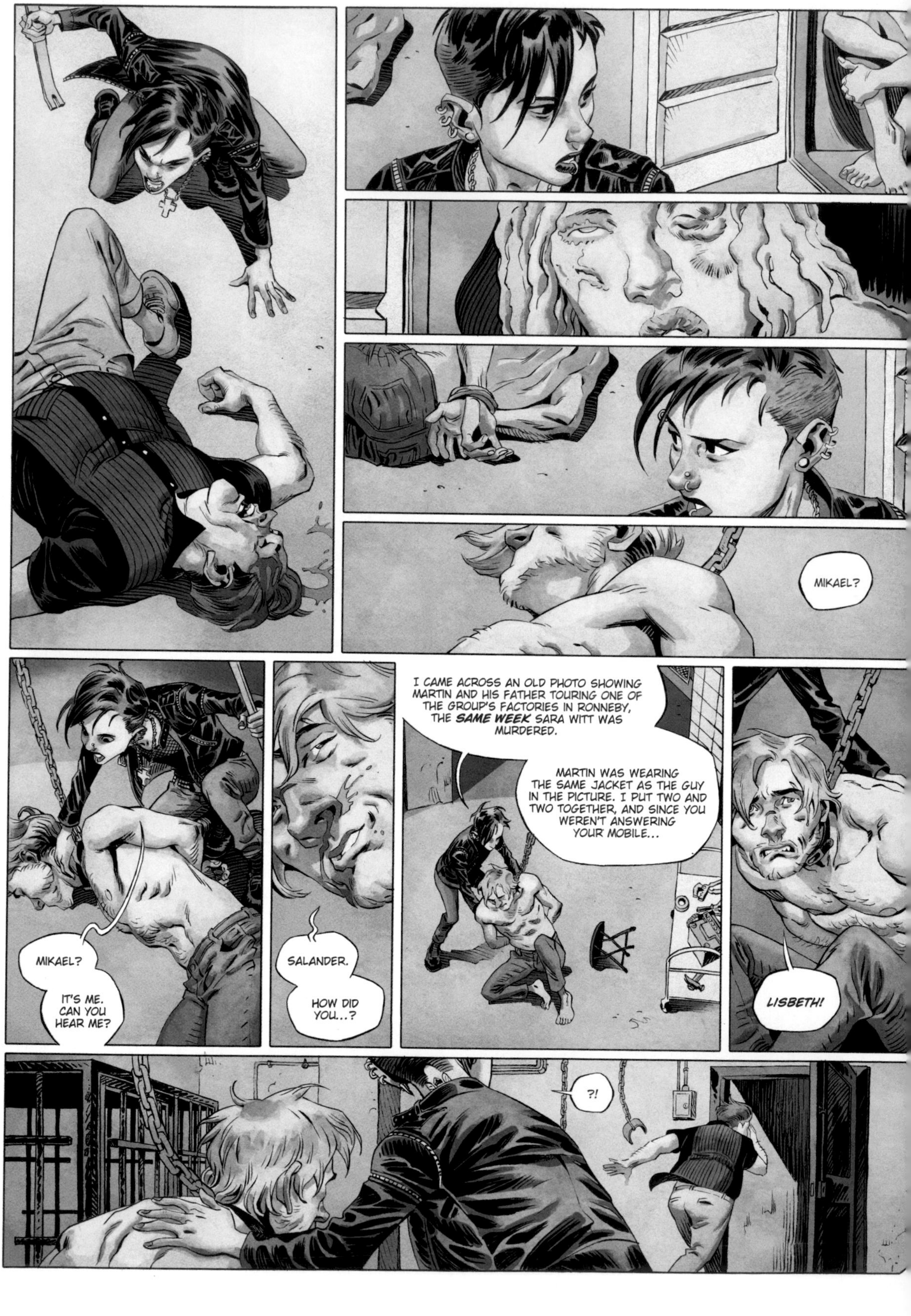

MIKAEL?
MIKAEL?
IT'S ME. CAN YOU HEAR ME?
SALANDER.
HOW DID YOU...?
I CAME ACROSS AN OLD PHOTO SHOWING MARTIN AND HIS FATHER TOURING ONE OF THE GROUP'S FACTORIES IN RONNEBY, THE **SAME WEEK** SARA WITT WAS MURDERED.
MARTIN WAS WEARING THE SAME JACKET AS THE GUY IN THE PICTURE. I PUT TWO AND TWO TOGETHER, AND SINCE YOU WEREN'T ANSWERING YOUR MOBILE...
LISBETH!
?!

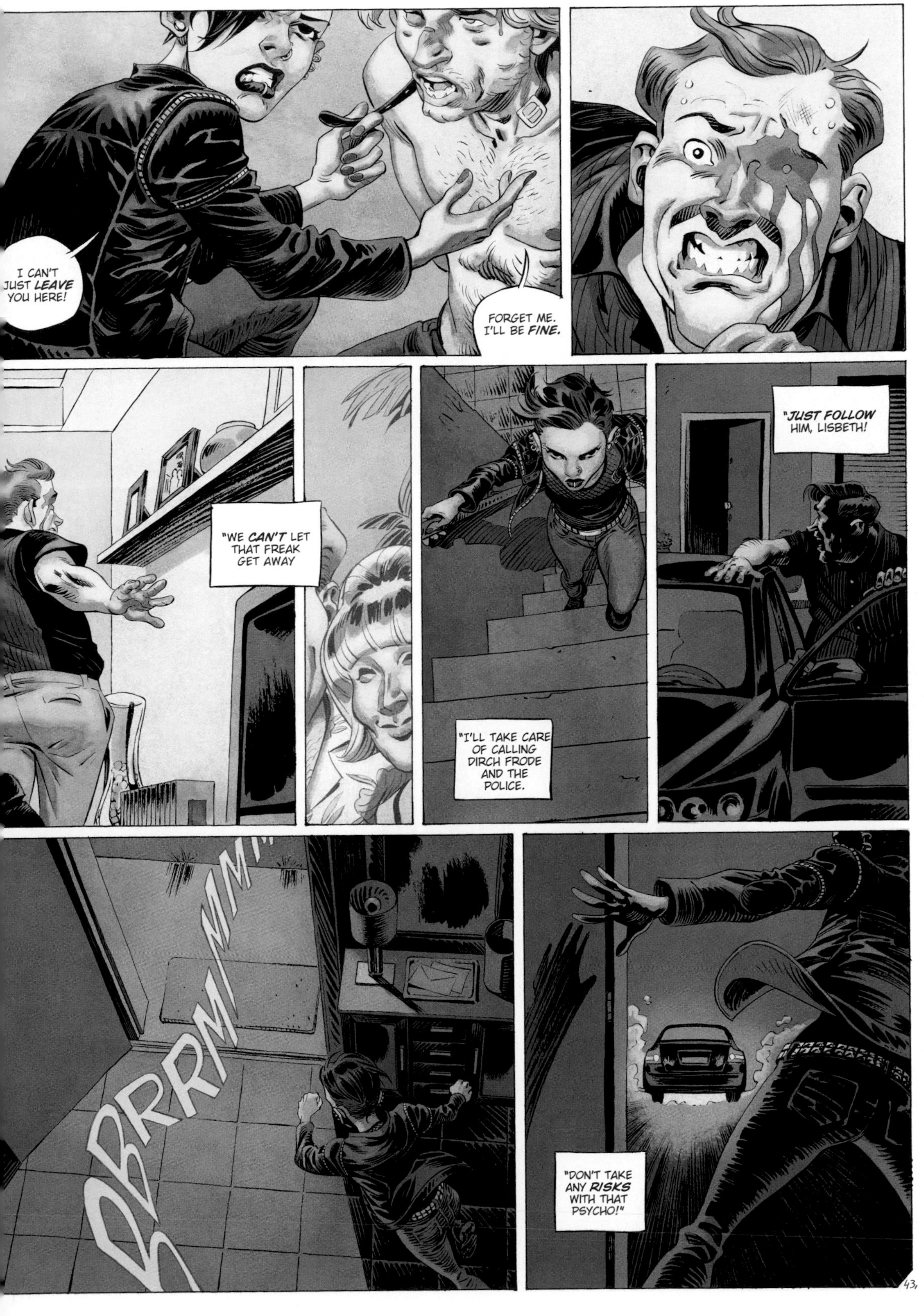
I CAN'T JUST *LEAVE* YOU HERE!
FORGET ME. I'LL BE *FINE.*
"WE *CAN'T* LET THAT FREAK GET AWAY
"I'LL TAKE CARE OF CALLING DIRCH FRODE AND THE POLICE.
"*JUST FOLLOW* HIM, LISBETH!
BBRRMMMMM
"DON'T TAKE ANY *RISKS* WITH THAT PSYCHO!"

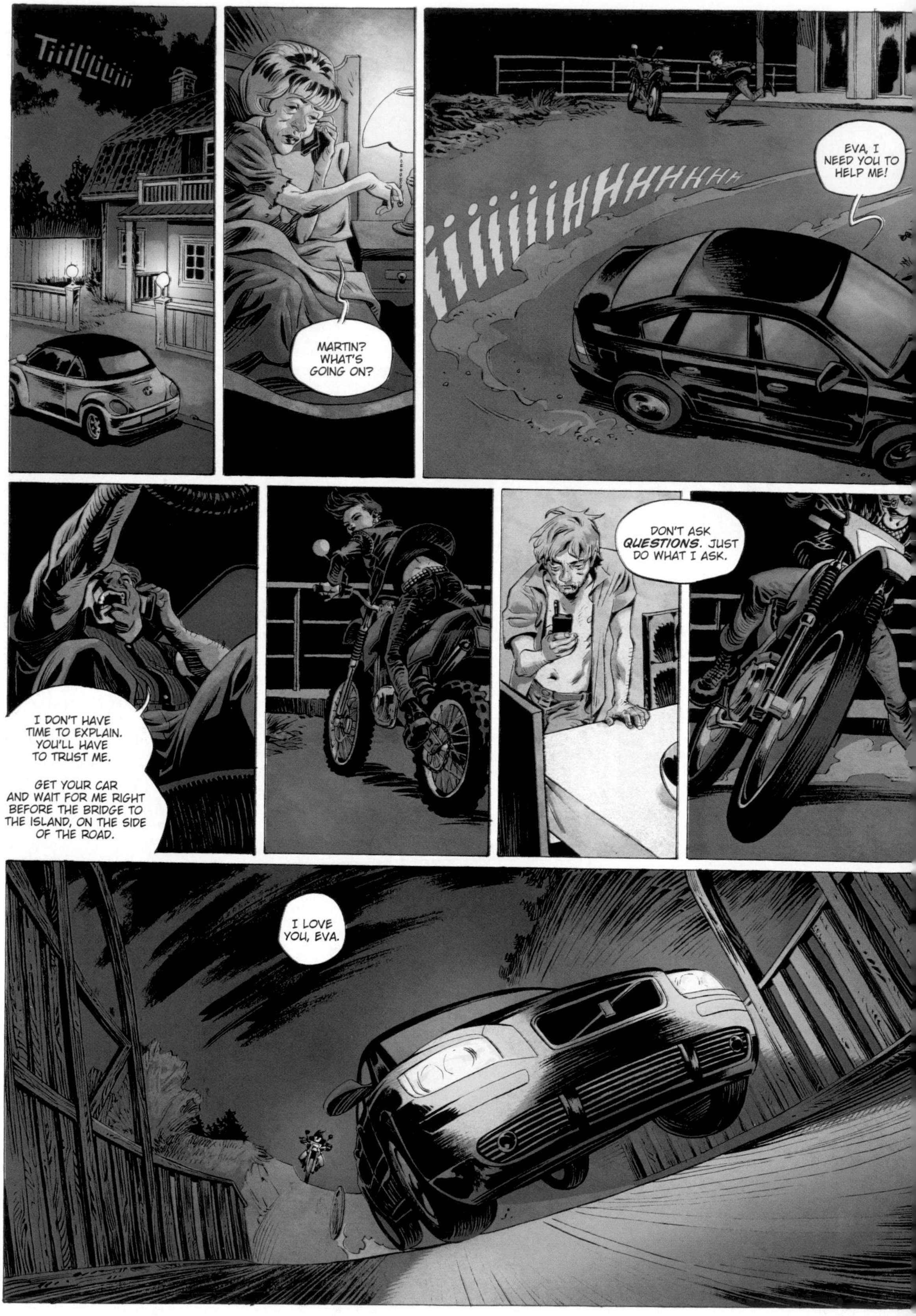
TIILIIIIII
MARTIN? WHAT'S GOING ON?
IIIIIIIHHHHHHHHH
EVA, I NEED YOU TO HELP ME!
I DON'T HAVE TIME TO EXPLAIN. YOU'LL HAVE TO TRUST ME.
GET YOUR CAR AND WAIT FOR ME RIGHT BEFORE THE BRIDGE TO THE ISLAND, ON THE SIDE OF THE ROAD.
DON'T ASK QUESTIONS. JUST DO WHAT I ASK.
I LOVE YOU, EVA.

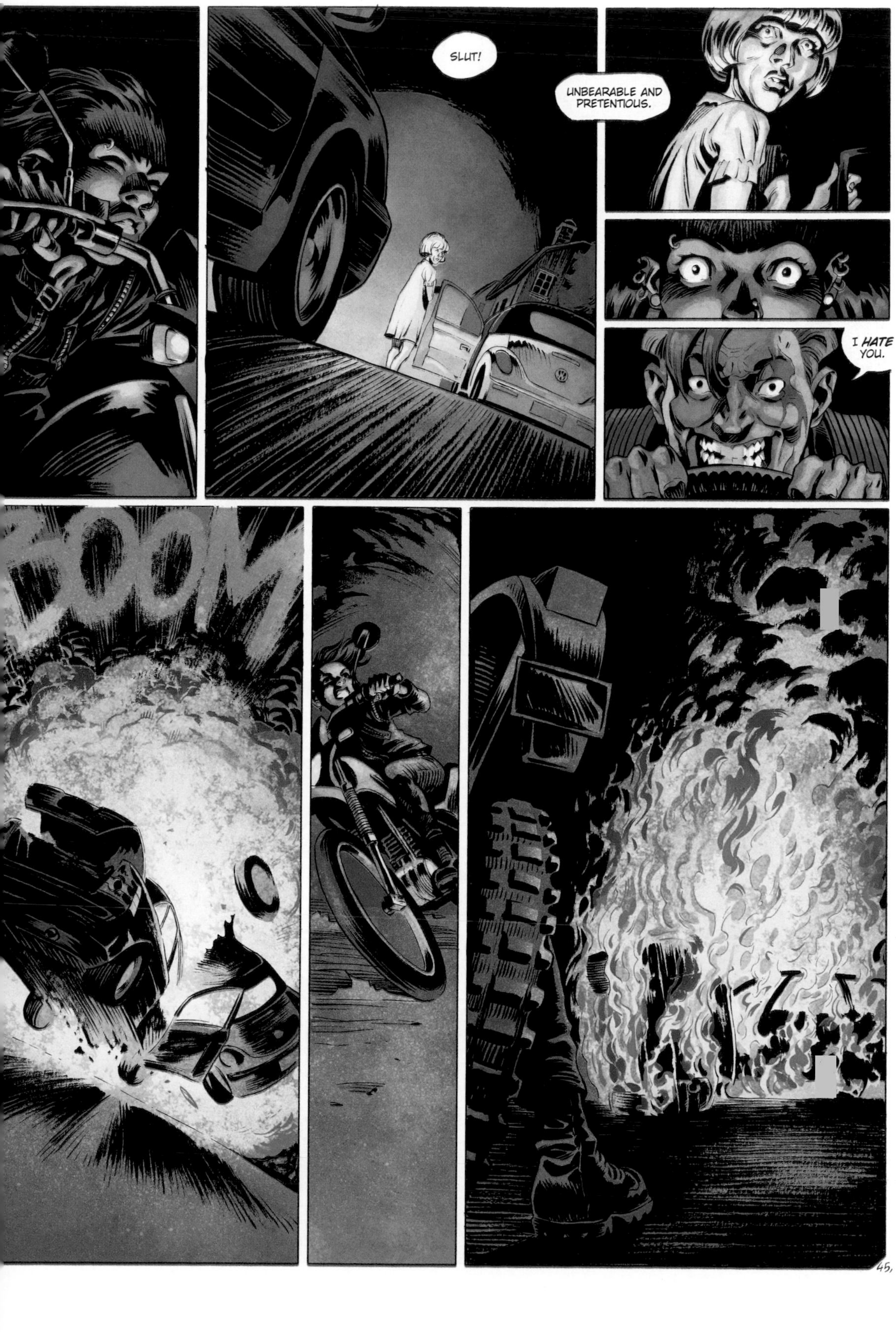
SLUT!
UNBEARABLE AND PRETENTIOUS.
I HATE YOU.
BOOM

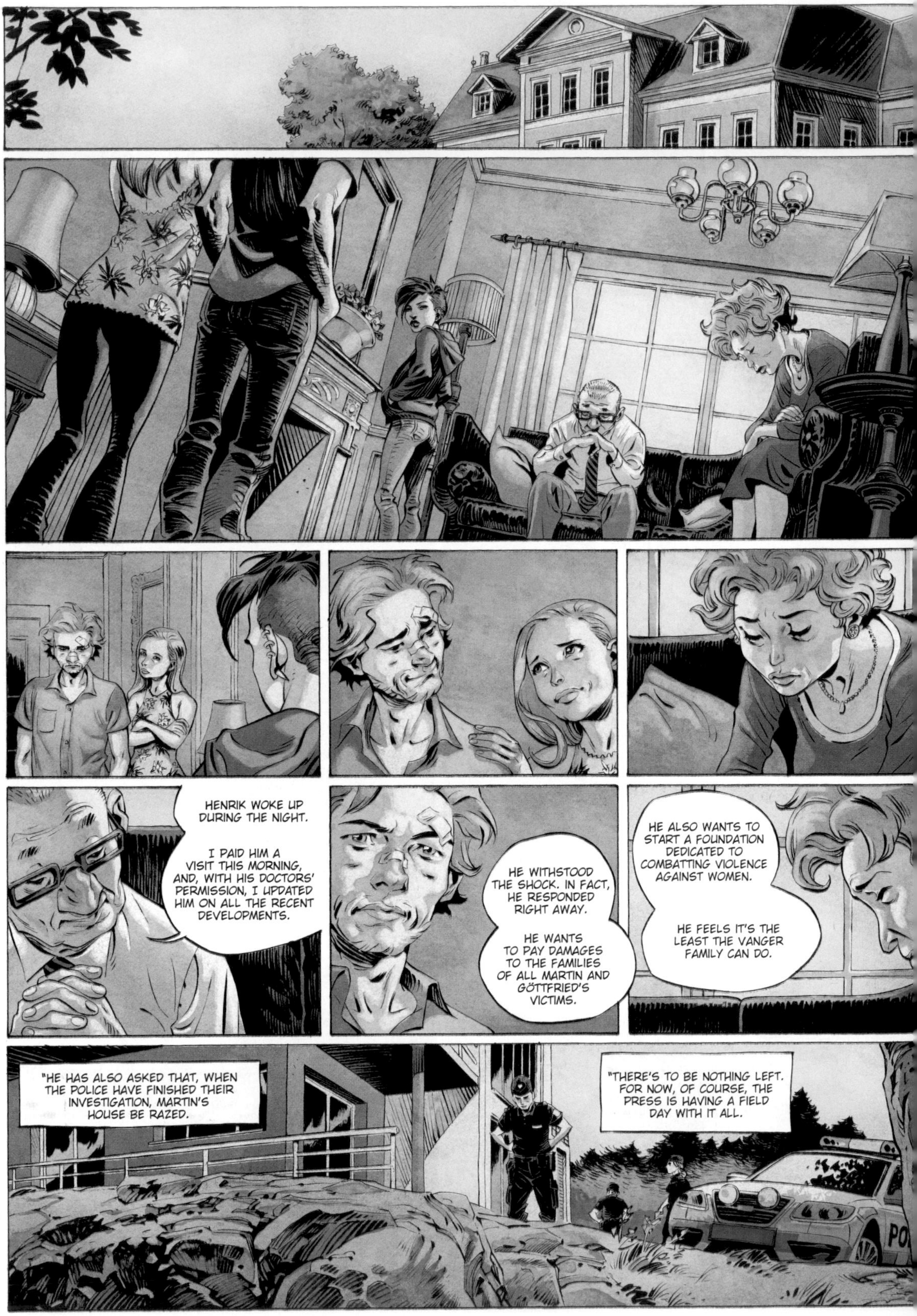
HENRIK WOKE UP DURING THE NIGHT.
I PAID HIM A VISIT THIS MORNING, AND, WITH HIS DOCTORS' PERMISSION, I UPDATED HIM ON ALL THE RECENT DEVELOPMENTS.
HE WITHSTOOD THE SHOCK. IN FACT, HE RESPONDED RIGHT AWAY.
HE WANTS TO PAY DAMAGES TO THE FAMILIES OF ALL MARTIN AND GÖTTFRIED'S VICTIMS.
HE ALSO WANTS TO START A FOUNDATION DEDICATED TO COMBATTING VIOLENCE AGAINST WOMEN.
HE FEELS IT'S THE LEAST THE VANGER FAMILY CAN DO.
"HE HAS ALSO ASKED THAT, WHEN THE POLICE HAVE FINISHED THEIR INVESTIGATION, MARTIN'S HOUSE BE RAZED.
"THERE'S TO BE NOTHING LEFT. FOR NOW, OF COURSE, THE PRESS IS HAVING A FIELD DAY WITH IT ALL.

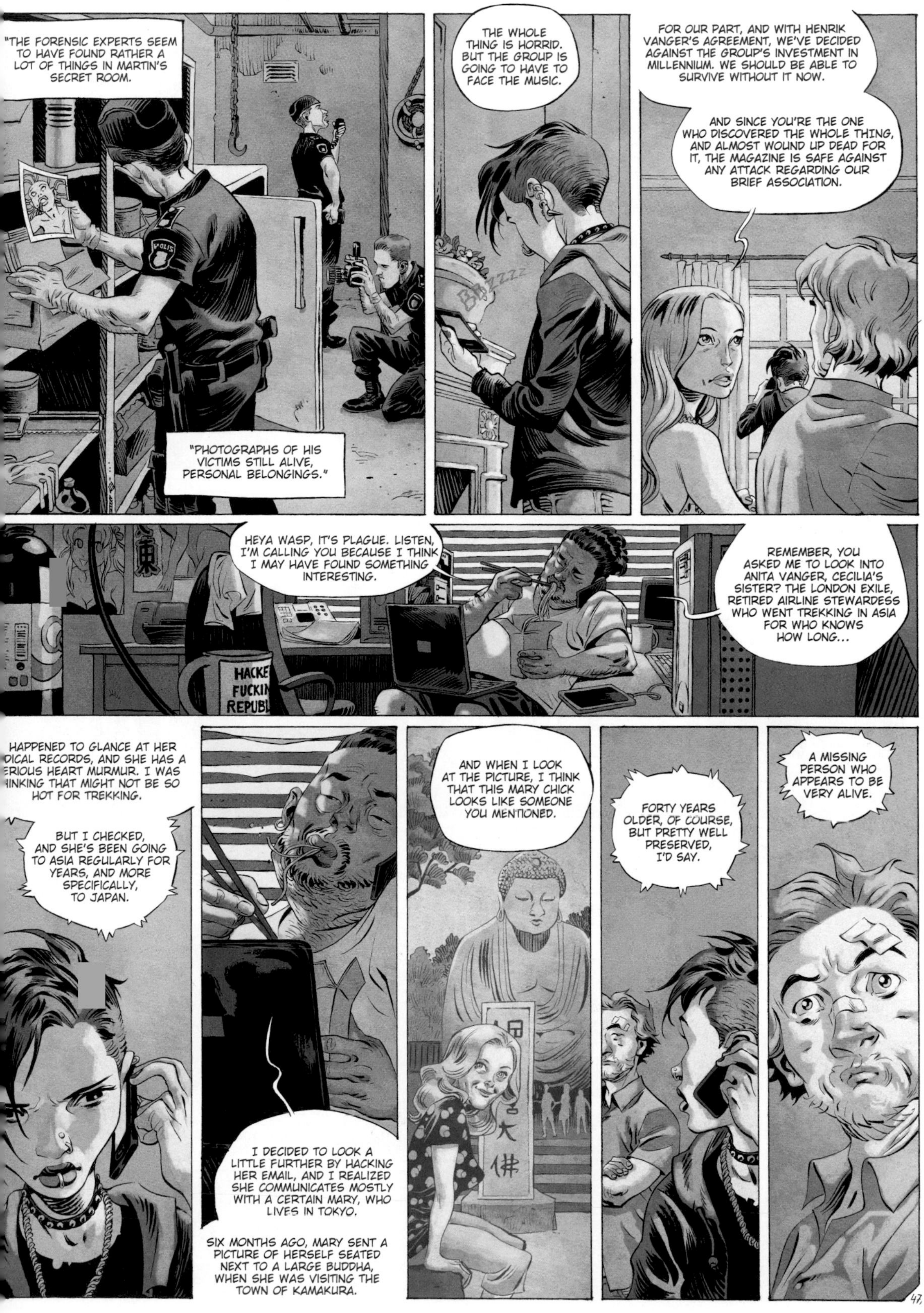
"THE FORENSIC EXPERTS SEEM TO HAVE FOUND RATHER A LOT OF THINGS IN MARTIN'S SECRET ROOM.
POLIS
"PHOTOGRAPHS OF HIS VICTIMS STILL ALIVE, PERSONAL BELONGINGS."
THE WHOLE THING IS HORRID. BUT THE GROUP IS GOING TO HAVE TO FACE THE MUSIC.
BZZZZZ
FOR OUR PART, AND WITH HENRIK VANGER'S AGREEMENT, WE'VE DECIDED AGAINST THE GROUP'S INVESTMENT IN MILLENNIUM. WE SHOULD BE ABLE TO SURVIVE WITHOUT IT NOW.
AND SINCE YOU'RE THE ONE WHO DISCOVERED THE WHOLE THING, AND ALMOST WOUND UP DEAD FOR IT, THE MAGAZINE IS SAFE AGAINST ANY ATTACK REGARDING OUR BRIEF ASSOCIATION.
HEYA WASP, IT'S PLAGUE. LISTEN, I'M CALLING YOU BECAUSE I THINK I MAY HAVE FOUND SOMETHING INTERESTING.
HACKE FUCKIN REPUBL
REMEMBER, YOU ASKED ME TO LOOK INTO ANITA VANGER, CECILIA'S SISTER? THE LONDON EXILE, RETIRED AIRLINE STEWARDESS WHO WENT TREKKING IN ASIA FOR WHO KNOWS HOW LONG...
HAPPENED TO GLANCE AT HER DICAL RECORDS, AND SHE HAS A ERIOUS HEART MURMUR. I WAS HINKING THAT MIGHT NOT BE SO HOT FOR TREKKING.
BUT I CHECKED, AND SHE'S BEEN GOING TO ASIA REGULARLY FOR YEARS, AND MORE SPECIFICALLY, TO JAPAN.
I DECIDED TO LOOK A LITTLE FURTHER BY HACKING HER EMAIL, AND I REALIZED SHE COMMUNICATES MOSTLY WITH A CERTAIN MARY, WHO LIVES IN TOKYO.
SIX MONTHS AGO, MARY SENT A PICTURE OF HERSELF SEATED NEXT TO A LARGE BUDDHA, WHEN SHE WAS VISITING THE TOWN OF KAMAKURA.
AND WHEN I LOOK AT THE PICTURE, I THINK THAT THIS MARY CHICK LOOKS LIKE SOMEONE YOU MENTIONED.
大佛
FORTY YEARS OLDER, OF COURSE, BUT PRETTY WELL PRESERVED, I'D SAY.
A MISSING PERSON WHO APPEARS TO BE VERY ALIVE.

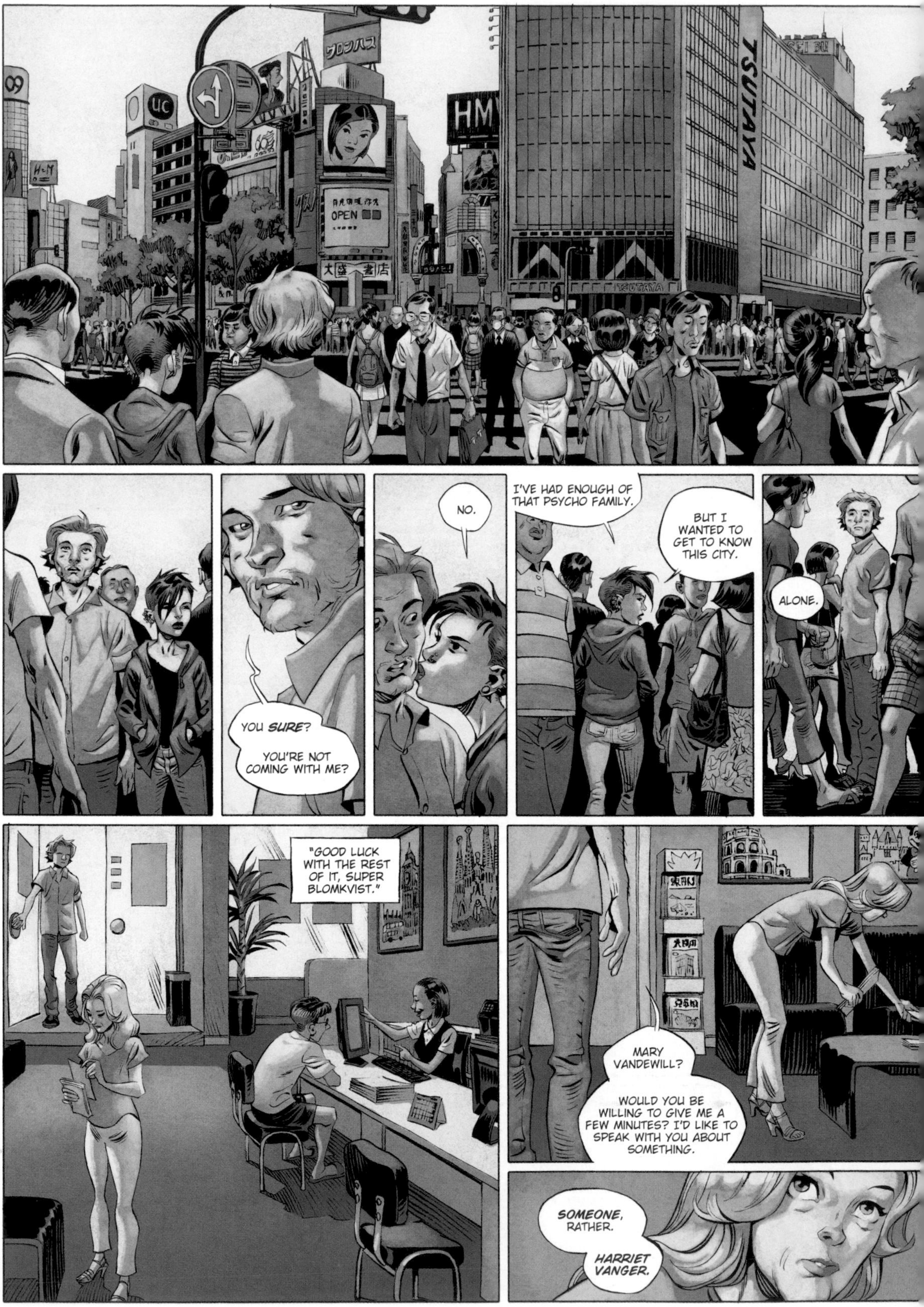
HMV
TSUTAYA
OPEN
TSUTAYA
YOU SURE?
YOU'RE NOT COMING WITH ME?
NO.
I'VE HAD ENOUGH OF THAT PSYCHO FAMILY.
BUT I WANTED TO GET TO KNOW THIS CITY.
ALONE.
"GOOD LUCK WITH THE REST OF IT, SUPER BLOMKVIST."
MARY VANDEWILL?
WOULD YOU BE WILLING TO GIVE ME A FEW MINUTES? I'D LIKE TO SPEAK WITH YOU ABOUT SOMETHING.
SOMEONE, RATHER.
HARRIET VANGER.

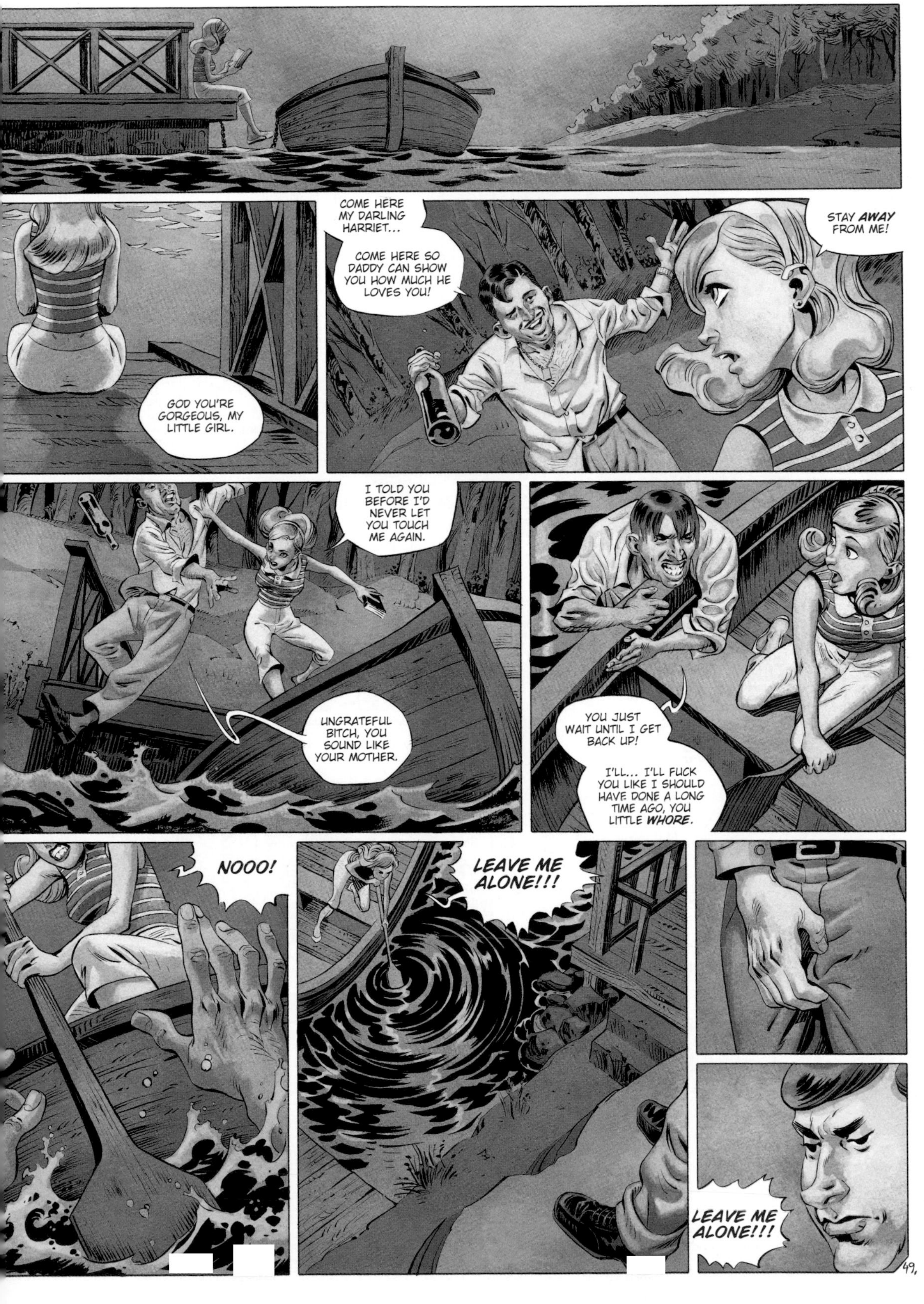

GOD YOU'RE GORGEOUS, MY LITTLE GIRL.
COME HERE MY DARLING HARRIET...
COME HERE SO DADDY CAN SHOW YOU HOW MUCH HE LOVES YOU!
STAY AWAY FROM ME!
I TOLD YOU BEFORE I'D NEVER LET YOU TOUCH ME AGAIN.
UNGRATEFUL BITCH, YOU SOUND LIKE YOUR MOTHER.
YOU JUST WAIT UNTIL I GET BACK UP!
I'LL... I'LL FUCK YOU LIKE I SHOULD HAVE DONE A LONG TIME AGO, YOU LITTLE WHORE.
NOOO!
LEAVE ME ALONE!!!
LEAVE ME ALONE!!!

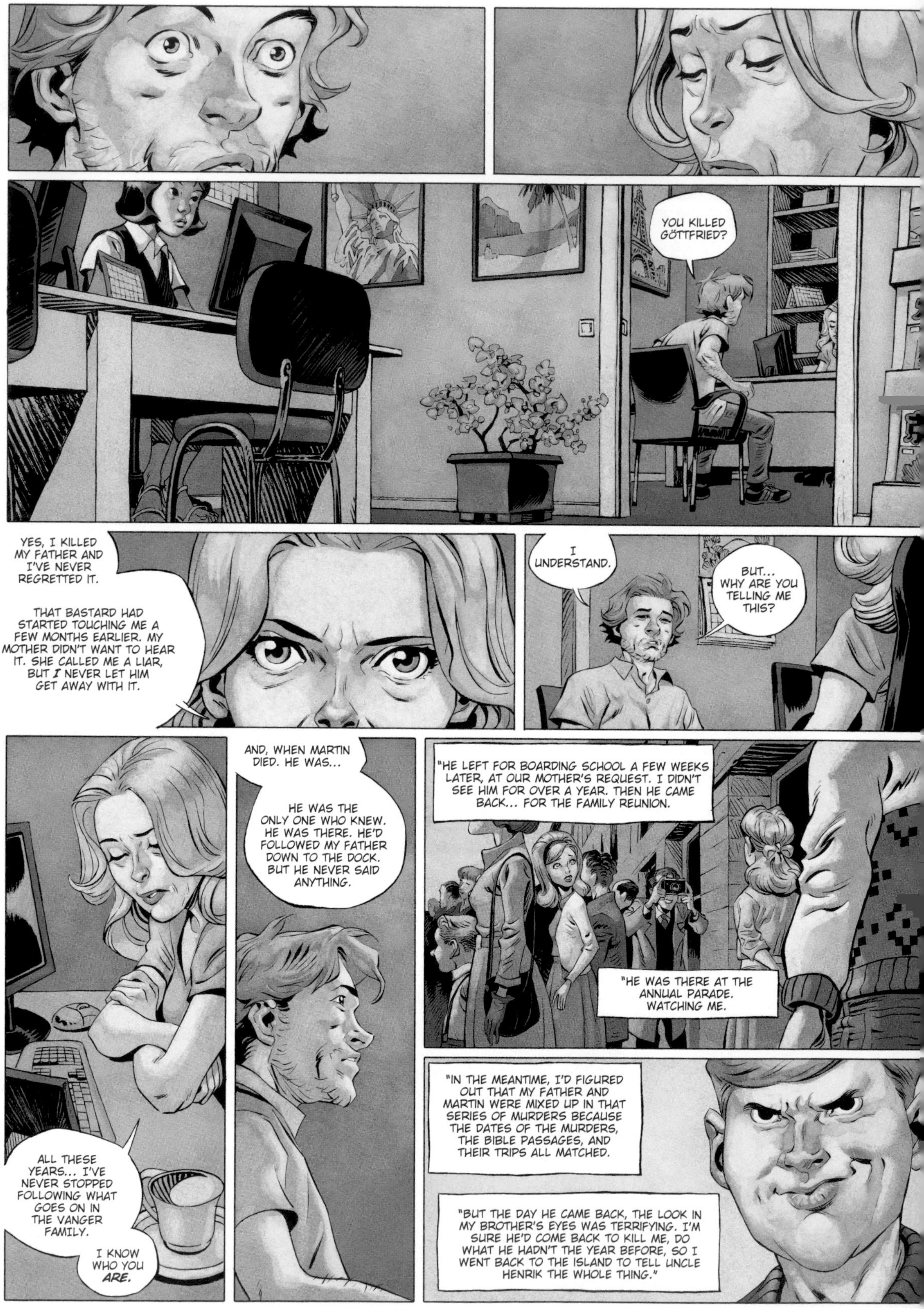
YOU KILLED GÖTTFRIED?
YES, I KILLED MY FATHER AND I'VE NEVER REGRETTED IT.
THAT BASTARD HAD STARTED TOUCHING ME A FEW MONTHS EARLIER. MY MOTHER DIDN'T WANT TO HEAR IT. SHE CALLED ME A LIAR, BUT *I* NEVER LET HIM GET AWAY WITH IT.
I UNDERSTAND.
BUT... WHY ARE YOU TELLING ME THIS?
AND, WHEN MARTIN DIED. HE WAS...
HE WAS THE ONLY ONE WHO KNEW. HE WAS THERE. HE'D FOLLOWED MY FATHER DOWN TO THE DOCK. BUT HE NEVER SAID ANYTHING.
ALL THESE YEARS... I'VE NEVER STOPPED FOLLOWING WHAT GOES ON IN THE VANGER FAMILY.
I KNOW WHO YOU ***ARE.***
"HE LEFT FOR BOARDING SCHOOL A FEW WEEKS LATER, AT OUR MOTHER'S REQUEST. I DIDN'T SEE HIM FOR OVER A YEAR. THEN HE CAME BACK... FOR THE FAMILY REUNION.
"HE WAS THERE AT THE ANNUAL PARADE. WATCHING ME.
"IN THE MEANTIME, I'D FIGURED OUT THAT MY FATHER AND MARTIN WERE MIXED UP IN THAT SERIES OF MURDERS BECAUSE THE DATES OF THE MURDERS, THE BIBLE PASSAGES, AND THEIR TRIPS ALL MATCHED.
"BUT THE DAY HE CAME BACK, THE LOOK IN MY BROTHER'S EYES WAS TERRIFYING. I'M SURE HE'D COME BACK TO KILL ME, DO WHAT HE HADN'T THE YEAR BEFORE, SO I WENT BACK TO THE ISLAND TO TELL UNCLE HENRIK THE WHOLE THING."

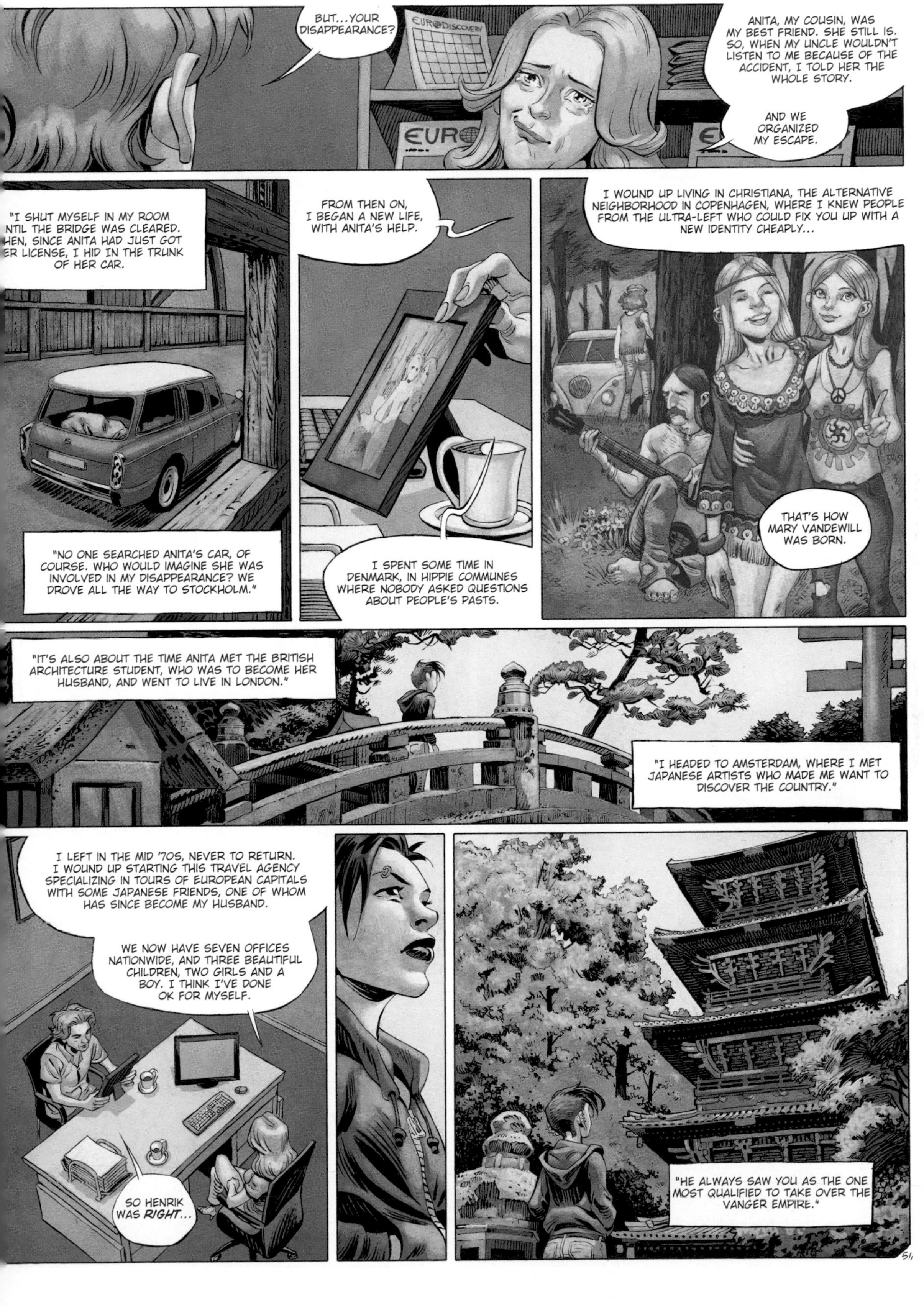

BUT...YOUR DISAPPEARANCE?
EURODISCOVERY
EURO
ANITA, MY COUSIN, WAS MY BEST FRIEND. SHE STILL IS. SO, WHEN MY UNCLE WOULDN'T LISTEN TO ME BECAUSE OF THE ACCIDENT, I TOLD HER THE WHOLE STORY.
AND WE ORGANIZED MY ESCAPE.
"I SHUT MYSELF IN MY ROOM
NTIL THE BRIDGE WAS CLEARED.
HEN, SINCE ANITA HAD JUST GOT
ER LICENSE, I HID IN THE TRUNK
OF HER CAR.
"NO ONE SEARCHED ANITA'S CAR, OF COURSE. WHO WOULD IMAGINE SHE WAS INVOLVED IN MY DISAPPEARANCE? WE DROVE ALL THE WAY TO STOCKHOLM."
FROM THEN ON, I BEGAN A NEW LIFE, WITH ANITA'S HELP.
I SPENT SOME TIME IN DENMARK, IN HIPPIE COMMUNES WHERE NOBODY ASKED QUESTIONS ABOUT PEOPLE'S PASTS.
I WOUND UP LIVING IN CHRISTIANA, THE ALTERNATIVE NEIGHBORHOOD IN COPENHAGEN, WHERE I KNEW PEOPLE FROM THE ULTRA-LEFT WHO COULD FIX YOU UP WITH A NEW IDENTITY CHEAPLY...
THAT'S HOW MARY VANDEWILL WAS BORN.
"IT'S ALSO ABOUT THE TIME ANITA MET THE BRITISH ARCHITECTURE STUDENT, WHO WAS TO BECOME HER HUSBAND, AND WENT TO LIVE IN LONDON."
"I HEADED TO AMSTERDAM, WHERE I MET JAPANESE ARTISTS WHO MADE ME WANT TO DISCOVER THE COUNTRY."
I LEFT IN THE MID '70S, NEVER TO RETURN. I WOUND UP STARTING THIS TRAVEL AGENCY SPECIALIZING IN TOURS OF EUROPEAN CAPITALS WITH SOME JAPANESE FRIENDS, ONE OF WHOM HAS SINCE BECOME MY HUSBAND.
WE NOW HAVE SEVEN OFFICES NATIONWIDE, AND THREE BEAUTIFUL CHILDREN, TWO GIRLS AND A BOY. I THINK I'VE DONE OK FOR MYSELF.
SO HENRIK WAS *RIGHT*...
"HE ALWAYS SAW YOU AS THE ONE MOST QUALIFIED TO TAKE OVER THE VANGER EMPIRE."

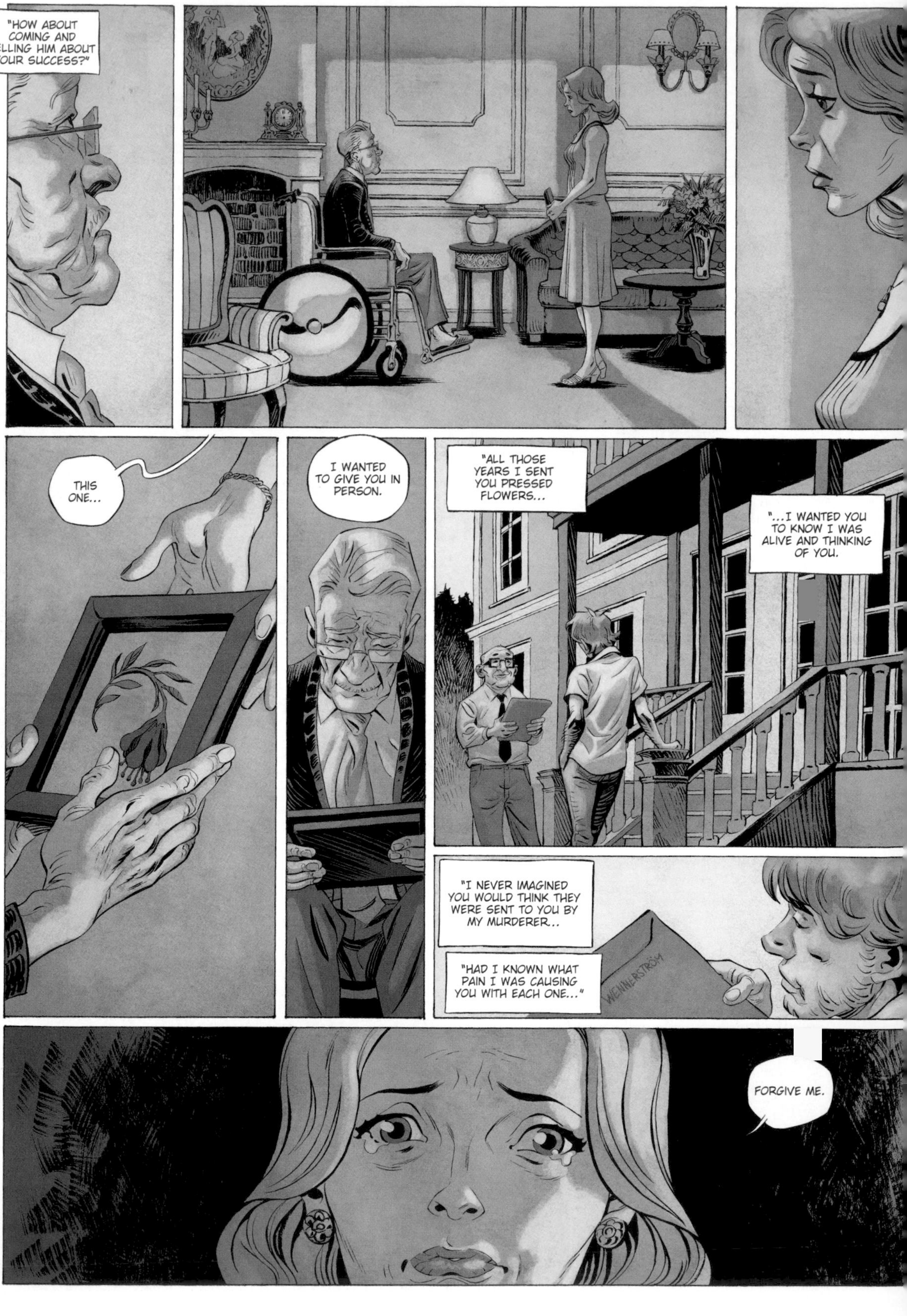
"HOW ABOUT COMING AND TELLING HIM ABOUT YOUR SUCCESS?"
THIS ONE...
I WANTED TO GIVE YOU IN PERSON.
"ALL THOSE YEARS I SENT YOU PRESSED FLOWERS...
"...I WANTED YOU TO KNOW I WAS ALIVE AND THINKING OF YOU.
"I NEVER IMAGINED YOU WOULD THINK THEY WERE SENT TO YOU BY MY MURDERER...
"HAD I KNOWN WHAT PAIN I WAS CAUSING YOU WITH EACH ONE..."
WENNERSTRÖM
FORGIVE ME.

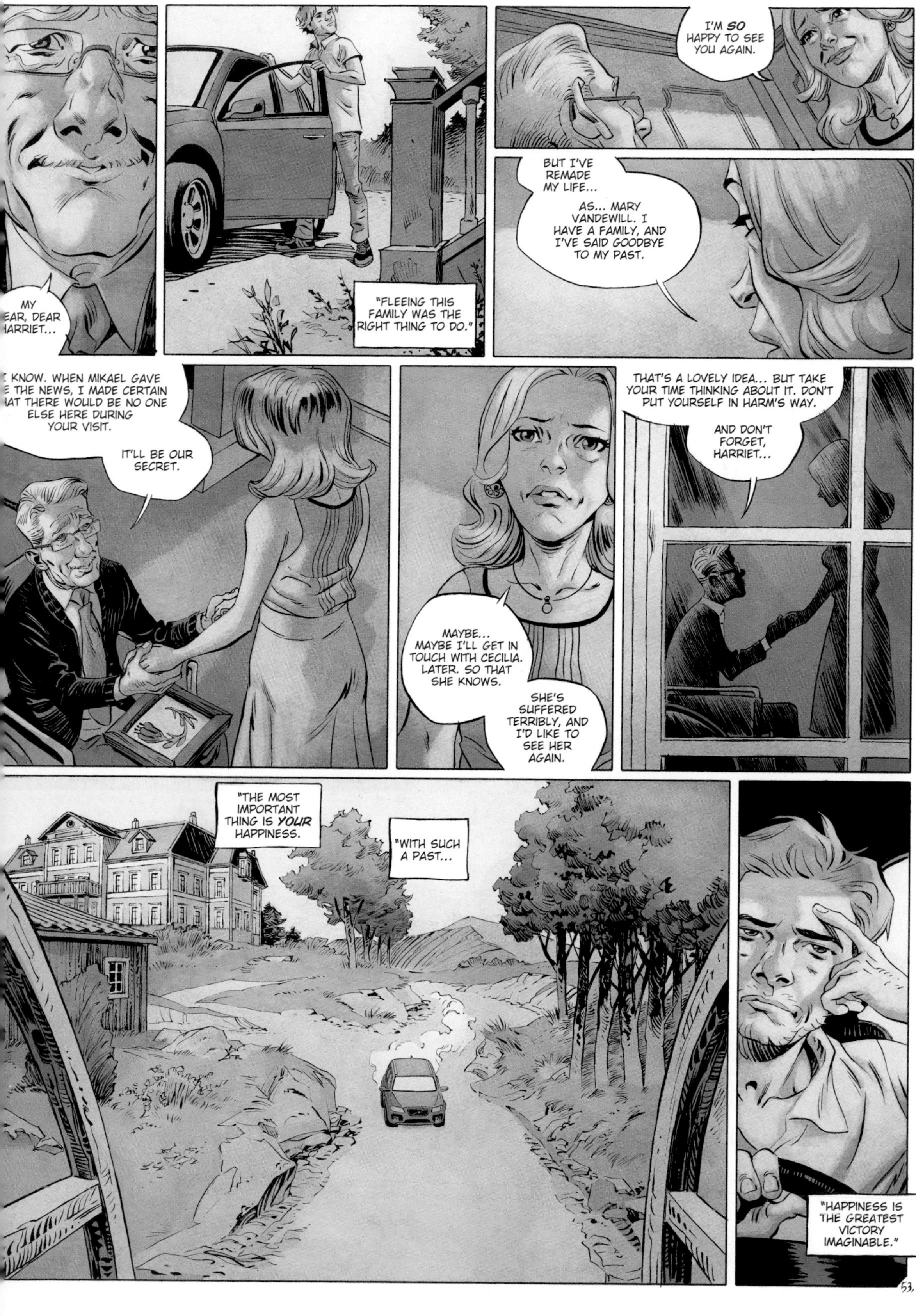
I'M *SO* HAPPY TO SEE YOU AGAIN.
MY EAR, DEAR ARRIET...
"FLEEING THIS FAMILY WAS THE RIGHT THING TO DO."
BUT I'VE REMADE MY LIFE...
AS... MARY VANDEWILL. I HAVE A FAMILY, AND I'VE SAID GOODBYE TO MY PAST.
KNOW. WHEN MIKAEL GAVE THE NEWS, I MADE CERTAIN AT THERE WOULD BE NO ONE ELSE HERE DURING YOUR VISIT.
IT'LL BE OUR SECRET.
MAYBE... MAYBE I'LL GET IN TOUCH WITH CECILIA. LATER. SO THAT SHE KNOWS.
SHE'S SUFFERED TERRIBLY, AND I'D LIKE TO SEE HER AGAIN.
THAT'S A LOVELY IDEA... BUT TAKE YOUR TIME THINKING ABOUT IT. DON'T PUT YOURSELF IN HARM'S WAY.
AND DON'T FORGET, HARRIET...
"THE MOST IMPORTANT THING IS *YOUR* HAPPINESS.
"WITH SUCH A PAST...
"HAPPINESS IS THE GREATEST VICTORY IMAGINABLE."

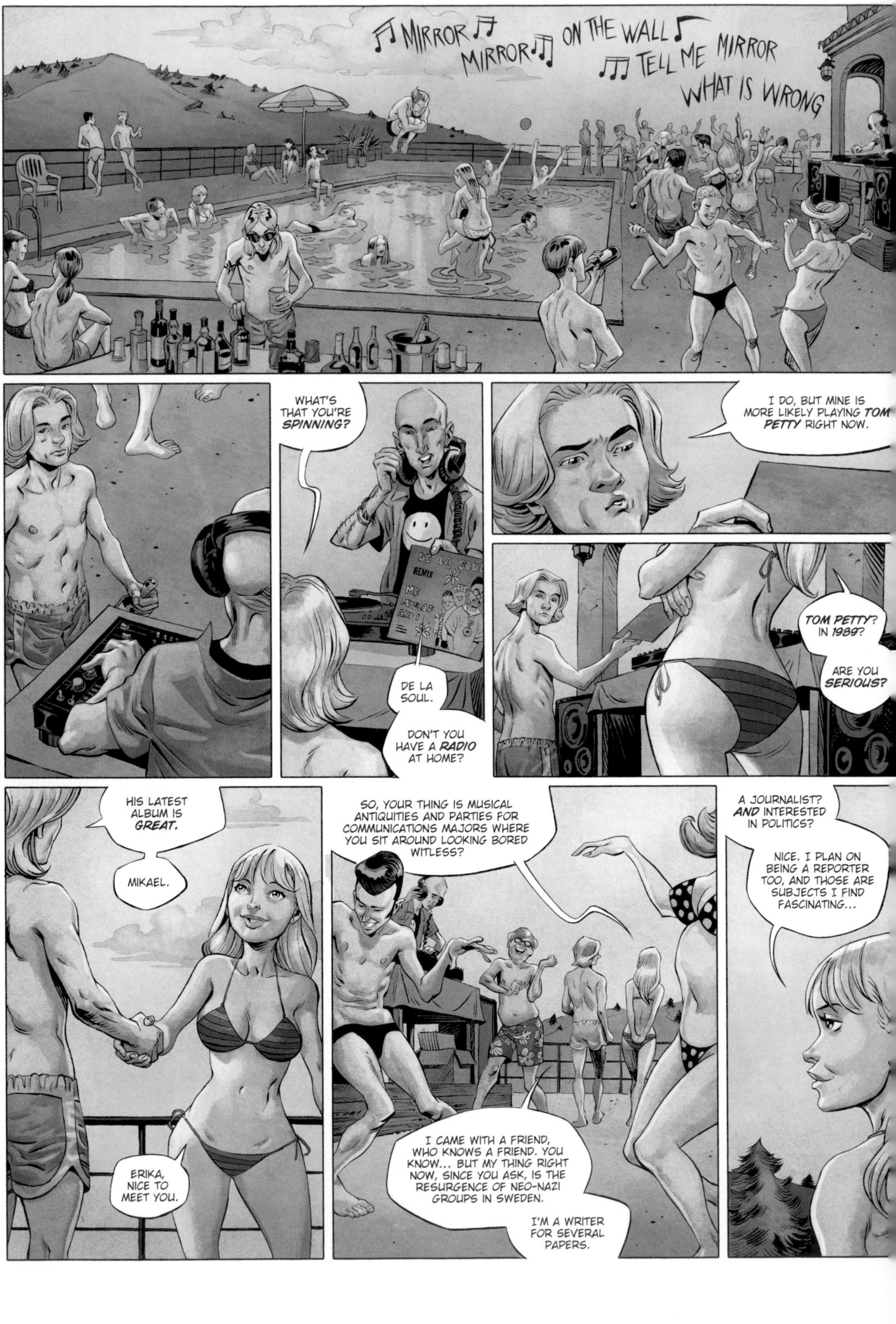
MIRROR MIRROR ON THE WALL TELL ME MIRROR WHAT IS WRONG
WHAT'S THAT YOU'RE SPINNING?
DE LA SOUL REMIX ME MYSELF AND I
DE LA SOUL.
DON'T YOU HAVE A RADIO AT HOME?
I DO, BUT MINE IS MORE LIKELY PLAYING TOM PETTY RIGHT NOW.
TOM PETTY? IN 1989?
ARE YOU SERIOUS?
HIS LATEST ALBUM IS GREAT.
MIKAEL.
ERIKA, NICE TO MEET YOU.
SO, YOUR THING IS MUSICAL ANTIQUITIES AND PARTIES FOR COMMUNICATIONS MAJORS WHERE YOU SIT AROUND LOOKING BORED WITLESS?
I CAME WITH A FRIEND, WHO KNOWS A FRIEND. YOU KNOW... BUT MY THING RIGHT NOW, SINCE YOU ASK, IS THE RESURGENCE OF NEO-NAZI GROUPS IN SWEDEN.
I'M A WRITER FOR SEVERAL PAPERS.
A JOURNALIST? AND INTERESTED IN POLITICS?
NICE. I PLAN ON BEING A REPORTER TOO, AND THOSE ARE SUBJECTS I FIND FASCINATING...

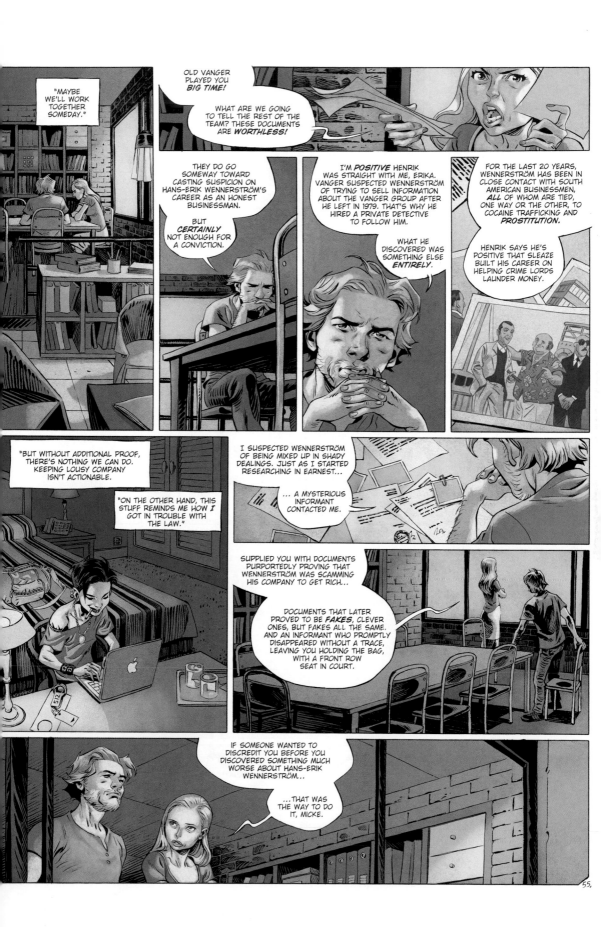

"MAYBE WE'LL WORK TOGETHER SOMEDAY."

OLD VANGER PLAYED YOU *BIG TIME!*

WHAT ARE WE GOING TO TELL THE REST OF THE TEAM? THESE DOCUMENTS ARE *WORTHLESS!*

THEY DO GO SOMEWAY TOWARD CASTING SUSPICION ON HANS-ERIK WENNERSTRÖM'S CAREER AS AN HONEST BUSINESSMAN.

BUT *CERTAINLY* NOT ENOUGH FOR A CONVICTION.

I'M *POSITIVE* HENRIK WAS STRAIGHT WITH ME, ERIKA. VANGER SUSPECTED WENNERSTRÖM OF TRYING TO SELL INFORMATION ABOUT THE VANGER GROUP AFTER HE LEFT IN 1979. THAT'S WHY HE HIRED A PRIVATE DETECTIVE TO FOLLOW HIM.

WHAT HE DISCOVERED WAS SOMETHING ELSE *ENTIRELY.*

FOR THE LAST 20 YEARS, WENNERSTRÖM HAS BEEN IN CLOSE CONTACT WITH SOUTH AMERICAN BUSINESSMEN, *ALL* OF WHOM ARE TIED, ONE WAY OR THE OTHER, TO COCAINE TRAFFICKING AND *PROSTITUTION.*

HENRIK SAYS HE'S POSITIVE THAT SLEAZE BUILT HIS CAREER ON HELPING CRIME LORDS LAUNDER MONEY.

"BUT WITHOUT ADDITIONAL PROOF, THERE'S NOTHING WE CAN DO. KEEPING LOUSY COMPANY ISN'T ACTIONABLE.

"ON THE OTHER HAND, THIS STUFF REMINDS ME HOW *I* GOT IN TROUBLE WITH THE LAW."

I SUSPECTED WENNERSTRÖM OF BEING MIXED UP IN SHADY DEALINGS. JUST AS I STARTED RESEARCHING IN EARNEST...

... A MYSTERIOUS INFORMANT CONTACTED ME.

SUPPLIED YOU WITH DOCUMENTS PURPORTEDLY PROVING THAT WENNERSTRÖM WAS SCAMMING HIS COMPANY TO GET RICH...

DOCUMENTS THAT LATER PROVED TO BE *FAKES*, CLEVER ONES, BUT FAKES ALL THE SAME. AND AN INFORMANT WHO PROMPTLY DISAPPEARED WITHOUT A TRACE, LEAVING YOU HOLDING THE BAG, WITH A FRONT ROW SEAT IN COURT.

IF SOMEONE WANTED TO DISCREDIT YOU BEFORE YOU DISCOVERED SOMETHING MUCH WORSE ABOUT HANS-ERIK WENNERSTRÖM...

...THAT WAS THE WAY TO DO IT, MICKE.

55.

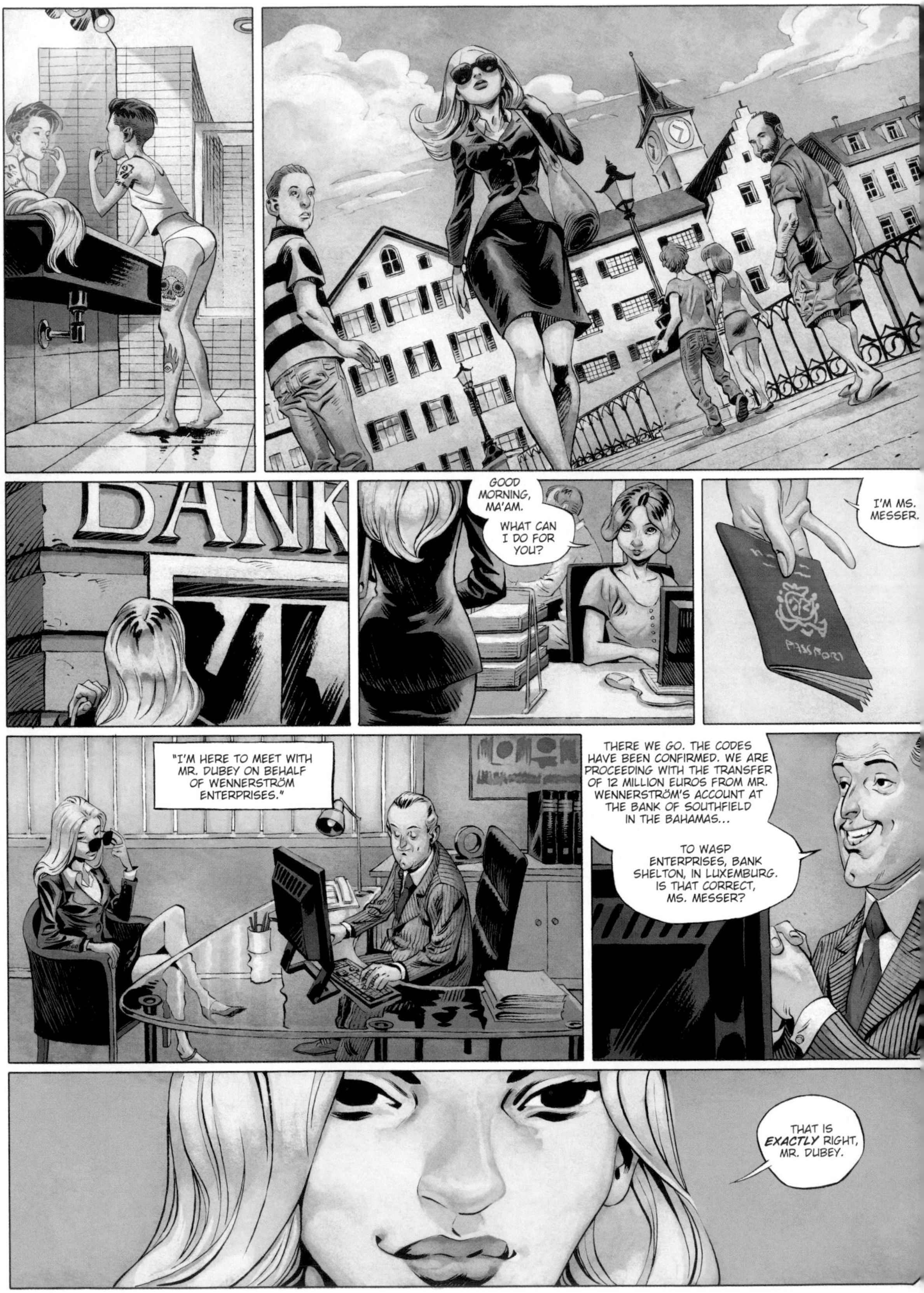
GOOD MORNING, MA'AM.
WHAT CAN I DO FOR YOU?
I'M MS. MESSER.
"I'M HERE TO MEET WITH MR. DUBEY ON BEHALF OF WENNERSTRÖM ENTERPRISES."
THERE WE GO. THE CODES HAVE BEEN CONFIRMED. WE ARE PROCEEDING WITH THE TRANSFER OF 12 MILLION EUROS FROM MR. WENNERSTRÖM'S ACCOUNT AT THE BANK OF SOUTHFIELD IN THE BAHAMAS...
TO WASP ENTERPRISES, BANK SHELTON, IN LUXEMBURG. IS THAT CORRECT, MS. MESSER?
THAT IS *EXACTLY* RIGHT, MR. DUBEY.

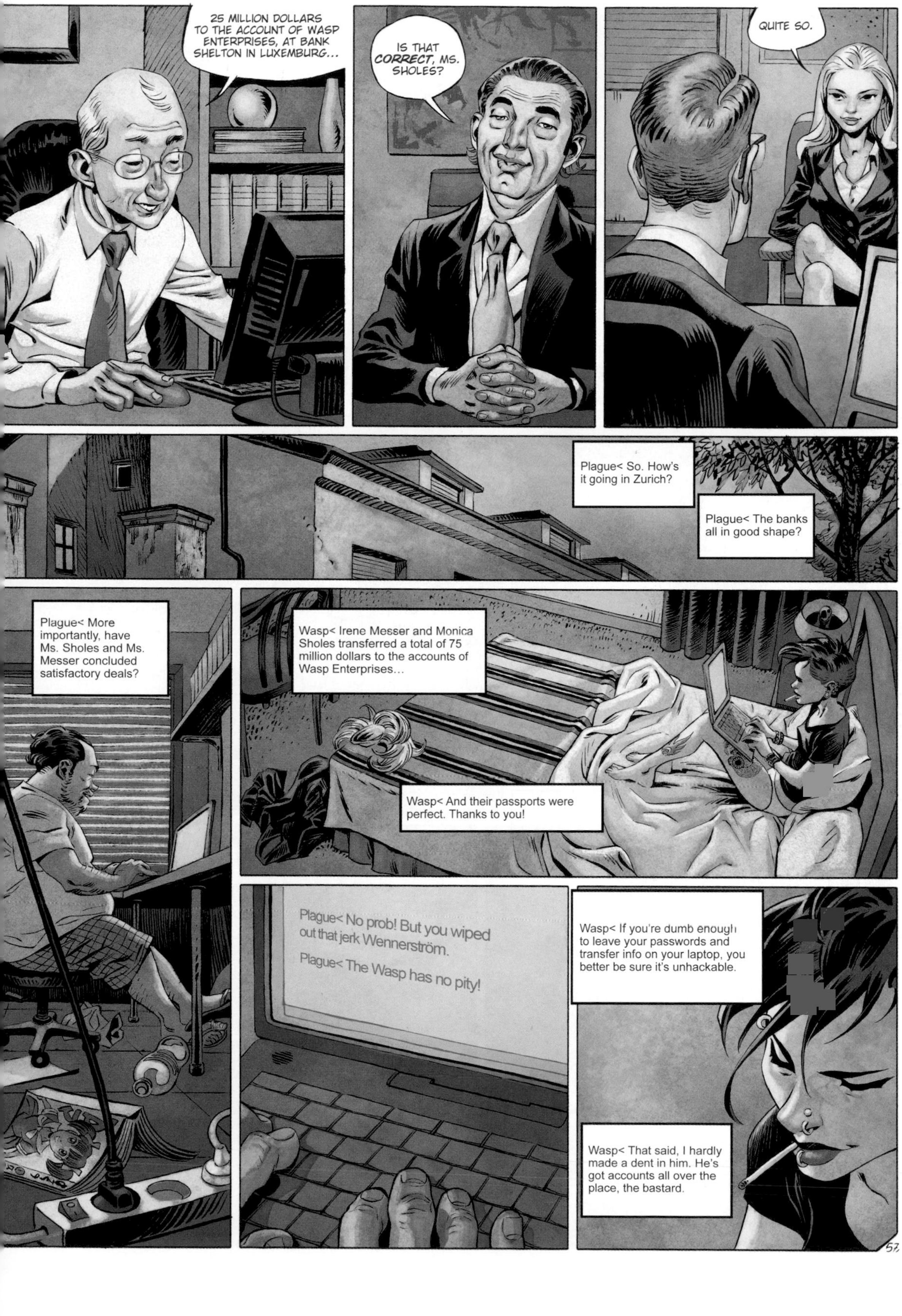
25 MILLION DOLLARS TO THE ACCOUNT OF WASP ENTERPRISES, AT BANK SHELTON IN LUXEMBURG...
IS THAT CORRECT, MS. SHOLES?
QUITE SO.
Plague< So. How's it going in Zurich?
Plague< The banks all in good shape?
Plague< More importantly, have Ms. Sholes and Ms. Messer concluded satisfactory deals?
Wasp< Irene Messer and Monica Sholes transferred a total of 75 million dollars to the accounts of Wasp Enterprises…
Wasp< And their passports were perfect. Thanks to you!
Plague< No prob! But you wiped out that jerk Wennerström.
Plague< The Wasp has no pity!
Wasp< If you're dumb enough to leave your passwords and transfer info on your laptop, you better be sure it's unhackable.
Wasp< That said, I hardly made a dent in him. He's got accounts all over the place, the bastard.

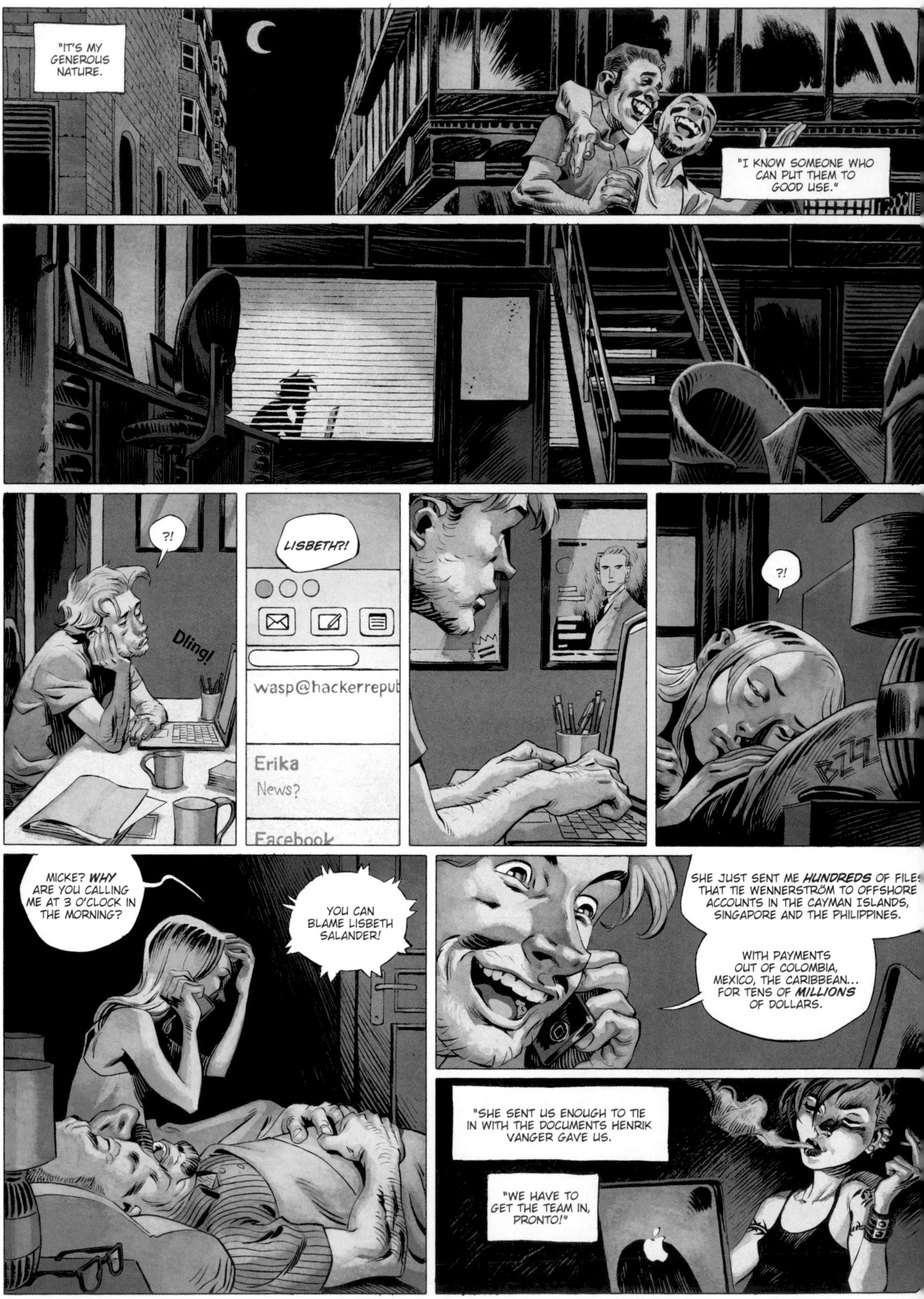

"IT'S MY GENEROUS NATURE.
"I KNOW SOMEONE WHO CAN PUT THEM TO GOOD USE."
?!
Dling!
LISBETH?!
wasp@hackerreput
Erika
News?
Facebook
?!
BZZZ
MICKE? WHY ARE YOU CALLING ME AT 3 O'CLOCK IN THE MORNING?
YOU CAN BLAME LISBETH SALANDER!
SHE JUST SENT ME HUNDREDS OF FILES THAT TIE WENNERSTRÖM TO OFFSHORE ACCOUNTS IN THE CAYMAN ISLANDS, SINGAPORE AND THE PHILIPPINES.
WITH PAYMENTS OUT OF COLOMBIA, MEXICO, THE CARIBBEAN... FOR TENS OF MILLIONS OF DOLLARS.
"SHE SENT US ENOUGH TO TIE IN WITH THE DOCUMENTS HENRIK VANGER GAVE US.
"WE HAVE TO GET THE TEAM IN, PRONTO!"

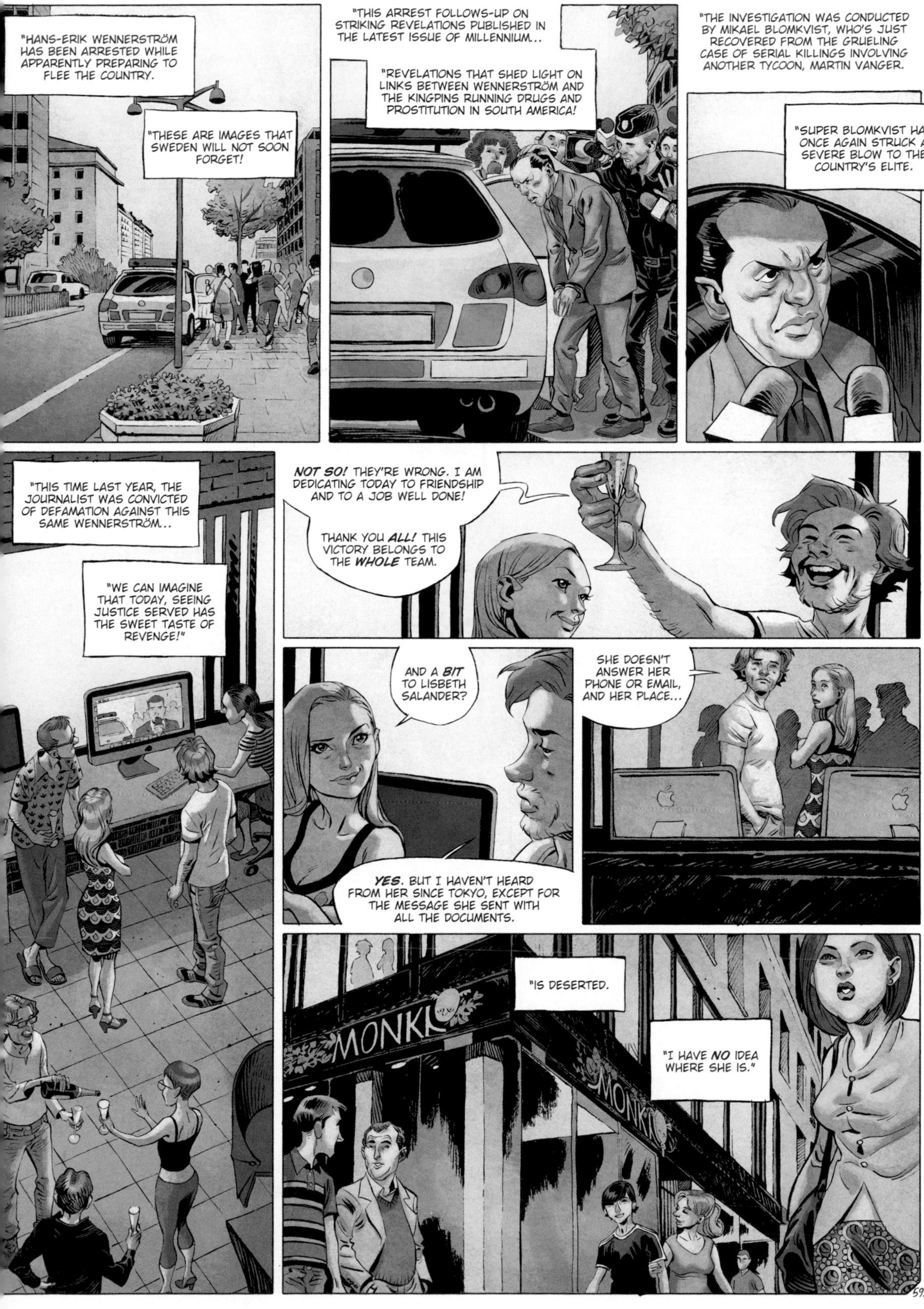

"HANS-ERIK WENNERSTRÖM HAS BEEN ARRESTED WHILE APPARENTLY PREPARING TO FLEE THE COUNTRY.
"THESE ARE IMAGES THAT SWEDEN WILL NOT SOON FORGET!
"THIS ARREST FOLLOWS-UP ON STRIKING REVELATIONS PUBLISHED IN THE LATEST ISSUE OF MILLENNIUM...
"REVELATIONS THAT SHED LIGHT ON LINKS BETWEEN WENNERSTRÖM AND THE KINGPINS RUNNING DRUGS AND PROSTITUTION IN SOUTH AMERICA!
"THE INVESTIGATION WAS CONDUCTED BY MIKAEL BLOMKVIST, WHO'S JUST RECOVERED FROM THE GRUELING CASE OF SERIAL KILLINGS INVOLVING ANOTHER TYCOON, MARTIN VANGER.
"SUPER BLOMKVIST HAS ONCE AGAIN STRUCK A SEVERE BLOW TO THE COUNTRY'S ELITE.
"THIS TIME LAST YEAR, THE JOURNALIST WAS CONVICTED OF DEFAMATION AGAINST THIS SAME WENNERSTRÖM...
"WE CAN IMAGINE THAT TODAY, SEEING JUSTICE SERVED HAS THE SWEET TASTE OF REVENGE!"
NOT SO! THEY'RE WRONG. I AM DEDICATING TODAY TO FRIENDSHIP AND TO A JOB WELL DONE!
THANK YOU *ALL!* THIS VICTORY BELONGS TO THE *WHOLE* TEAM.
AND A *BIT* TO LISBETH SALANDER?
YES. BUT I HAVEN'T HEARD FROM HER SINCE TOKYO, EXCEPT FOR THE MESSAGE SHE SENT WITH ALL THE DOCUMENTS.
SHE DOESN'T ANSWER HER PHONE OR EMAIL, AND HER PLACE...
"IS DESERTED.
"I HAVE *NO* IDEA WHERE SHE IS."
MONKI

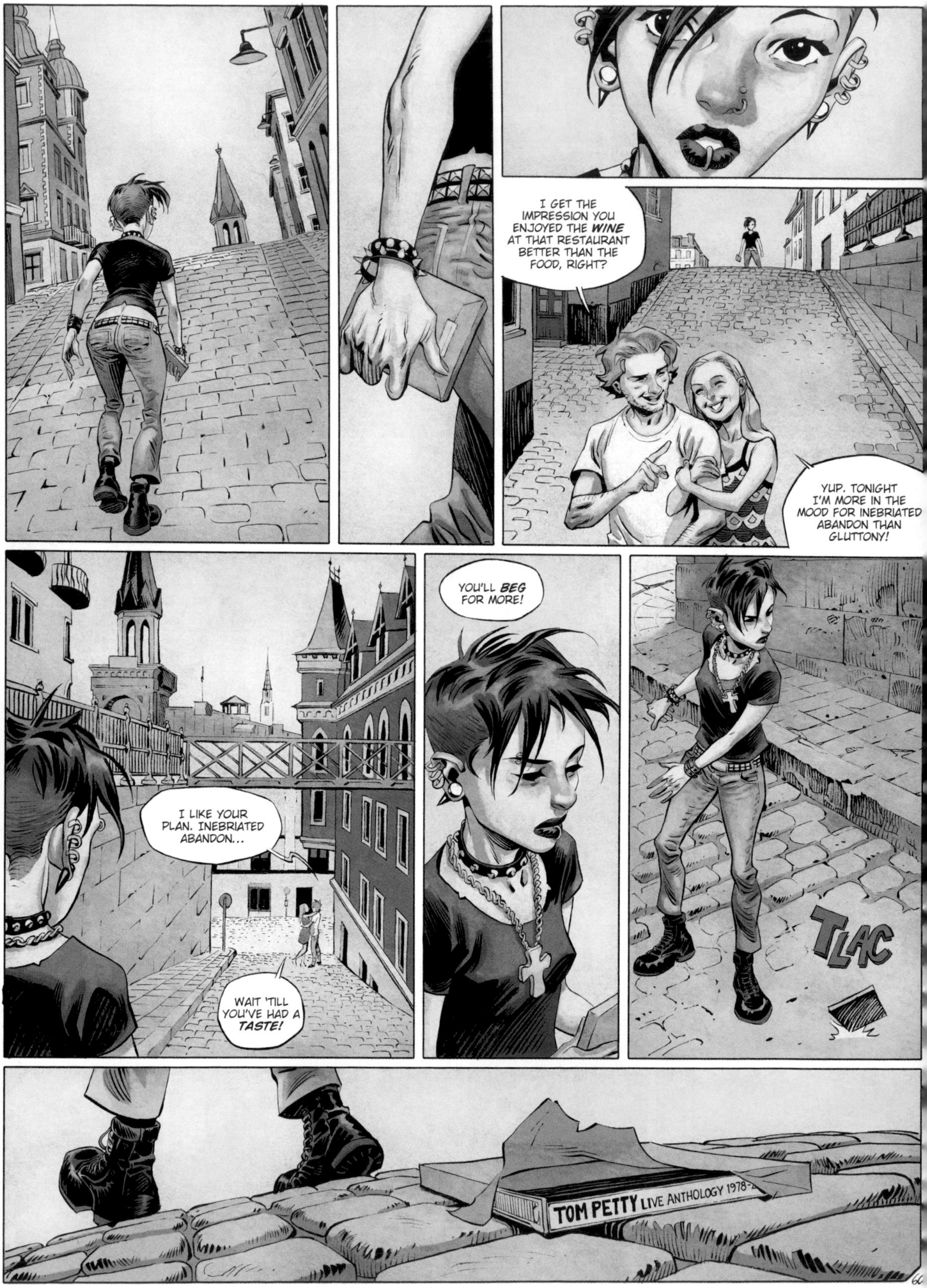
I GET THE IMPRESSION YOU ENJOYED THE WINE AT THAT RESTAURANT BETTER THAN THE FOOD, RIGHT?
YUP. TONIGHT I'M MORE IN THE MOOD FOR INEBRIATED ABANDON THAN GLUTTONY!
I LIKE YOUR PLAN. INEBRIATED ABANDON...
WAIT 'TILL YOU'VE HAD A TASTE!
YOU'LL BEG FOR MORE!
TLAC
TOM PETTY LIVE ANTHOLOGY 1978-

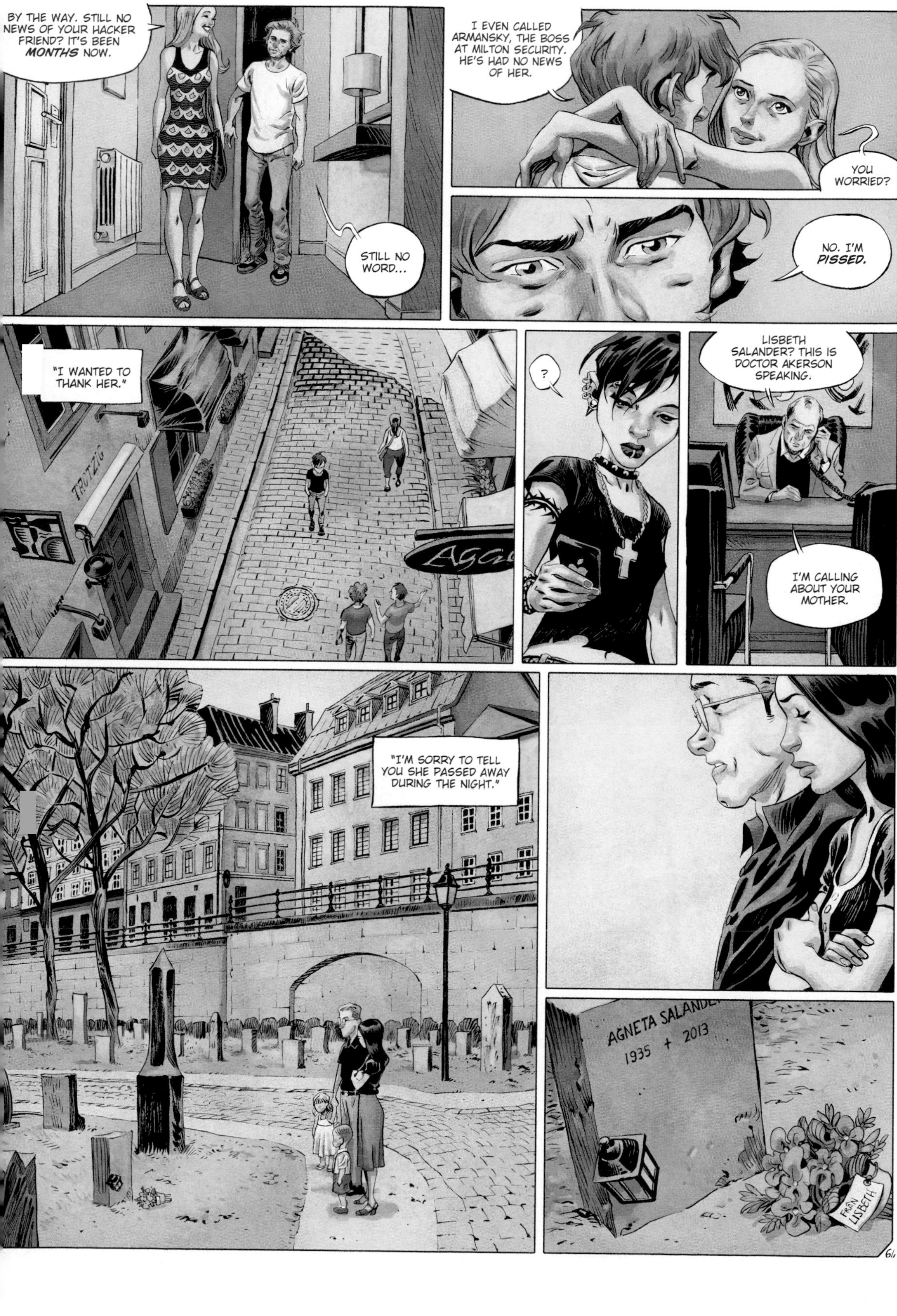
BY THE WAY. STILL NO NEWS OF YOUR HACKER FRIEND? IT'S BEEN MONTHS NOW.
STILL NO WORD...
I EVEN CALLED ARMANSKY, THE BOSS AT MILTON SECURITY. HE'S HAD NO NEWS OF HER.
YOU WORRIED?
NO. I'M PISSED.
"I WANTED TO THANK HER."
TROTZIG
?
LISBETH SALANDER? THIS IS DOCTOR AKERSON SPEAKING.
I'M CALLING ABOUT YOUR MOTHER.
"I'M SORRY TO TELL YOU SHE PASSED AWAY DURING THE NIGHT."
AGNETA SALANDE
1935 + 2013
FRÅN LISBETH

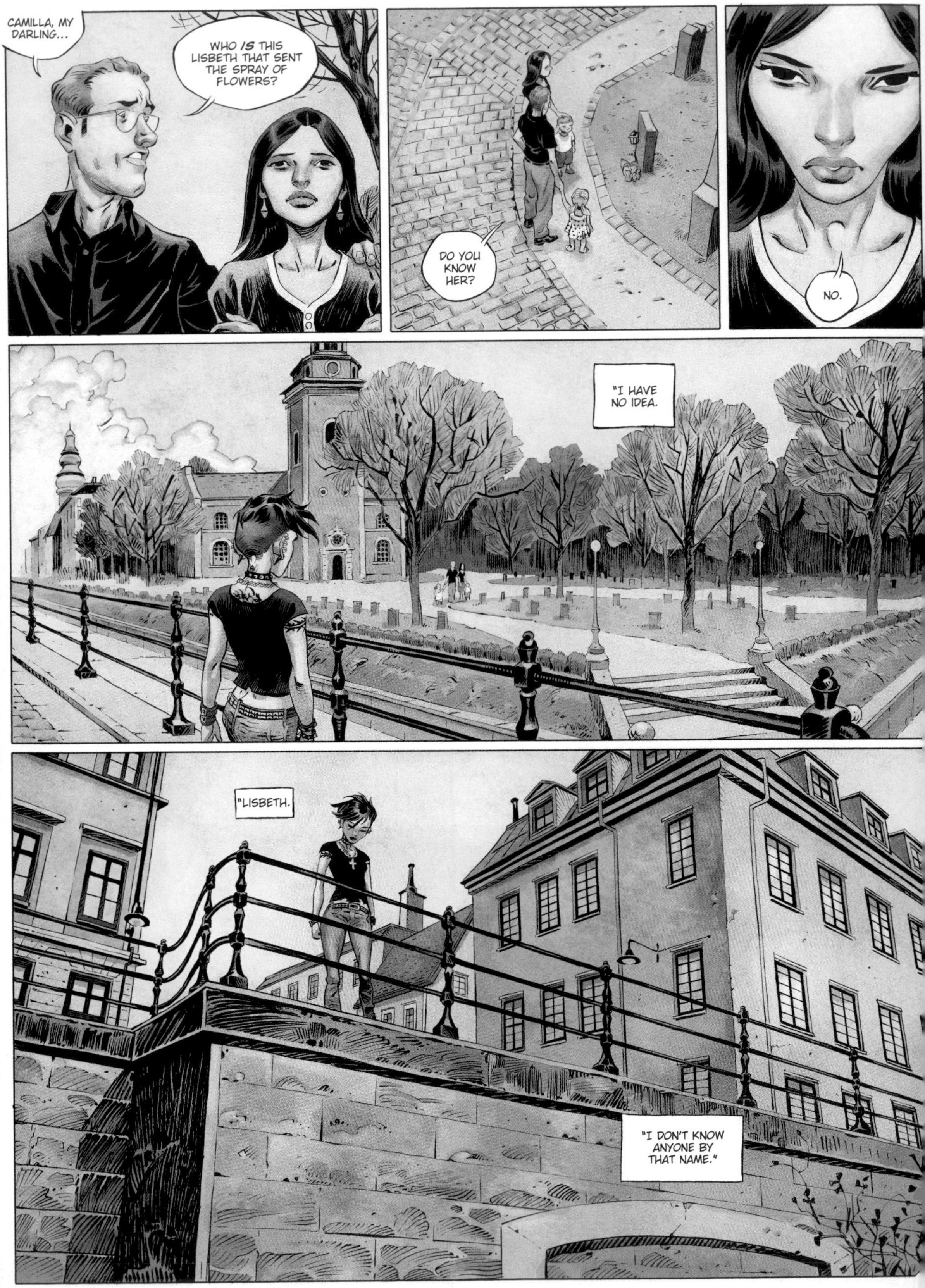
CAMILLA, MY DARLING...
WHO IS THIS LISBETH THAT SENT THE SPRAY OF FLOWERS?
DO YOU KNOW HER?
NO.
"I HAVE NO IDEA.
"LISBETH.
"I DON'T KNOW ANYONE BY THAT NAME."

MILLENNIUM

THE GIRL WITH THE DRAGON TATTOO

COVERS GALLERY

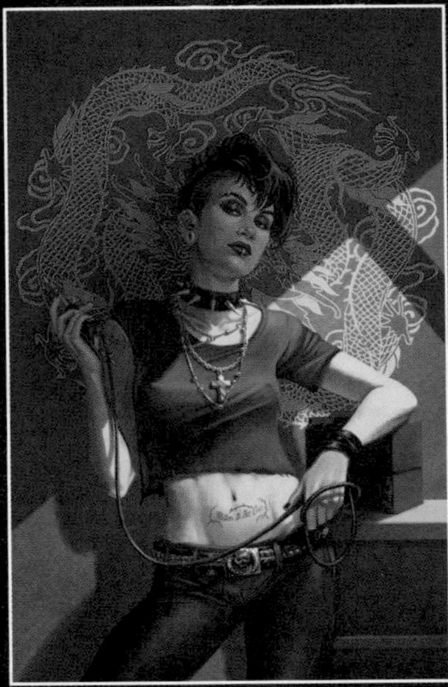

1 COVER A by **Claudia Ianniciello**

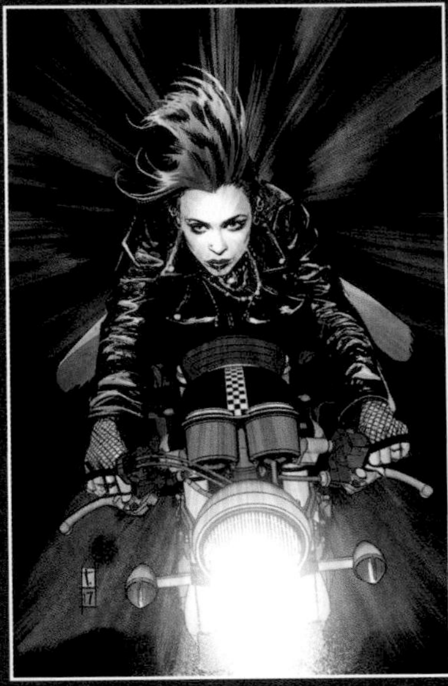

1 COVER B by **Tomm Coker**

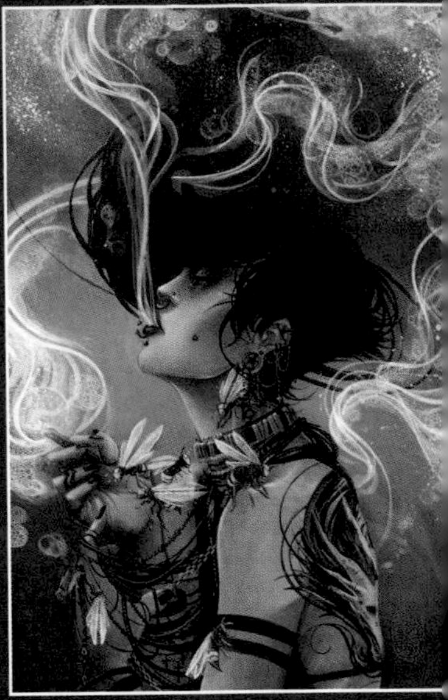

1 COVER C by **Nen Chang**

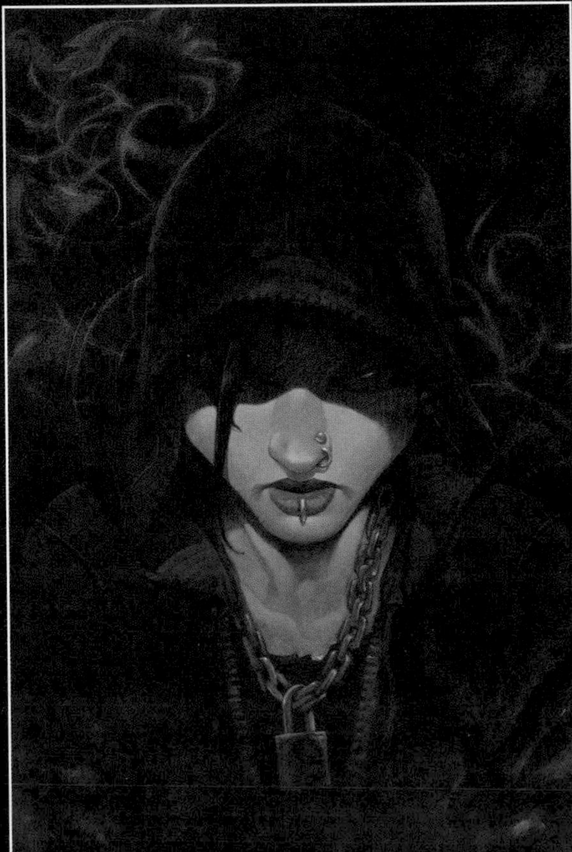

1 COVER D by **Homs**

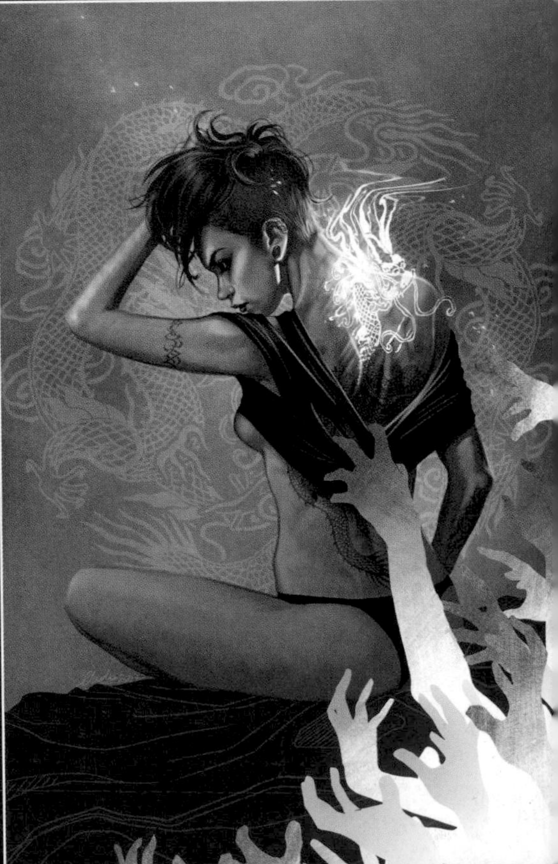

2 COVER A by **Claudia Ianniciello**

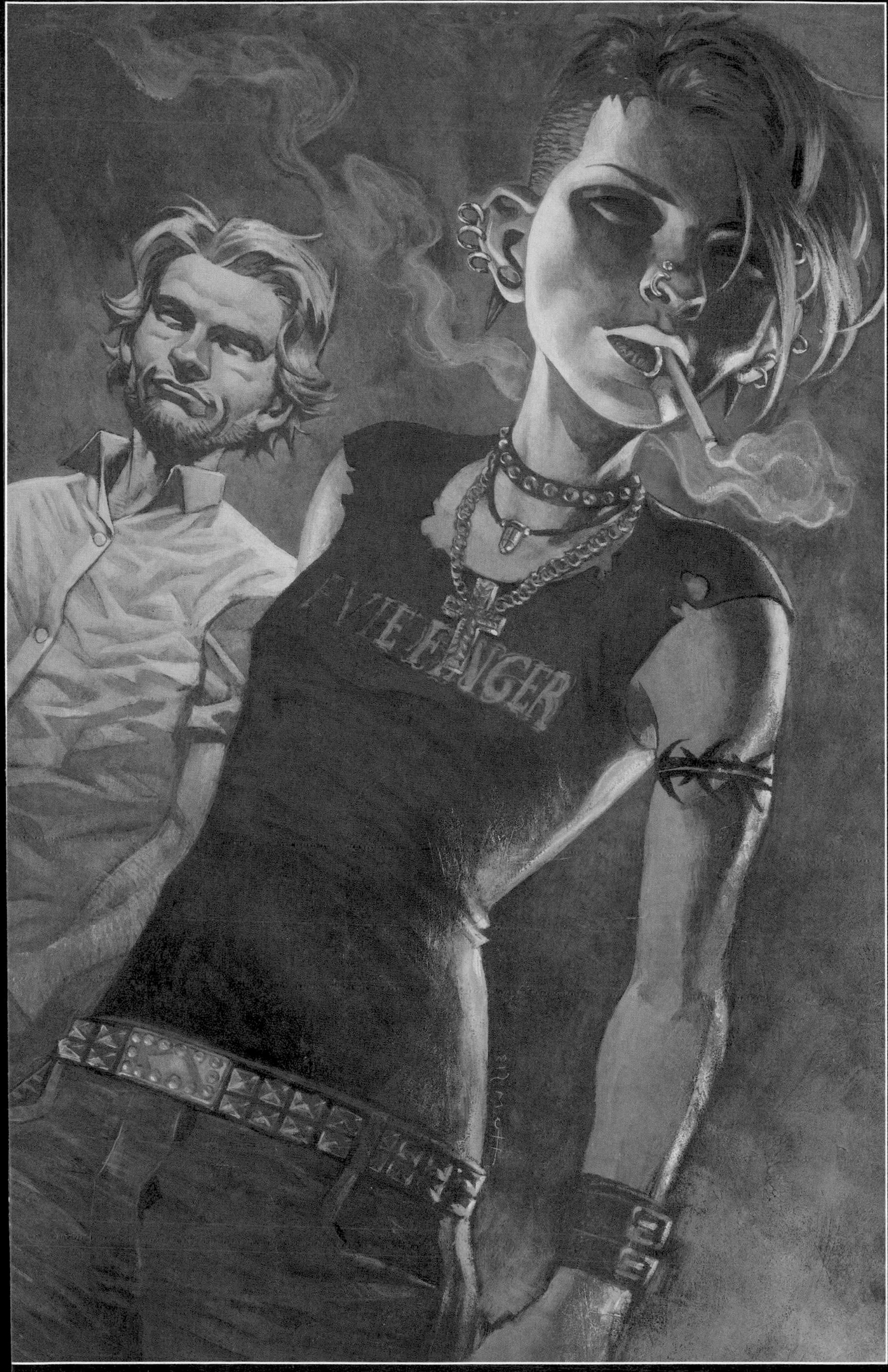

2 COVER B by Homs

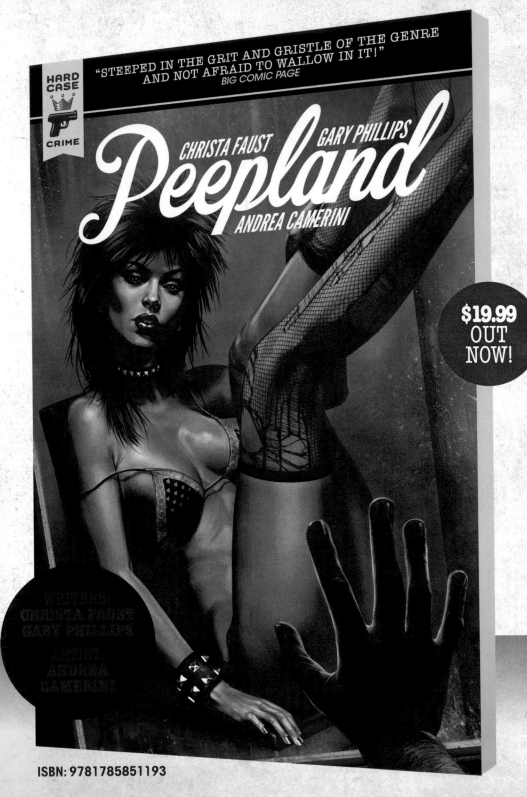

COLLECTIONS!

THE GIRL WITH THE DRAGON TATTOO

CREATOR BIOS

SYLVAIN RUNBERG

Sylvain Runberg is a French writer who divides his time between Stockholm, Provence, and Paris. He has a diploma in Plastic Arts and an MA in Political History. Before he started writing, Sylvain Runberg worked for publishing house Humanoides Associés (editor of Moebius & Enki Bilal).

His first book was launched in 2004 and since then Runberg has had more than 70 books published by some of the largest French publishers (Glénat, Le Lombard, Dupuis, Dargaud, Casterman, Soleil, Futuropolis etc,...) and is now translated into 18 languages, having sold in total over a million copies worldwide.

Sylvain is best known for his comics adaptation of the Stieg Larsson's *Millennium* trilogy, which has been published in six volumes with the illustrators Homs and Man. The adaptation has been acclaimed by both French and European media and readers and is already published in 13 other countries. Further to that success, Runberg has been trusted by Dupuis and the rights holders of *Millennium* to write an exclusive continuation of the comics series called the *Millennium Saga*.

Runberg is currently working on several new comics and TV projects that will be published in years to come.

HOMS

Homs is a Spanish comic artist who has worked for US companies like Marvel, but also for European publishers like Dupuis. Cutting his teeth on Marvel Comics titles such as *Blade*, *Red Sonja*, and *Marvel Westerns*, Homs' work has also appeared in magazine *Heavy Metal*, and in the Spanish anthologies *Barcelona TM* and *Revolution Complex*.

Since 2010 he has focused on work for the European market. Together with writer Frank Giroud, he was responsible for the 'L'Angelus' storyline in the *Secrets* series for Dupuis in 2010-2011. He collaborated with Sylvain Runberg to make a comic adaptation of Stieg Larsson's hit novel series *Millennium* in six parts for Dupuis. His most recent work includes *SHI* for Dagaud.